Elmer H. Stoffelbach

THE JUNIOR-COLLEGE MOVEMENT

BY

LEONARD V. KOOS

PROFESSOR OF SECONDARY EDUCATION
UNIVERSITY OF MINNESOTA

GINN AND COMPANY
BOSTON · NEW YORK · CHICAGO · LONDON
ATLANTA · DALLAS · COLUMBUS · SAN FRANCISCO

𝕿𝖍𝖊 𝕬𝖙𝖍𝖊𝖓𝖆𝖚𝖒 𝕻𝖗𝖊𝖘𝖘

GINN AND COMPANY · PRO-
PRIETORS · BOSTON · U.S.A.

PREFATORY NOTE

This volume essays a comprehensive but, at the same time, compact consideration of a movement which seems destined, like the advent of the junior high school, to affect profoundly the organization of our American system of education. The endeavor has been to present content of such a character and in such form as to prove useful to those who desire to make themselves conversant in a general way with the movement, and likewise to those who seek information on how best to encourage its development in a state or other system of schools or to administer junior-college work in a particular locality.

The factual basis drawn upon for present purposes is the findings of an extended investigation of the movement carried forward by the writer under subventions from the Commonwealth Fund of New York City and from the University of Minnesota. The two-volume report of this investigation has been issued as a Research Publication of the University, Education Series, No. 5.

L. V. K.

CONTENTS

THE JUNIOR–COLLEGE MOVEMENT

CONTENTS

LIST OF DIAGRAMS

[ix]

THE JUNIOR-COLLEGE MOVEMENT

LIST OF DIAGRAMS

[xi]

THE JUNIOR–COLLEGE MOVEMENT

I

SCOPE AND VARIETY OF THE MOVEMENT

I. Its Growth and Present Scope

The junior college a recent development. During the last two decades there have appeared upon the educational scene two new units asking for recognition in our system of education. Singularly enough, and without apparent conjunction of intention on the part of their friends, both have been brought before the American audience bearing in the names most frequently applied to them the word "junior." This is, however, not without analogous reason, since each is designed to provide education for those who in their stages of training are in the vicinage of the beginning years of the institution of which it is the namesake. For one of them, the junior high school, the writer has already attempted an evaluation, and has set down what seemed to him to be the basic principles of guidance in its development. A similar but more comprehensive evaluation of the other, the junior college, is here essayed.

Of the two movements which are referred to, the one lower in the system—and probably in part because it is lower in the system—has taken greater hold and is to be found in greater numbers in most sections of the country. The junior college, however, has grown at a rapid rate, and seems no less to merit such evaluation as is possible in its present state of development.

The present scope of the movement. It is no easy task to ascertain the exact number of examples of a new educational unit. Those who may be appealed to in any state for lists of junior colleges are sometimes unaware of the existence of all such institutions. A few schools may have been discontinued or may have metamorphosed into four-year colleges. In some instances there is unwillingness of authorities in charge to supply the items of information asked for. Inquiries extending over a period of nine months indicate, however, that by the end of the school year 1921–1922 the number of junior colleges of the three main types, public, state, and private, had mounted to approximately two hundred. During the succeeding school years the number has increased, so we may with assurance say at this writing that it is well over this mark.

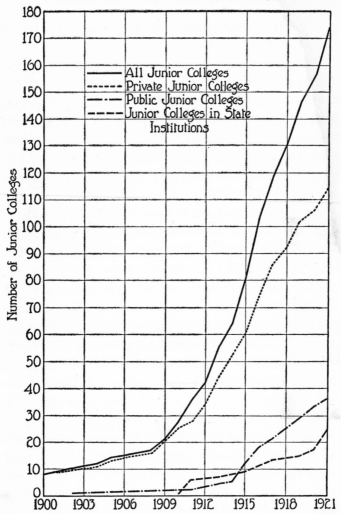

FIG. 1. Number of junior colleges in operation in each successive
year from 1900 to 1921 inclusive

II. Types of Junior Colleges

A. PUBLIC JUNIOR COLLEGES

Growth and present status. The increase in the number of junior colleges maintained by city, high-school, or junior-college districts, hereafter to be referred to as "public junior colleges," has been nothing short of notable. The first of these institutions to come into existence is the one maintained in connection with the township high school at Joliet, Illinois. Another was established about the same time in Goshen, Indiana, but has since been discontinued. It was not until 1911 that others of the group considered were established, the period of most rapid development beginning in 1915. As far as may be accurately ascertained thirty-six institutions of this type were in operation during 1921–1922. One of these has since been discontinued, but at least nine, despite the financial difficulties of the times, were added during 1922–1923, bringing the total to at least forty-five or fifty. Establishment of additional units is under consideration in a number of other communities.

The control of these units. Since they are nearly always maintained in connection with city and high-school districts, the units are under the direction and control of local school authorities, except in so far as these solicit the guidance of the universities in the states of location. Certain of the junior colleges of

[4]

California have entered upon an affiliation with their state university which implies some measure of co-operative direction.

Almost exclusively these public junior colleges are housed with high-school units, although there are varying degrees of separation of administration, teaching faculty, student body, and social life in the two units. The only exceptions met with are in Kansas City, Missouri, where the upper unit, although a part of the public-school system, is housed in a separate structure at some distance from high-school units; and the junior college in Grand Rapids, Michigan. Some other communities maintaining junior colleges are considering the provision of separate housing, but many do not regard complete separation as desirable.

The chief factor of growth. The facts of control and housing of this type of junior college direct attention to what seems a chief factor (although not at all the only factor) in their development, that they are upward extensions of our public-school system; a step in evolution which is a natural one in communities that have in something like a satisfactory manner taken care of education on the lower levels. The first step was the provision of the work of the common school, next to follow was the high school, and last to come is what many school authorities concerned are inclined to believe is the culmination of the local school system—the junior college.

THE JUNIOR-COLLEGE MOVEMENT

B. STATE INSTITUTIONS

Growth and present status. Under the second type, those maintained as state institutions or as parts of state institutions, may be grouped a wide variety of junior colleges. Most of the units, however, are maintained in connection with normal schools and teachers' colleges. This was the last of the types to come into existence, but its representatives have increased in numbers with considerable rapidity since their first appearance. A spurt of growth for 1921 was caused entirely by developments in California, and here the increase was in part at the expense of junior colleges in high-school districts, which were taken over by state teacher-training institutions.

The total number of these units on state foundations in 1921–1922 was twenty-four. Of these, six only were not operated in connection with normal schools and teachers' colleges. Without question this number of state institutions would be somewhat larger if to it were added normal schools and teachers' colleges which, without making formal announcement of offering junior-college or regular college curricula, permit or encourage students who plan to go on to other higher institutions to carry academic work to the exclusion or almost to the exclusion of professional courses. This does not refer to those teacher-training institutions whose graduates pursuing regular two-

[6]

year professional curricula are granted two years of credit in colleges or universities to which they transfer. Such institutions are not here regarded as belonging properly to the junior-college movement, despite the fact that their catalogues sometimes refer to them as junior colleges.

Control. For junior colleges in normal schools and teachers' colleges the control, with one exception, is lodged in whatever authorities direct the institutions of which they are a part. These are the state normal-school board or, in a small proportion of instances, the special board in charge of a particular normal school. The exception is the Southern Branch of the University of California, which is in charge of the parent institution. The control of the six remaining units varies between state boards of education, as with Idaho Polytechnic Institute, and boards in charge of a special type of education, as with Grubbs Vocational College[1] and John Tarleton Agricultural College in Texas, operating under the same board as does the Agricultural and Mechanical College.

The chief factor of growth. The outstanding factor in the growth of junior colleges in normal schools and teachers' colleges (the prevailing group in this type) is the motive of expansion from the normal-school to a more widely functioning status. Since the goal selected for the normal school is more often than any

---

[1] Recently renamed the North Texas Agricultural College.

[7]

other the full-fledged teachers' college, to provide the academic work for junior-college curricula is looked upon as a stepping-stone to the status sought, and consequently as at least temporarily desirable.

C. PRIVATE JUNIOR COLLEGES

Growth and present status. Of the three types of junior colleges the private seem to have come into existence soonest and to have increased in numbers at the most rapid rate. A small number were reported to have been in existence before or at the opening of the century, but it is unlikely that they were established with anything like a consciousness of the relationship of such establishment to a junior-college movement. It may even be that in a few instances the answer to the writer's inquiry on this point was made on the erroneous assumption that what was asked for was the date of establishment of the institution, rather than of the junior-college curriculum. In other instances there must have been in operation in these early years an advanced curriculum two years in length which, at the inception of the movement proper, logically classified as a junior-college offering. In at least two instances there were institutions patterned to some extent after the German *Gymnasium*, which presumably carries the student to the end of our second college year.

The growth of this type has been so rapid through-out the period since the opening of the century that despite the rapid development of the other types they still maintain their numerical supremacy at the present time, since they now constitute fully two thirds of all units bearing this name.

Control. Approximately a hundred (which means three fourths) of the total number of private institutions were reported as operating under the auspices of some church or other religious group. A wide range of denominational frequency is represented, beginning with the Methodist Episcopal Church and including considerable numbers with Lutheran, Baptist, Catholic, Presbyterian, Latter-Day Saints, Christian, and Episcopal connections, not to mention a scattering of others. The remainder are reported by authorities in charge as being under "private" auspices. Approximately half of these are strictly private-venture schools.

Secondary-school association. Like the junior colleges in city and high-school districts, but unlike those in state institutions, most of this group are maintained in association with institutions of secondary-school grade. In some cases the two junior-college classes are known as junior and senior years, and the two high-school years immediately below as freshman and sophomore years.

The chief factor of development. Although, as with the two preceding types, the factors of development of private junior colleges have been various, the chief force has probably been the movement for standardization of higher institutions. Not being in a position, on account of inadequate teaching staff, facilities, and resources, to qualify as standard four-year colleges, many less well-established institutions have taken recourse to the junior-college status as a means of finding a recognized place in the school system. In a small proportion of instances the growth has had something akin to that of the stronger public high school, which through sheer vigor, both scholastic and financial, has tended to rise into the higher levels of education. Then, too, there is the group of weaker but aspiring secondary schools, which look upon the junior-college status as one step above the high-school level and therefore that much nearer the goal of the standard college, to which they hope to evolve during the passage of a few to several years. Lastly, there is the small group already mentioned, which were established as presumable equivalents of German *Gymnasia*. But by far the most common factor is the first one cited.

D. THE JUNIOR COLLEGE IN UNIVERSITIES

The fourth type is the one which at this writing is to be found as a lower division including the first two years in six universities of the West and Mid-West. Although bearing significant relationships to other types, it is reserved for further description in Chapter VII.

III. GEOGRAPHICAL DISTRIBUTION OF JUNIOR COLLEGES

The distribution in general. The geographical distribution of two hundred and seven junior colleges of the three types is shown in the accompanying map of the United States. Among the general impressions gained from a cursory examination of the map are (1) the widespread representation of the movement (eleven only of the forty-eight states contain no junior colleges) ; (2) the greater prevalence in the Southern, Mid-Western, and Pacific-coast states; (3) the appearance of public junior colleges primarily in the Mid-West and California; (4) the appearance of the smaller number of junior colleges as state institutions in a distribution almost fully as widely scattered; (5) the rather general distribution of private units to almost all sections of the country, but with a considerable degree of concentration in Missouri and the Southern states, a full half being in the South; and (6) a much smaller representation in New England and the middle Atlantic states than elsewhere.

IV. JUNIOR-COLLEGE ENROLLMENTS

Their size. Numbers enrolled in junior colleges in 1921–1922 ranged widely, from as few as six or seven students to well over a thousand. The middle case for public institutions (when they are arranged in the

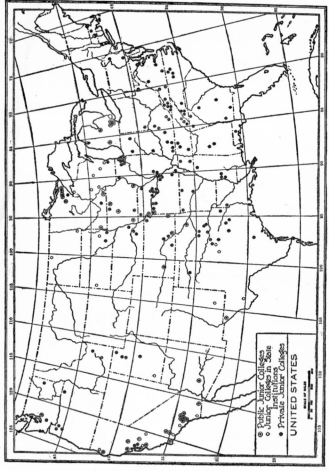

FIG. 2. Map showing distribution of junior colleges by types

order of size from least to greatest) was 59; for state institutions, 78; for private units, 44. The ranges in enrollments of the middle 50 per cent when thus arranged are, respectively, 39 to 151, 28 to 195, and 28 to 72. These figures show that private junior colleges run somewhat smaller than do the other types.

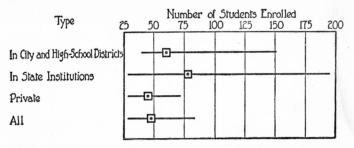

Fig. 3. Median enrollments, and range of enrollments of the middle 50 per cent, of each type and of all types of junior colleges. (The length of line represents the range of the middle 50 per cent; the square locates the median)

Total enrollments. The full count of junior-college registration in 1921–1922 for all units of the three types was, respectively, over 5000, somewhat more than 3500, and something short of 8000. When these figures are added they mount to a grand total of more than 16,000 students, or, roughly, the equivalent of the enrollment in two large state universities—no inconsiderable number. The enrollment during 1922–1923 was in all likelihood well up toward 20,000.

V. Coeducation and Segregation in Junior Colleges

A final detail in this preliminary description of the status of the junior-college movement concerns the distribution of the several types as to men's, women's, and coeducational institutions. Public and state units are seldom if ever segregated institutions, whereas in almost three fifths of the cases private junior colleges are not coeducational. Of the segregated units approximately three fourths are for women and the remaining fourth for men.

VI. The Movement Merits Consideration

In the brief span of approximately two decades an educational institution practically unknown at the opening of the century has multiplied to such an extent that at the close of the period the total number of its representatives is well in excess of two hundred. Exclusive of the units to be found in universities, these junior colleges group roughly under three widely differing types: public junior colleges, those in state institutions, and schools on private foundations. Within each group there are variations. These junior colleges are to be found in one or more of their three forms in more than three fourths of the states and in all sections of the country. They range in enrollment from a mere handful of students to more than a thousand, and the grand total of registration in them is already far in excess of that of two large state universities. There can be no doubt that a movement which develops through these variations and to such proportions during such a brief period of time is deserving of more scrutiny than it has had, both for the purpose of evaluating it and, in the event of its being found a desirable addition to the educational system, for marking out appropriate lines of its future development.

The first step toward this evaluation, taken in the next chapter, is to ascertain the nature of the expectations of the movement by its friends—the current conceptions of the special purposes of the junior college.

II

CURRENT CONCEPTIONS OF THE SPECIAL PURPOSES OF THE JUNIOR COLLEGE

I. Canvassing for the Purposes

Many who take thought for the first time of the function of the junior college are inclined to look upon this new unit in the school system solely as a sort of isthmus connecting the mainland of elementary and secondary education with the peninsula of professional and advanced academic training. A canvass of the special purposes of this recent addition to our educational institutions shows, on the other hand, that many of its friends expect much more of it than that it shall be a mere "neck of land between two larger bodies of land." In large part these friends of the junior college look upon it as an institution with a function far more extensive than that just described, affecting much larger proportions of the population and influencing profoundly the organization of education on levels above and below.

What is presented in this chapter touching the special purposes of the junior college has been compiled from an analysis of a wide variety of materials.

[16]

Among these materials were, first, twenty-two articles and addresses published in educational periodicals or, in a few instances, as parts of volumes. Most of the statements used appeared in print within the last decade. Among those whose contributions to the literature on the junior college were used are Angell, Bolton, J. Stanley Brown, Claxton, Coursault, Harper, Hill, Judd, Lange, Vincent, and Zueblin, not to mention a number of others. The materials used may be assumed to be more or less complete statements of the writers' conceptions of the meaning of this new movement.

A second body of materials was collected from the catalogues or bulletins issued by the junior colleges now in operation, in so far as these were supplied to the writer upon request directed to the head of each school reported by the United States Bureau of Education[1] as maintaining a junior college. For the most part these catalogues were issued for the school year 1920–1921, but in a few instances bulletins published a year or two earlier were used. The total number of institutions represented is fifty-six, twenty-three being public and thirty-three private. Seven of these here classified as public institutions are among those considered as state institutions in the foregoing chapter, four of them being in normal schools. The remainder are junior colleges maintained in connection

[1] *Bureau of Education Bulletin No. 33* (1920), pp. 95–96.

with city, union-district, township, or county high schools. Of the private junior colleges seventeen are in Southern states and sixteen in other states.

The term "special purposes" as here used nowhere appears in the materials entering into the compilation. What have been so classified are what the articles and bulletins designate as the "advantages of," "opportunities of," "values of," "arguments for," etc. the junior college. As may be seen from the following explanation, such statements, indicating as they do the aspirations entertained for the junior college by its friends, are readily transmutable into "special purposes."

Twenty-one more or less distinct purposes were found during the canvass. The original distribution contained almost fifty, but a careful consideration of meanings reduced the number more than half. These figures alone indicate a wide variety of functions expected to be performed by the junior college, an indication which is emphasized by a cursory examination of the purposes themselves or of the groups under which they may be classified.

Before proceeding to the elucidation of each special purpose, mention should be made of some difficulties met with in the attempts at classification. In studies of this sort meanings shade into one another almost imperceptibly; one cannot be certain that violence has not sometimes been done by placing a particular statement under some particular category, thus to some extent misrepresenting the meaning intended by the author. It is also at times impossible to take account of all interrelationships of purposes expressed or implied. Such minor difficulties, however, cannot appreciably affect the general conclusions of this study of special purposes, since the larger meanings stand out unequivocally.

II. The Purposes Found

Group I. Purposes affecting especially the two years under consideration. The first function to come up for mention, *offering two years of work acceptable to colleges and universities,* is the one most commonly put forward in the catalogues, but not in the remaining literature. This is the purpose which looks to the interests of students planning to go on to the higher levels of training, the isthmian function already referred to. From the emphasis we may anticipate that this function will be more nearly certain of performance than any of those following it in the list.

The next two purposes (2 and 3) are among those which would make it possible for the junior college to serve the interests of those who are "not going on." The former urges for such students *the provision of opportunities for "rounding out their general education,"* opportunities which are not given if the work offered is only that regarded as preliminary to some form of advanced training. Those who have been interpreted as subscribing to this purpose are inclined to assume that for the student who is not going on education would be left at loose ends if he concluded his training with work suited to the first purpose. It is worth noting that the college catalogues do not posit this purpose as frequently as does the literature.

The third purpose refers to *preparation for occupations, the final training for which would be given during junior-college years*. If occupations for which the final training can be completed during what are commonly accepted as secondary-school years are classified as *trades*, and if those for which such training can be completed only with four or more years of work beyond the high school are classified as *professions*, what is advocated here is training for *semiprofessions*. Whenever the fields in which such training is to fall are named by the first two groups, they are agriculture, industry, home economics, and commerce. Teaching is the sole occupation named in the catalogues of private junior colleges. The usual statements in these catalogues, which come from private junior colleges in Missouri and the Southern states, are to the effect that the state departments grant certificates to teach upon the completion of some or all of the work of the two years if the candidate includes courses in education.

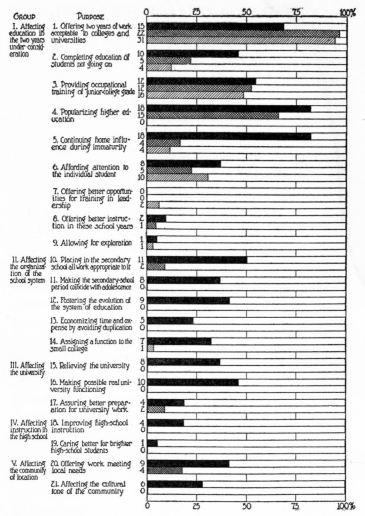

GROUP	PURPOSE		

GROUP

I. Affecting education in the two years under consideration

II. Affecting the organization of the school system

III. Affecting the university

IV. Affecting instruction in the high school

V. Affecting the community of location

PURPOSE

1. Offering two years of work acceptable to colleges and universities · 15 / 22 / 31

2. Completing education of students not going on · 10 / 5 / 4

3. Providing occupational training of junior-college grade · 12 / 12 / 16

4. Popularizing higher education · 18 / 15 / 0

5. Continuing home influence during immaturity · 18 / 4 / 4

6. Affording attention to the individual student · 8 / 5 / 10

7. Offering better opportunities for training in leadership · 0 / 0 / 2

8. Offering better instruction in these school years · 2 / 2 / 1

9. Allowing for exploration · 1 / 1

10. Placing in the secondary school all work appropriate to it · 11 / 2

11. Making the secondary-school period coincide with adolescence · 8 / 0

12. Fostering the evolution of the system of education · 9 / 0

13. Economizing time and expense by avoiding duplication · 5 / 0

14. Assigning a function to the small college · 7 / 1

15. Relieving the university · 8 / 0

16. Making possible real university functioning · 10 / 0

17. Assuring better preparation for university work · 4 / 2

18. Improving high-school instruction · 4 / 0

19. Caring better for brighter high-school students · 1 / 0

20. Offering work meeting local needs · 9 / 4

21. Affecting the cultural tone of the community · 6 / 0

FIG. 4. Special purposes of the junior college. (Black, per cent in statements in educational literature ; cross-hatching, in public junior-college catalogues ; single-hatching, in private junior-college catalogues)

Under a fourth purpose, *popularizing higher education*, have been classified statements bearing on the lowering of the cost of education on this level or bringing it nearer the home of the student. These have been generalized in this way because cost and proximity are to be regarded as factors very influential in determining the proportions of the population who will avail themselves of higher educational opportunities. It is significant to note that although this function is recognized in large proportions of the literature and of the catalogues of public junior colleges, it is left unmentioned in the catalogues of private institutions. It is not difficult to see vital relationships between this purpose and the second and third, especially in view of the greater range of interests and mentality which must come to be represented in the larger proportion of the population that will be enrolled in these years of higher education if the junior-college plan is at all commonly introduced.

Continuing home influences during immaturity (purpose 5) is proposed by a large proportion of those making the statements in educational literature, but by a much smaller proportion of the catalogues. Whenever this purpose is put forward in catalogues of private junior colleges, it refers to influences which are *like* those of the home, rather than being those of the home itself. Some of the statements specifically take cognizance of the "critical period" represented by these years in the student's life, a period especially dangerous if he attends the larger universities, where the fostering agencies are said not to be so well organized and administered as in the smaller institutions. Closely associated with this purpose and, indeed, at times scarcely to be distinguished from it are those grouped under the sixth purpose, which emphasize what may be termed the *social control of the individual in small groups*. The other aspect of attention to the individual student—the predominant one—concerns *individual attention during instruction* owing to the smaller classes. Frequently mentioned is the fact that such attention cannot be afforded in the larger schools. The next purpose (7), *offering better opportunities for training in leadership*, proposed in a few catalogues, seems to be put forward by those who feel that the small college, with its smaller enrollment than the large university, gives to all students better opportunities for experiences which constitute "laboratory work" in leadership.

The last two purposes in Group I, *offering better instruction in these school years* and *allowing for exploration*, are not often named either in the literature or in the catalogues. The acceptance of the former as a special purpose is justified by those who propose it, on the ground of their belief that the best teachers of the secondary school are assigned to junior-college work, whereas the teachers of less experience and lower ranks often give instruction to freshmen and sophomores in colleges and universities.

Group II. Purposes affecting the organization of the school system. From this point in the list the purposes are not commonly recognized in the junior-college catalogues; they are put forward almost exclusively by those expressing themselves through the literature canvassed. It is to be expected that those who contributed to the literature would attempt more nearly complete statements of the functions of the new unit than would those who prepared the catalogues.

The next four purposes (10–13), although having something in common, are sufficiently distinct to justify their being separately listed. They all point toward the reorganization of the school system by urging the upward extension of the secondary school. The first of these would accomplish this, its adherents maintain, by *placing in the secondary school all work of secondary-school grade.* Those who call attention to this advantage mention the fact that the high school in its upper years and the first two years of college or university have much of their curricula in common. Courses in mathematics and in the foreign languages are used as cases in point. Those who propose the second purpose of this group (11) complain that our four-year high school covers only a portion of the full period of adolescence, and recommend that in order to adapt the organization to the periods of change in the nature of youth the secondary school must begin earlier and, at the other end, must include two additional school years. The third (12) stresses the historical fact that our public-school system has shown a consistent tendency to develop by extension at the top, and that the next "logical" step in its evolution is the addition of the freshman and sophomore years of college. This purpose will be seen to have much in common with the fourth in Group I. The next purpose in Group II, *economizing time and expense by avoiding duplication* (13), is not unlike the first purpose in this group (10), but it emphasizes more especially the avoidance of waste to be achieved through the changes made.

The last purpose (14) in the group calls attention to the service performed for the smaller and weaker colleges by *making a place for them in our system of education.* The statements included here speak of the impracticability of the aspirations of many of these small colleges to become high-class four-year institutions, and stress the appropriateness of their becoming strong junior colleges in a system of which this two-year unit is an organic part.

Group III. Purposes affecting the university. The next two purposes, *relieving the university* (15) and *making possible real university functioning* (16), are opposite aspects of the same situation. Statements classified under the former argue that the organization of the junior college will remove many or all underclassmen from the university and will free the latter to a large extent from the obligation of carrying forward extension work on the freshman and sophomore level; whereas statements classified under the latter contend that being thus freed from work on the lower level, the university will be in a position to function as a university—that is, it may devote itself exclusively to work on the higher level. This release will react favorably upon the character of instruction and will tend to encourage research, one of the functions of a university which suffers from the overload of freshman and sophomore work. Those who propose the next purpose (17) look to see an *improvement in the preparation of students for university work*, but they fail to mention the grounds for their hopes. These may be implicit in purposes 6, 8, and 9, as already presented.

Group IV. Purposes affecting instruction in the high school. The expectation that the establishment of the junior college will *affect high-school instruction favorably* (18) rests, in the minds of those who propose it, on the general fact that a higher unit of the educational system always exercises an influence on the standards of a lower unit where the two institutions are closely associated. The single recognition of the next purpose (19) refers to the better opportunity of *serving the interest of the more capable student* who arrives at his fourth high-school year with less than four units of credit to earn for graduation. With junior-college work offered in the high school, he may progress without loss of time.

Group V. Purposes affecting the local community. The last purpose but one (20) appears to be one of the not uncommon expectations, namely, that the junior college will be able to *offer courses adapted to local needs*, the particular needs whenever mentioned being vocational or social; and the last (21) anticipates that the establishment of a junior college will *affect the level of cultural interests of the local community* to a degree now manifest in many college towns throughout the country.

III. Purposes at Once Requiring Scrutiny and Supplying Criteria

As already intimated, this survey of the current conceptions of the special purposes of the junior college reveals the fact that although the first function in the minds of many advocates is the offering of two years of work acceptable to higher institutions, the ambitions entertained for it far exceed this original service. These comprehend types of training better suited to the needs of the increasing proportion of the population which the junior college is expected to attract, especially general and occupational types of training adapted to the needs of students who will not continue their education beyond the work of these two years. All these types of training are to be provided under conditions which will foster, better than can prevalent conditions, the intellectual and social welfare of individual students. Advocates of the junior college anticipate that its general introduction will affect profoundly, but in constructive ways, the organization and functioning of our system of education: it will permit the consummation of the secondary school, will assure the small college an unquestionable function in the educational system, and will encourage the university to differentiate its activities from those of the lower schools, much of whose work it is now called upon to do. They also look for the junior college, through courses offered and through its cultural influences, to be highly serviceable to the local community. Other hopes are entertained for the junior college, but these are the predominant ones.

These aspirations outline an ambitious program for this new unit—so ambitious, indeed, that the special purposes as catalogued cannot be accepted forthwith. However, they furnish a cross section of the educational consciousness which has given rise to the movement, and at the same time they supply a set of tentative criteria, the validity of which is scrutinized in subsequent portions of this volume.

III

THE JUNIOR COLLEGE IN ITS ISTHMIAN
FUNCTION—THE OFFERING

I. The Plan of Inquiry

The chapter immediately preceding shows that the claim put forward on which there is the nearest approach to full agreement among the three groups of sources used is *offering two years of work acceptable to colleges and universities.* The meaning of this claim has already been made clear as applying to students who plan to continue their education into the advanced academic or professional courses beyond the junior-college level. It is the aim of the two chapters next following to examine into the feasibility of performing in junior colleges this isthmian function. The process of scrutiny will be made in the following manner: (1) testing out the assumption as far as it concerns two years of "college work" in the sense of the first two years of work in the usual college of letters and science; (2) inquiring into the feasibility of giving effectively in junior colleges the first two years of work in training toward the professions, both in pre-professional curricula (for example, pre-legal and pre-medical) and in the freshman and sophomore years of professional curricula open to the student upon completion of his high-school work (for example, agriculture or engineering); (3) comparing instructors and instruction in junior colleges with those on the same level in other higher institutions; and (4) reporting on the extent to which colleges are now willing to accept the product of this new unit in the educational system. The third and fourth portions, more especially the former, have been included because acceptability to other higher institutions cannot be decided on the basis solely of whether the work is offered or even actually going forward, but is to be evaluated also by considering who gives it and how effectively it is done.

II. THE JUNIOR COLLEGE AND THE FIRST TWO YEARS OF COLLEGE WORK

The junior-college offering. A careful analysis of the work offered in twenty-three public and thirty-five private junior colleges, as shown in their catalogues, gives an average total number of 255.0 semester-hours of work for the former group, 192.0 for the latter, and 214.6 for all the fifty-eight institutions represented. When from the group classified here as public are removed seven operating on state foundations, the average amount of work offered drops to 219 semester-hours, whereas removing from the private group three institutions at that time listing work beyond the second college year brings its average down to 160.4.

A comparison of the amounts of work offered by the two groups in each of the several fields discovers interesting similarities and differences. In English, for example, the average extent of the offering does not differ widely, being 17.7 and 16.0 semester-hours respectively. The same may be said for public speaking, modern foreign languages, psychology, and physical education. However, in offerings in mathematics, science, the social subjects, music, agriculture, commerce, engineering and industrial, and "other occupational" the public institutions exceed the private, whereas in ancient languages, Bible and religion, education, and home economics the latter outdo the former.

The percentage distribution for all units represented in the analysis shows the largest proportion of the offering devoted to modern foreign language. Next in order follow science, the social subjects, English, ancient languages, and mathematics. Fields receiving little emphasis when measured in this way are public speaking, Bible and religion, philosophy, psychology, physical education, music, art, agriculture, and "other occupational" subjects. Lines of work whose extent of recognition lies between that for these two extremes are commerce, home economics, engineering and industrial courses, and education.

When the percentages for both ancient and modern foreign languages are added, they total more than a fourth of the total offering. When a similar addition is made for all occupational or near-occupational subjects, such as agriculture, commerce, education, engineering and industrial, etc., they include less than a fourth of the total offering.

The listed offerings and the work going forward. It is to be expected that the amount of work and the number of courses reported in the catalogues are sometimes in excess of what is actually being taught. Those who have had contact with schools during their early aspirational stages will know that classes in some courses do not always materialize.

Visits to junior colleges included a number of institutions represented in the analysis just summarized, and therefore it was possible to make a comparison of the work in progress during the school year and that listed in the catalogue, and thereby estimate the extent to which the former falls below the latter.

Of the junior colleges visited, the number on which the making of such a check was possible included nine public and five private schools—a total of fourteen. This constitutes almost a fourth of the fifty-eight junior colleges represented in the data so far presented in the current chapter, a proportion sufficiently large to be of considerable significance in passing judgment on the problem in hand.

THE OFFERING

Of the public junior colleges there were five with less work going forward during the year than was listed, two without a difference in this respect, and two with more work going forward than was listed.

TABLE I. CURRICULAR OFFERINGS DURING 1921–1922 OF TWENTY-THREE[1] PUBLIC AND THIRTY-FIVE PRIVATE JUNIOR COLLEGES

SUBJECTS AND SUBJECT-GROUPS	AVERAGE NUMBER OF SEMESTER-HOURS			AVERAGE PERCENTAGE OF TOTAL OFFERING		
	Public	Private	All	Public	Private	All
English	17.7	16.0	17.1	6.9	8.8	7.9
Public speaking	3.0	2.8	2.9	1.2	1.5	1.4
Ancient languages	12.8	19.5	16.9	5.9	10.2	7.9
Modern foreign languages .	42.1	38.6	40.0	16.5	20.1	18.6
Mathematics	19.3	13.6	15.9	7.6	7.1	7.4
Science	44.5	22.6	29.9	17.5	11.8	13.9
Social subjects	27.5	18.9	22.3	10.8	9.8	10.4
Bible and religion	0.0	3.9	2.3	0.0	2.0	1.1
Philosophy	2.4	1.9	2.1	0.9	1.0	1.0
Psychology	3.1	2.9	3.0	1.2	1.5	1.4
Physical education	2.7	2.4	2.5	1.0	1.3	1.2
Music	8.8	4.4	6.2	3.5	2.3	2.9
Art	3.1	4.9	4.2	1.2	2.6	2.0
Agriculture	5.8	1.1	3.0	2.3	0.6	1.4
Commerce	26.7	0.5	10.9	10.4	0.3	5.1
Education	5.3	9.7	7.9	2.1	5.1	3.7
Engineering and industrial .	16.6	10.7	13.1	6.5	5.6	6.1
Home economics	9.8	16.0	12.5	3.8	8.3	5.8
Other occupational	3.8	0.7	1.9	1.5	0.4	0.9
All subjects	255.0	192.0	214.6	99.9	100.3	100.1

As the total amount of work listed in all the nine catalogues was 2025 semester-hours, and the algebraic

[1] Seven of these were state institutions, four being in normal schools.

sum of corrections was 192½, it appears that the average per cent of unfavorable difference is 9.5. If this difference were found to apply to all public junior colleges, it would mean a reduction of the average of 255.0 previously reported by almost 25 semester-hours, bringing it down to 225 or 230 semester-hours. Of the private junior colleges there were three with less work going forward, one without a difference, and the other with an increase. The total amount of work listed is 985 semester-hours; the sum of the corrections is 53 semester-hours, an average of 5.4 per cent. If this difference were found to apply to all junior colleges of the private group, it would mean a reduction of the average total of 192.0 semester-hours to something more than 180 hours of work actually going forward. While reductions in both groups are appreciable, they cannot be regarded as large enough to discredit the findings of the study made.

A tabulation of the particular courses not going forward shows that the total number for both public and private institutions, not making allowance for additional courses going forward and not in published lists, is sixty-five. These are scattered throughout the entire offering and manifest little or no tendency to locate in particular fields or especially in the more advanced subjects.

It seems safe to conclude that neither the average amount of reduction nor the extent of disappearance of particular courses is large enough to warrant discrediting to any large extent the results of any subsequent conclusions involving the description of the junior-college offerings that has been given.

College offerings in freshman and sophomore years. The next step in the study of the feasibility of giving in junior colleges the first two years of college work is a comparison of the analysis of work just presented with that available during freshman and sophomore years in standard colleges of liberal arts. To arrive at some adequate description of the latter a similar analysis was made of the work in a large number of such institutions, one hundred and fourteen being of the separate college type and twenty of them colleges of liberal arts in institutions of the university type. All units included are on approved lists of some recognized standardizing agency. Except in sections where all or almost all colleges were included, as with New England and the Western states, resort was had to random selection. Both colleges and universities were selected with a view to securing lists geographically representative of the entire country.

With one exception the *amounts* of work offered in each of the subject-groups in the colleges of liberal arts exceed those in junior colleges. The difference is especially notable for the colleges in universities, but there are also appreciable differences for the separate units. The only academic subject in which the amounts are almost equivalent is mathematics. Here the offerings in public junior colleges at least compare favorably with those in the other institutions. The single exception of excess for the new unit is in the materials that have been grouped under occupational. These include agriculture, commerce, engineering and industrial, home economics, and "other occupational."

The averages of total numbers of semester-hours of work offered are in harmony with expectations warranted by data on individual subjects or subject-groups. The total college offerings in the first two years exceed those in all junior colleges by fully 50 per cent. The excess over public junior colleges is somewhat smaller. The offerings in these years in university colleges of liberal arts are more than double those in public junior colleges. When it is recalled that the averages for junior colleges are to some extent reduced when subtractions are made for courses listed but not going forward, the comparison becomes even more unfavorable. Were there no qualifying considerations such as are afforded below, the results of the comparison so far made would operate as a serious argument against the feasibility of the junior-college plan.

Percentage distributions of the work offered show a much greater approximation to equivalence among the types of institutions being compared. Subject-groups in which the colleges and universities have

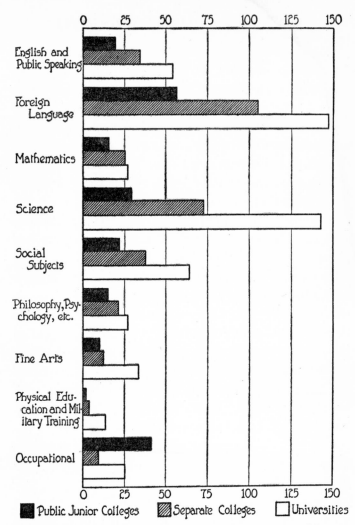

FIG. 5. Average number of semester-hours offered in each subject or subject-group in public junior colleges and in the first two years of separate colleges and colleges of liberal arts in universities

significant excesses are foreign language and science, the separate colleges leading in the former and the universities in the latter. Private institutions tend to bring up the average for junior colleges in the former group and tend to pull it down in the latter. Many private institutions are without equipment for college courses in science other than general inorganic chemistry; this is not as characteristic of institutions of the public type. The percentage distributions of academic subjects show that the junior colleges are making endeavors, and consistent progress, in the direction of affording curricular materials which will meet the requirements here being considered.

The proportion of occupational material in junior colleges far eclipses that in the other institutions. The smaller proportion in private than in public junior colleges would be more than made up if work in the field of education were removed from the group in which it has been included and introduced at this point. The explanation of this larger proportion for junior colleges is to be found in the wider service that some junior colleges are endeavoring to render than that of merely providing the first two years of work in colleges of liberal arts. For example, some public institutions are also endeavoring to give the first two years of engineering or other professional curricula, while in both groups there are occasional examples of efforts in the direction of affording some occupational training for

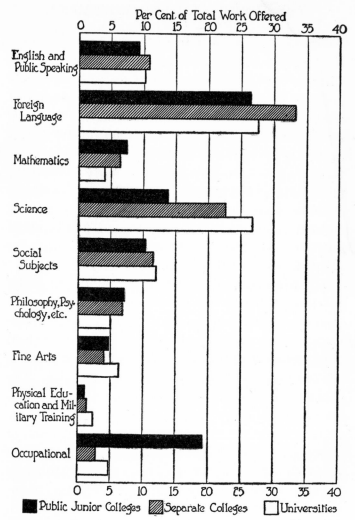

FIG. 6. Percentages of the offerings in each subject and subject-group in the total offering in public junior colleges and in the first two years of separate colleges and colleges of liberal arts in universities

those who do not plan to continue their education beyond the junior-college level.

A study of the range of work actually taken by the students. Since it may be thought that a canvass of offerings may hardly be looked upon as an adequate test of whether junior colleges do or can qualify on the aspiration of providing the first two years of college work, a study has been made (a summary of the findings of which is here reported) of the work actually taken by a group of two hundred randomly selected students during their first two years of attendance upon a college of liberal arts, in this instance the College of Science, Literature, and the Arts, of the University of Minnesota. The aim of the special inquiry in this instance was to secure some measure of the degree to which all the work actually taken by these students is or is not spread evenly over the entire range of work included in their curricula.

The method of this special inquiry will require a word of explanation through illustrative application, for which the subject of mathematics is used. A total of five hundred and forty quarter-hours of work in this field[1] were taken by the two hundred students referred to. The courses represented included only higher algebra (five credits), solid geometry (five credits), college algebra (five credits), trigonometry

---

[1] The computation does not include the courses in commercial algebra and the mathematics of investment, which were introduced under occupational.

(five credits), analytic geometry (five credits), and calculus (five credits). These courses may be seen to represent a total range of 30 credit-hours. Three of them (namely, solid geometry, analytic geometry, and calculus) were taken by 2 per cent (four students) or less of the two hundred students. As these represent a range of fifteen credits, they constitute 50 per cent of the total range of work in this field. As these three courses were taken by one, three, and one, respectively, of the two hundred students, the total amount of credit covered by them is 25 quarter-hours. This amount is 4.6 per cent of the total of 540 hours taken in mathematics. The three remaining courses— higher algebra, college algebra, and trigonometry— registered 37, 19, and 47, respectively, of these students, involving 515 credit-hours, or 95.4 per cent of all the work taken in mathematics. There is thus a marked contrast between the proportion of range of work in mathematics represented in the courses taken by 2 per cent or less of the students and the proportion of the total credit covered by these courses when weighted by the number of students by whom they are taken. A half of the credit range of the courses accounts for less than a twentieth of the total credit involved.

Data for the remaining subjects and subject-groups disclose similar, although not always equivalent, contrasts. The only subject-groups that show larger proportions of total credit for courses infrequently taken are foreign language, fine arts, and occupational, for which the percentages are, respectively, 10.6, 15.5, and 17.2. The difference in the cases of fine arts and occupational is primarily attributable to the fact that it is rare for a large number of students to take *any single* course in these lines.

When courses pursued by 5 per cent or less are included, the proportions of the total credit covered increase notably only in the three subject-groups, two of these being music and the occupational. Conclusions drawn for the problem in hand would have additional corroboration from the contrasts if space could be spared here for the data resulting from such computations.

The figures for all subjects show that in the total of $17,495\frac{1}{2}$ quarter-hours of work taken by the two hundred students, a *range* of $1070\frac{1}{2}$ hours of courses is represented. For those accustomed to the semester plan it may be more meaningful to say that a total range of 713.7 semester-hours of different courses is represented. This amount exceeds the range of offering in the average college by almost 400 hours and that of the average university by somewhat less than 200 hours. However, of this total range $540\frac{1}{2}$ quarter-hours, or slightly more than 50 per cent, are taken by 2 per cent or less of the two hundred students, and $679\frac{1}{2}$ quarter-hours, or 63.5 per cent, by 5 per cent or

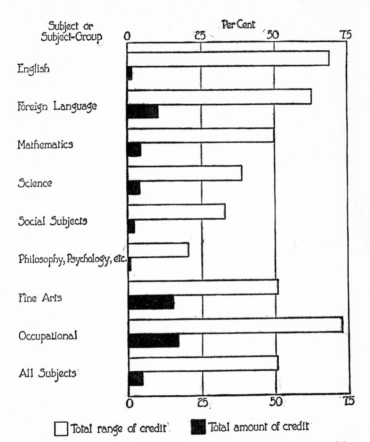

Subject or Subject-Group

	Per Cent
	0 25 50 75

English

Foreign Language

Mathematics

Science

Social Subjects

Philosophy, Psychology, etc.

Fine Arts

Occupational

All Subjects

0   25   50   75

☐ Total range of credit   ■ Total amount of credit

Fig. 7. Percentages (1) of the total range of credit represented by courses taken by 2 per cent or less of two hundred students, and (2) of the total amount of credit in these courses

less. In terms of semester-hours this means that if the courses represented were removed from the offering in this institution, the total represented in remaining courses taken by larger numbers of students would be reduced to 353.4 and 260.7 hours respectively. Thus only 4.8 per cent and 12.0 per cent, respectively, of the total credit would be involved. Therefore it does not seem to be beyond the bounds of reasonable expectation to assume that the total offering of regular college work in junior colleges can be kept to something like 250 semester-hours without sacrificing the interests of those who contemplate completion of a four-year liberal-arts curriculum. The lower total of semester-hours just referred to, 260.7, is not far in excess of the average for public junior colleges as previously indicated, even when this is reduced by 10 per cent for courses not going forward. In view of the recency of the junior-college movement and the modest enrollment of many units, with relatively small proportions in the second year, and in view of the fact that the offerings to freshmen and sophomores in standard colleges, as analyzed for this study, are padded by courses seldom if ever taken by underclassmen, the writer feels secure in concluding that the stronger junior colleges—if not already prepared to do so—will shortly be able, as far as the curriculum is concerned, to realize their ambition of offering the first two years of college work.

THE OFFERING

The appropriate offering for the purpose in question. It remains to afford this conclusion of feasibility the additional corroboration of suggesting within the scope of approximately 225 to 250 semester-hours a junior-college offering likely to meet the requirements of the situation. Since the analysis of work actually taken as here reported concerns an institution in the Middle West, the work suggested is that which would be more adaptable to the needs of the same section, although it will be seen to be adaptable, with minor modifications, to most other sections. The proposals are based on careful consideration of the offerings and prescriptions in the colleges of liberal arts spoken of in earlier portions of this chapter. The courses listed are for the most part those appearing with greatest frequency in the offerings of separate colleges, more especially institutions in the Middle West. The amounts of credit assigned are likewise determined in most instances by the typical numbers of semester-hours assigned to them in the college offerings. The list is not presented to be defended against other proposals, but as one likely to meet, for a group of students representing a legitimate range of liberal-arts needs and interests, the requirements of the function under consideration. In order to meet the requirements of many colleges and universities the usual offering in physical training should be added to the list.

English and Public Speaking	*Semester-Hours*	
Freshman rhetoric	6	
Advanced composition	4	
English literature	4	
American literature	4	
Shakespeare	6	
General public speaking	2	
Extempore speaking	2	
		28

Foreign Language		
Elementary French	8	
Second-year French (intermediate)	8	
Advanced French	6	
Survey of French literature	4	
French conversation	4	
Elementary German	8	
Second-year German (intermediate)	8	
		46

Mathematics		
Higher algebra	3	
Solid geometry	2	
Trigonometry	3	
College algebra	3	
Analytic geometry	4	
Differential and integral calculus	6	
		21

Science		
General inorganic chemistry	8	
Qualitative chemistry	4	
Quantitative chemistry	4	
Organic chemistry	8	
General botany	8	
General zoölogy	8	
Physiology	4	
Heredity, evolution, genetics	3	
Vertebrate zoölogy	6	
General physics	10	
		63

Social Subjects	Semester-Hours	
Modern Europe	6	
Medieval Europe	6	
American history	6	
English history	6	
Greek history	3	
Roman history	3	
Economic history	3	
Principles of economics	6	
American government and politics	5	
Comparative government	4	
Introduction to sociology	6	
		54
Philosophy and Psychology		
Introduction philosophy	3	
Ethics	3	
Logic	3	
General psychology	4	
		13
Total		225

The estimate of total range of credit involved in offering the courses listed is seen to be 225 semester-hours. Some may see portions of the offering which might be dispensed with in particular situations. Among these might be one of the courses in literature listed under English, the most advanced course in French, as much as from 5 to 10 semester-hours of the offerings in science, two or three courses in history, and one in the philosophy group. Such a reduction would bring the total down to something like 200 semester-hours or slightly less, but each step in curtailment might affect disadvantageously a group of students whose interests command recognition. The desirable situation implies avoiding an offering that is in essence a fully prescribed curriculum; it demands one sufficiently elastic to permit preparation for a variety of arrangements of the upper-class curriculum of the liberal-arts college.

Some may feel that the offering should include other courses found available with considerable frequency for freshmen and sophomores in standard colleges, but not listed here, and that these should be either added to those suggested or, in certain instances, substituted for some of those named. Among such courses there are, under English and public speaking, the novel, the short story, nineteenth-century poetry, and argumentation and debate; under foreign language, French or German conversation and Spanish; under science, general biology, plant physiology or morphology, elementary physics, astronomy, and geology; and in social subjects, money and banking, municipal government, etc. It would not be difficult to recommend fifty to seventy-five more semester-hours of work drawn from this supplementary list which might fit the needs of no negligible number of students contemplating continuation in colleges of liberal arts.

The offering as listed includes in foreign languages four college years of French and two of German. Most colleges add work in Latin and Spanish to this offering. Courses in the former have been omitted because relatively few students in the typical Mid-Western college are at present enrolled in classes in Latin, and because in junior colleges where it is offered classes infrequently materialize. Spanish is omitted because it is felt that work in two modern foreign languages will suffice. If Spanish is substituted for German, the extent of the offering in foreign language might need to be increased, because students now often enter college with two high-school years of Spanish. The disappearance of German from high-school programs obviates the necessity of offering more than two years of that language in the junior college. Since college freshmen in the Middle West seldom offer more than two years of French for entrance, in some situations it would be gratuitous to offer more than the three college years of that language.

III. THE JUNIOR COLLEGE AND PREPROFESSIONAL REQUIREMENTS

The problem and the procedure in studying it. The second aspect of the feasibility of giving in the junior college two years of work acceptable to colleges and universities is, like that just canvassed, one of major importance to the junior-college movement. The question here is, Can the junior college offer and give effectively the first two years of work in training toward the professions, both in preprofessional curricula (for example, pre-legal and pre-medical) and in the freshman and sophomore years of professional

[49]

curricula open to the student upon completion of his high-school work (for example, agriculture and engineering)? Unable to give this work, the friends of the junior college could hardly lay claim to be fostering a unit that will play more than a minor rôle in the educational system. It is perhaps needless to point out that, in addition to being important, the study of this aspect of the problem must be at least fully as complex and difficult as that which has just been canvassed.

With the aim of providing a basis for answering this question with something like finality, an extended study was made of such curricula in a wide variety of professional lines—in point of fact, eighteen. Most of the occupations not included are infrequently represented in higher institutions or are fairly well represented by the curricula for some other profession which has been included. A few of those included concern a relatively small proportion of any possible student body in junior colleges generally, either now or in the future.

A total of two hundred and thirty curricula are represented in the tabulations made to canvass the feasibility of providing in the junior college the offering necessary to qualify on the criterion in question. This is an average of more than twelve curricula for each of the lines represented. The numbers of curricula per professional line are not, however, equal, as they range from four to twenty-eight. The smaller numbers of curricula are to be explained usually by the relatively small numbers of institutions offering training for the occupations, but occasionally by the small proportions of catalogues used in which the curricula were reported in detail or by years. The curricula used are those of standard institutions in all sections of the country. Most of these are universities on private or public foundations; but for lines like agriculture and home economics it was necessary to draw upon larger state agricultural and mechanical colleges, some of which, in range and character of work offered, will compare favorably with some institutions known as universities.

Distinction between general and special subjects and courses. To facilitate consideration of the feasibility of giving in junior colleges the work listed, it was found desirable to divide it into two large groups which are designated as *general* and *special*, marking out, at least roughly, a distinction between the materials of general and specialized education. Under the former class have been grouped most prescribed work in English; foreign language; mathematics through calculus; most courses in the social studies, including only first courses in economics; philosophy; psychology; and all courses in "pure" science. Here have been counted also all elective portions of curricula where these may be selected from nonspecial fields. In the second class have been placed all such materials in the fields named as bore evidence of being for special groups or were clearly "applied" courses, such as "business" English, mathematics of investment, agricultural chemistry, educational psychology, etc. Here also were placed all courses in commerce in advance of the first course in economics. Far the larger proportion, however, of this class was made up of work in such special lines as pharmacy, education, agriculture, home economics, engineering, and the like.

TABLE II. AVERAGE NUMBERS OF SEMESTER-HOURS OF GENERAL AND SPECIAL WORK REQUIRED IN TWO YEARS OF PREPROFESSIONAL CURRICULA AND IN THE FIRST TWO YEARS OF PROFESSIONAL CURRICULA

PROFESSIONS	SEMESTER-HOURS	
	General	Special
1. Law	52.8	1.0
2. Medicine	60.0	0.0
3. Dentistry (two years)	64.2	0.3
4. Dentistry (one year)	30.4	0.0
5. Nursing	58.2	3.6
6. Pharmacy	32.4	31.2
7. Education	58.3	2.3
8. Commerce	47.1	12.6
9. Journalism	53.8	6.7
10. Agriculture	39.1	29.0
11. Forestry	36.4	34.0
12. Home economics	40.6	23.6
13. Civil engineering	44.1	23.5
14. Electrical engineering	45.2	23.1
15. Mechanical engineering	43.9	24.4
16. Chemical engineering	52.4	14.2
17. Chemistry	62.8	4.5
18. Mining	48.8	21.9
19. Architecture	33.3	33.8

Practically without exception what has been classed as general is comprehended by the minimum liberal-arts offering suggested for junior colleges near the close of the preceding section of the current chapter. This means that all general portions of these pre-professional requirements could be met by an offering of the sort proposed, the residual problem in meeting all the requirements of any particular preprofessional line here under consideration being that of providing in addition the special content.

All general requirements. (1) Assuming that the average total requirement, exclusive of physical and military training during the two junior-college years, is sixty semester-hours or slightly above (in some curricula in agriculture, engineering, etc. it runs as high as seventy), the study made shows that the following groups of students could meet all or essentially all of their requirements of the first two years, professional or preprofessional, in junior colleges with a general offering of the subjects and courses already specified: law, medicine, dentistry (two-year preprofessional or combination curricula), nursing (degree curricula), education, journalism, and chemistry. The requirement of the one-year pre-dental course could be fully met. (2) Approximately from two thirds to three fourths of the prescriptions in the following groups could be met: commerce, agriculture, home economics, and all engineering groups excepting chemical engineering and architecture. (3) A somewhat larger proportion could be met in chemical engineering. (4) In pharmacy, forestry, and architecture only about half of the requirements could be met. If no special work could be offered in junior colleges, students interested in the lines represented in (2), (3), and (4) as here grouped would need to transfer to the professional schools or other higher institutions at the end of the first year.

Further assurance that strong junior colleges of good size could meet the general requirements as far as here estimated is afforded by scrutiny of the present-day junior-college offerings themselves, especially those of the public and state types. This assurance is provided not only by the amounts of work given in each of the main fields, as already shown in the preceding section of this chapter, but also by the tests of particular courses in each of these fields, space for the presentation of which could not be spared in this volume.

Special requirements. From what has already been indicated the professions requiring consideration under the head of special requirements are commerce; pharmacy; agriculture; forestry; home economics; civil, electrical, mechanical, and chemical engineering; mining; and architecture.

The average amount of special work in the curricula ˎin commerce is 12.6 semester-hours, and this requirement is more frequently distributed to courses in accounting and commercial geography and less frequently to courses in money and banking, statistics, the theory of investments, and business English. There can be little question of the practicability of providing fully for the group of students who plan to continue work in university schools of commerce upon the completion of their junior-college work. Stronger public junior colleges are already giving the equivalent, in amount at least, of the necessary special courses.

The average amount of special work in curricula in pharmacy is practically half the total work the enrolled student takes during his first two years. This high average resulted from a tabulation of the first two years of three-year (two cases) and four-year (six cases) curricula. Those conversant with curricula in this field will know that in these four-year and sometimes even in the three-year programs the professional work is often placed in the first two years, and the general work for the most part in the upper years. This reversal of the usual procedure in training for the professions is owing to the desire of those contemplating entrance to this occupation to achieve their objective in a short period of two years and their unwillingness to defer entrance to occupational activity until they have completed a four-year curriculum. Some of them, however, do subsequently aspire to a degree, and for them the longer curricula have been provided. This situation is probably not what those in charge of schools of pharmacy prefer. It is thus conceivable that these authorities would be ready to accept the general training if it were taken in junior colleges before the student entered upon the more strictly special work in the curricula in pharmacy.

Moreover, schools of pharmacy now in existence seem for the present to have no difficulty in caring for all those seeking to enter this occupation, and it does not appear necessary or desirable, therefore, for the junior college (except perhaps in an occasional local situation) to endeavor in the immediate future to give the amount of special training found to be prescribed in the first two years of three-year and four-year curricula in this field. Should pharmacy evolve to the professional level (this level being determined by the requirement for entrance of at least four years of training beyond high-school graduation), as leaders in the field are disposed to believe it will, the junior college will be in a position to serve it preprofessionally just as it can now serve law and medicine. Should this genuinely professional level prove unattainable, and preparation for pharmacy remain on its present typically semiprofessional level (involving only two years of training beyond the high school), the full advent of junior-college reorganization will allocate curricula in pharmacy to the junior-college units. In the latter event the relatively small proportion which students in this line bear to all those enrolled in higher institutions will make it necessary to establish the work in at most a very few junior-college centers in any state. Perhaps even a single center will suffice. Either eventuation can be served by the junior college, as it seems probable that rapid junior-college reorganization will even hasten the clarification of issues tending to confuse the problem of training for this line of work.

The average amounts of special work in the first two years of curricula in *agriculture, forestry,* and *home economics* do not differ widely, being, respectively, 29.0, 34.0, and 23.6 semester-hours. The courses more frequently entering to make up the special content for *agriculture* during freshman and sophomore years are agricultural chemistry, field or farm crops, horticulture, soils, live stock, and dairy and poultry husbandry, although there are many departures from this list. Most of these courses are of an elementary or introductory character. Although a few junior colleges are offering work of this nature, for the most part even the public junior colleges cannot qualify at the present writing, owing to the fact that they are usually to be found in cities of good size where there is little demand for special work of this kind. The proportion of students in any cross section of prospective enrollment in all lines the country over may be shown to be considerable, and any complete plan of junior-college reorganization cannot lose sight of them.

There is no reason to believe that the work concerned cannot be given in junior-college units especially equipped and manned for it. In any state system of junior colleges the needs of this group could be conserved by establishing this special line of work in association with strong high schools serving territory with interests of a rural and agricultural character.

The situation as to *forestry* differs from that in agriculture chiefly in that the proportion of students likely to be concerned is much more nearly negligible, and that as yet no junior college introduces this work into its total offering. Since it is desirable in certain states to provide training for this type of activity, that portion specifically occupational could be offered in one or two junior-college centers contiguous to the region most needing the service. Pending complete reorganization of secondary and higher education along junior-college lines, those students who plan to enter forestry would find it necessary to transfer from the junior college at the end of the first year.

Public junior colleges would need practically to double their average offerings in *home economics* to take care adequately of the first two years of four-year curricula in this field. The offerings in private junior colleges are already almost adequate in extent and character, a situation explained by the fact that these institutions are so predominantly for women only. As junior colleges come to extend the materials of instruction for those young women who will conclude their education in the junior-college period, they will open up more work in this field and will at the same time bring completely within the realm of feasibility the giving of the first two years of curricula in home economics.

As the *engineering* group of students constitute a large proportion of any large total number of students taking work on the level of the first two college years —approximately a seventh or eighth of all—their needs must be met in any thoroughgoing reorganization involving universal institution of the junior-college plan. Although the first two years of the curriculum in chemistry can be cared for with little or no difficulty by an offering exclusively general in character, a full eighth of the lower half of the curriculum in chemical engineering is special, a third of those in civil, electrical, and mechanical engineering and in mining is special, and half of that in architecture is special. The special content of a graphic nature is descriptive geometry and a greater or less amount of mechanical, machine, or engineering drawing and design; the more common types of shop and related work are woodworking, forging, foundry, machine shop, and pattern-making; and the almost usual courses in engineering proper are surveying, mechanics, and, often, materials of construction. A comparison of these prescriptions with the junior-college offerings shows that the latter, although a little short, approximate the special requirements of all but the curricula in mining and architecture. Even though they do not fully qualify, the situation is flattering when the youth of the junior-college movement is considered. The apparent partial lacks are foundry practice in the list of shop courses, and in mechanics and materials of construction in the list of engineering courses. The facts that even these are given in some junior colleges (albeit a small number), and that many in the engineering field do not question the practicability of giving the work in strong junior-college units, give promise that under proper supervision the junior college can and will do all the work of the first two years of most engineering curricula. The exceptions most likely to present themselves are mining and architecture. As with forestry, the numbers and proportions of students concerned are not large, and there is no reason to believe that the solution of the problem of making the work available cannot be similar to that suggested in discussing forestry.

Before leaving consideration of the group of engineering professions, reference should be made to current movements to lengthen the periods of training beyond their present typical duration. As this comes to be achieved the unspecialized content at the lower end of the curricula is almost certain to be enlarged, and as this enlargement takes place the giving in junior colleges of the first two years of work will become increasingly feasible.

Summary. From the presentation just concluded it may be assumed that strong junior colleges should find no insurmountable difficulty in endeavoring to provide satisfactorily for the following professional groups:

A. By two years of work exclusively or almost exclusively general rather than special:

1. Law (pre-legal or combination curricula)
2. Medicine (pre-medical or combination curricula)
3. Dentistry (pre-dental or combination curricula)
5. Nursing (pre-nursing or combination curricula)
7. Education (pre-education or first two years of four-year or five-year curricula)
9. Journalism
17. Chemistry

B. By two years of work usually for the most part general, but also in considerable part special, usually the first two years of four-year curricula:

8. Commerce
10. Agriculture
12. Home economics
13. Civil engineering
14. Electrical engineering
15. Mechanical engineering
16. Chemical engineering.

C. By a one-year professional curriculum exclusively general, until the two-year preprofessional curriculum is fully established:

4. Dentistry (pre-dental curriculum)

D. By one year of general work applicable to professional curricula, until the place of the occupation in question either as a profession or as a semiprofession is established.

6. Pharmacy (in the case of some four-year curricula in pharmacy two years of such general work should be acceptable)

E. By one year of general work applicable to professional curricula, until the junior-college plan is thoroughly established and particular junior-college units (few in number because of the small proportion of students concerned) are specially equipped and manned to give the two full years of work, or until curricula are modified to prescribe a larger proportion of work of a general nature:

11. Forestry
18. Mining
19. Architecture

With the more general availability of opportunities of education on the junior-college level, it is almost certain that the first two years of curricula in the lines here found to contain considerable special material will move in the direction of more general content, as is already true for the older professions. In the meantime the special offerings will need to be made if the student is to remain in the junior college for two years and also complete the professional curricula in the scheduled period of years.

It is well to point out again the fact that the description here provided is in terms of the typical requirements, rather than of the variations from the typical. The fact of variation complicates for the adviser of students in the junior college the task of recommending courses to meet the requirements of a number of different higher institutions. It complicates even more the work of planning a satisfactory junior-college offering. Giving in the junior college the special content in all these professional lines will be much facilitated by a better standardization of the curricula in them. This process of standardization is itself likely to be accelerated by the advent of the junior-college plan.

IV

THE JUNIOR COLLEGE IN ITS ISTHMIAN FUNC-
TION—INSTRUCTORS AND INSTRUCTION

I. Training, Experience, Teaching-Load, and Remuneration of Instructors

Importance of the comparison. As was made clear near the opening of the foregoing chapter, in which consideration was given to the feasibility of offering in the junior college two years of work acceptable to colleges of liberal arts, there is implicit in the claim the belief that the work can be effectively done in the new unit. A few of the sources drawn upon for the current conceptions of special purposes of the junior college went even farther than merely to imply it, as may be seen in Chapter II, which shows that at least a few friends of the junior college made so bold as to assert that it would offer better instruction in these school years than is afforded in other higher institutions, the chief ground cited for the conviction being that the more seasoned high-school instructors selected for junior-college work are more effective teachers than are the younger, less experienced instructors often employed in colleges and universities.

Whatever may be the merit of this particular contention, it is clearly essential to an evaluation of the movement that as complete and unbiased an inquiry into junior-college instruction as could be made without sacrificing other vital portions should be included. No educational unit could long justify its existence without effective teaching; and if junior-college teaching shows no promise of becoming efficient, to the degree at least of the instruction afforded on this level by its predecessors in the field, there would be meager occasion to argue for the extension of the movement on other grounds.

Three chief methods were used in this portion of the investigation: first, a comparison as to training, experience, teaching-load, and remuneration of junior-college instructors with those giving instruction on the same level in colleges and universities; second, a comparison of the instruction itself by means of a large amount of classroom visitation; third, a comparison of the efficiency of junior-college graduates in their first year of work in universities and colleges subsequently attended with that of students who had completed their first two years of work in a university. The method throughout, be it noted, is one of comparison.

The highest degrees held. One measure of the extent of preparation of an instructor, albeit a rough one, is the highest degree he holds. In a comparison of junior-college teachers with college and university teachers, when those giving instruction in special subjects like home economics, art, music, and physical training are omitted from both groups, a small percentage in the former group are found to be without degrees, whereas in the college and university group there are none without such academic recognition. These exceptions among junior-college instructors are for the most part those who have had especially large amounts of preparation in fields they are teaching; for example, a small proportion of the teachers of French who are native to the language. Instructors in public junior colleges and Northern private junior colleges on the one hand, and those in colleges and universities on the other, in roughly equivalent proportions hold masters' as their highest degrees. There is, however, a striking difference between the percentages holding bachelors' and doctors' degrees. Junior colleges have practically none of the latter, the difference being almost balanced by the larger percentage of those holding only bachelors' degrees in the junior-college groups. As between public and Northern private junior colleges, the former have some extent of advantage.

A more nearly valid criterion for assisting in passing judgment on the satisfactoriness of preparation of junior-college teachers is a comparison with respect to the highest degrees held by those teachers in

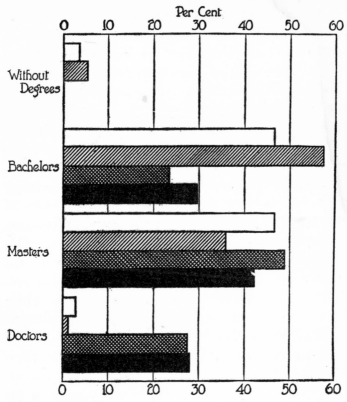

FIG. 8. Percentages of instructors without degrees and with bachelors', masters', and doctors' degrees as the highest held. (In outline, public junior colleges; single-hatching, private junior colleges; cross-hatching, separate four-year colleges; black, universities)

colleges and universities who teach work taken exclusively by students on the junior-college level (that is, by freshmen and sophomores), and who teach no

[67]

courses taken characteristically by juniors and seniors. Of the college groups so restricted 40.9 per cent held bachelors' as their highest degrees, 40.9 per cent held masters' degrees, and only 18.2 per cent held doctors' degrees. Of the university group 33.8 per cent held bachelors' degrees, 55.4 per cent masters' degrees, and 10.8 per cent doctors' degrees. These distributions are much more nearly like that for public junior colleges, although they are still somewhat superior to it. They indicate that, when measured by degrees held by this group of instructors only, the standards operative in higher institutions are less unattainable for junior colleges.

High-school and junior-college teachers compared as to highest degrees held. It would probably be granted without argument that for teachers in junior colleges the percentages holding advanced degrees are larger than for those in standard high schools. Nevertheless, to illustrate the extent of difference, some reference is here made to a study recently completed by Hutson,[1] of the training of a large number of teachers in the high schools of Minnesota, a state which has for many years maintained relatively high standards of preparation for high-school teachers. This study shows that in high schools with thirty or more

[1] P. W. Hutson, The Training of the High-School Teachers of Minnesota. Master's thesis on file in the Graduate School of the University of Minnesota and published by the College of Education as No. 3 of the Educational Monograph Series.

teachers only 10 per cent have advanced degrees, and in high schools with eleven to twenty-nine teachers only 3.1 per cent are so equipped. It shows also, by citation from the results of an investigation made by Dean M. E. Haggerty, that almost all teachers of academic subjects in high schools of the state have been the recipients of bachelors' degrees. These facts, compared with those pertaining to teachers in junior colleges, indicate that instructors in these new institutions, as measured by degrees held, constitute a selected group, and that large proportions are well on their way from the typical level of training regarded as essential for high-school teaching to that considered desirable for instruction of collegiate rank.

Numbers of years of training received. A second measure of the total extent of preparation for teaching in the institutions represented is the total number of years of training received, including all undergraduate and graduate periods, not omitting summer sessions. The results are in harmony with the facts pertaining to the highest degrees held, in that they indicate the superiority in extent of training of instructors in colleges and universities as compared with those in junior colleges, and in that instructors in public junior colleges are again somewhat better trained than those in Northern private units.

As in the instance of the highest degrees held, a special study was made of those college and university instructors who were not giving instruction to upper-classmen, but to students on the junior-college level only. The median number of years of post-high-school training received by this group of college instructors is 5.4, approximately a year less than for the whole group of college teachers giving instruction to students in these years. The difference for university teachers is much less marked, as the median for those giving instruction to students in junior-college years only is 6.0, whereas it is 6.3 for the whole group. The smaller difference for the university group is to be accounted for largely by the fact that some with considerable graduate training are part-time instructors who are satisfied with such a status in view of the possibility of making further progress toward advanced degrees while teaching.

Special preparation for the subjects taught and number of departments in which instructors teach. The question of preparation for teaching in junior colleges is not, however, solely one of degrees or the extent in years of the period of preparation. It is also a question of special preparation in the fields in which the teacher is giving instruction. If the basis of comparison in this instance is the proportion of instructors having an undergraduate major or more in the subjects taught (and this can surely not be regarded as too high a standard of preparation), we find that in public junior colleges and Northern private junior colleges approximately three fourths of the teachers have had this amount, the remainder having had less for a part or all of their teaching work. This proportion mounts to six sevenths for instructors in four-year colleges and to practically all in universities. The proportion leaves something still to be hoped for in

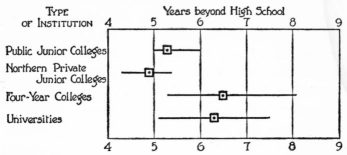

FIG. 9. Median and quartile numbers of years of training beyond the high school received by those teaching in junior colleges and in junior-college years of four-year colleges and universities. (The length of line represents the interquartile range—that is, the range of the middle 50 per cent; the square locates the median)

the training of teachers, not only in the new unit but also in the four-year colleges of liberal arts.

A phase of the problem of securing adequate preparation in subjects taught is the number of different departments in which the teacher is required to give instruction. This situation was also inquired into, the usual classification of departments in colleges being followed in the computations. Approximately three fifths of the instructors in public and Northern private junior colleges teach in one department only, something more than a fourth teach in two departments, with small percentages giving instruction in more. In four-year colleges the proportion teaching in a single department rises to three fourths, with something more than a fifth teaching in two departments. University instructors teach exclusively in one department. It appears that the junior college is not the only type of higher institution in which instructors must carry work in more than one department, standard four-year colleges also struggling with the problem of a spread of the teacher's work.

The facts so far presented touching the extent of preparation for subjects taught and the number of different departments in which teachers are required to give instruction lead naturally to the question of whether there are not variations among the subjects as to amounts of preparation; that is, whether in certain lines instructors are not characteristically better prepared than in certain others. An inquiry on this point shows that almost three fourths of the teachers of English in junior colleges have had either a graduate major or both graduate and undergraduate majors in that subject, and the proportions for French and chemistry are even greater. In three other subjects, namely, economics, political science, and sociology, the percentages are only 15.4, 10.0, and 37.5 respectively. This contrast presents a serious situation.

The difficulty seems to be one arising out of the relatively small extent of total offering in some subjects as compared with others. No one will desire to contend that these subjects in which teachers typically show meager preparation should be omitted from the offering, the curriculum to be restricted to English, foreign language, a few courses in science, and mathematics. Nor will there be advocates of having them taught by persons insufficiently prepared. The way out, if we are to have junior colleges, must lie in other directions.

Training in education. The last aspect of the training of instructors to be dealt with concerns the work they have had in the field of education. The differences here are notably in favor of the junior-college groups. The median amounts for teachers in public and Northern private junior colleges are 16.2 and 21.5 semester-hours respectively; for those in colleges and universities they are 5.0 and 1.8. This large difference is a reflection of the fact that the former have much more largely than the latter come from the ranks of high-school teachers, who must in most states and in most teacher-training institutions meet certain minimum requirements in the field.

The teaching-load. But general and special preparation of instructors is not the sole determinant of the feasibility of giving instruction in an educational institution. Consideration must be given also to conditions under which the work goes forward. One of these is the total amount of instructional activity required—the teaching-load. Where this is unduly large it is impossible for a teacher to do good work.

Computations show that the median load of instructors in public junior colleges which give work on this

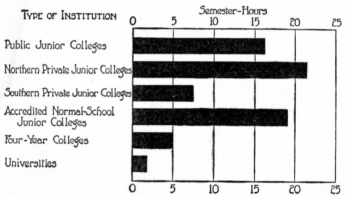

FIG. 10. Median numbers of semester-hours of work in education taken by each group of instructors

level only is 13.5 clock-hours per week, all laboratory work being weighted according to current practices. The range of the middle 50 per cent is 11.2 to 15.1 hours. The median load for teachers in Northern private junior colleges is 1.4 hours greater than in public institutions. The load for instructors in four-year colleges does not differ markedly from that for public junior colleges, whereas the load in universities is much lower than for all other groups studied.

Experience. Another factor generally conceded to be of some importance in evaluating possibilities of effective instruction on the junior-college level is the extent of the instructor's experience. Perhaps the most significant measure of experience which can be reported for the purposes of this volume is the number

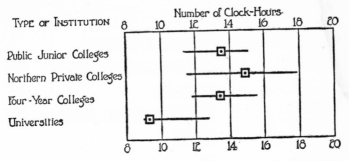

FIG. 11. Median and quartile clock-hours in the teaching-load of instructors in junior colleges, four-year colleges, and universities. (The length of line represents the interquartile range—that is, the range of the middle 50 per cent; the square locates the median)

of years in high schools, junior colleges, colleges, and universities only, excluding experience in rural or elementary institutions, and in other types which must have less meaning for teaching on the junior-college level. By this measure the teachers in public junior colleges take the superior position (with a median of 9.1 years), and this is because a larger proportion of them have had extended experience in high-school teaching before entering upon junior-college work. They are closely followed by instructors in four-year colleges (8.9 years). The lowest amount is that for teachers in universities (4.2 years), although it does not drop far below that for private junior colleges (5.0 years). It appears that a full half of the university group have had 4.2 or more years of related experience, which is far from saying that the majority of those who give instruction to underclassmen in universities are "inexperienced."

If experience in present and in related positions counts for anything in effectiveness of classroom procedure, we are justified in anticipating that in this respect teachers in public junior colleges will at least not fall below those in other higher institutions.

Remuneration. Last in this canvass of factors conditioning the effectiveness of instruction in the several types of institution represented comes the item of salaries received. The significant relationship here is, of course, that if junior-college salaries cannot compare favorably with those paid in colleges and universities, the new unit will not be able to secure instructors as well equipped in matters of training and satisfactory experience as are those employed in the older types of institution.

The tendency is for public junior colleges to pay better salaries than do private units, even after proper allowances are made for board and room, if these are provided as a part of the remuneration. Salaries in the former are appreciably but not markedly less than in four-year colleges and compare favorably with those of instructors teaching courses to under-classmen in universities, except as concerns the upper fourth of the salary distribution in these. The exceptions rise

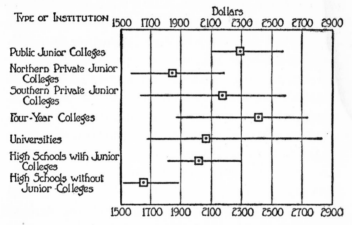

FIG. 12. Median and quartile annual salaries of instructors in junior colleges, four-year colleges, universities, high schools in districts maintaining junior colleges, and high schools in districts not maintaining junior colleges. (Length of line represents the interquartile range— the range of the middle 50 per cent; the square locates the median)

out of the fact that some men of high rank in universities have teaching responsibility for courses taken by freshmen and sophomores, with instances of salaries ranging up to $5000 and $6000.

A comparison of the figures for instructors in public junior colleges with those in high schools is likewise

[77]

illuminating. It shows that there is some tendency to difference between high-school and junior-college instructors in the same districts—a median difference of something like $250. High schools in cities of the same size and general region in which junior colleges are not maintained pay salaries considerably lower than do those with junior colleges, which leads to at least one conclusion of significance—that junior-college work is as a rule not introduced until a district has already taken care in a relatively satisfactory way of work on the lower level. It is worth noting that salaries in Northern private junior colleges range between those in high schools in districts maintaining junior colleges and those in high schools in districts not maintaining them.

The general conclusion from these facts as they concern public junior colleges is that salaries in them do not compare unfavorably with salaries in other higher institutions. It should not be impossible to secure at the figures cited some teachers who will do very well the work of junior-college instruction. On the other hand, it is desirable to raise the general level further to some extent: first, because for some years to come it will still be regarded as more honorific to be a member of a staff of a four-year college or a university, and, secondly, because the junior college does not afford, as does the university, the opportunity for further graduate study.

Summary and implications on training, experience, remuneration, etc. The trend of the facts presented is such as to afford assurance of the ultimate efficacy of instructional work in the junior college. In the matter of degrees held and duration of periods of training, to be sure, the colleges and universities lead the junior colleges at a considerable distance, but from the standpoint of the brief history of the movement the progress of the new unit is to be regarded as commendable. With respect to the special preparation of instructors for subjects taught, the junior colleges also make a fair showing, but they lag somewhat behind their predecessors in the collegiate field, the inadequacy lying for the most part in subjects of which the students take lesser amounts during their first two years of college work. Commendation for progress, however, should hardly be interpreted as signifying satisfaction with the status quo, and there should be continued insistence on an approach to and attainment of standards as these are seen to be operative in colleges and universities.

In training in the field of education, in experience, in teaching-load, and in salaries, instructors in junior colleges compare somewhat more favorably with those in other higher institutions than they do in the foregoing items. In training in the field of education the junior-college instructor notably surpasses the instructor in the college and university, and in experience he surpasses him appreciably. After all apologies are made for the varying quality of both, there remains an expectation that observation of much classroom work in both types of unit would demonstrate a somewhat superior instructional procedure for the junior college. The teaching-load is not essentially different in public junior colleges from what it is in four-year colleges, but it is somewhat larger than in universities. While remuneration is not as large for junior-college teachers, the present disparity is not discouraging. It will take no extraordinary elevation of salaries of the middle group as shown to assure something like successful competition with colleges and universities for instructors.

It must be admitted, as the reader has perhaps discerned, that the favorable light in which junior colleges are placed in the comparisons envelops the public institutions more than the private institutions. It must in all fairness be emphatically stated, however, that this is far from saying that all public junior colleges are superior in these respects to all private junior colleges. Some of the latter are clearly superior to certain of the former in most of the items on which facts have been presented. The conclusion to be drawn is that the trend of superiority is with the public unit.

This section should not be brought to a close without reference to certain implications of the facts presented. The first two of these concern the means of achieving further progress toward securing teachers with better preparation in some of the fields represented in an adequate junior-college offering. Both recommendations may well be used in identical instances. One of these recommendations is to encourage the establishment of only sizable junior-college units. Establishment of institutions with small enrollments either must obstruct the offering of many subjects essential to a desirable curriculum or else require their presentation by teachers inadequately prepared in them. Larger attendance will go far to remove both horns of this dilemma.

The second recommendation is that accrediting agencies should not merely acquiesce in but actually encourage the assignment of instructors to work on both junior-college and high-school levels. It is certainly preferable to require teaching in a single department in various grades, including the last two high-school and the freshman and sophomore college years, rather than to require a spread of the teaching-load to departments for which an instructor has had insufficient preparation. The argument of contamination of the instructor by contact with high-school standards of work is little more than bogeyism, and seems to ignore entirely the analogous contamination which the credulous might be induced to believe is experienced when one who teaches senior college classes gives instruction also to college freshmen and sophomores. The writer's observation of work done by those who teach on both levels leads him to believe that it can be done, and in many instances is now being done, without violation of "college standards," and that it often effects an elevation in the standards of high-school work—a value worth bearing in mind.

Above and beyond this advantage of fostering adequate preparation for a specialty by encouraging the teaching of a subject on both high-school and junior-college levels lies one suggested by the more extended training in educational subjects of teachers in junior colleges. Many of these—most of them, in fact—are also teaching courses in the high school and are therefore meeting the requirements of high-school certification in accredited schools, which now almost universally, in regions where public junior colleges are present, include training in the professional field referred to. Should there be an effort to apply a standard to junior colleges which would reduce the proportion of those giving instruction on both levels, there would almost certainly follow a reduction in the proportion meeting this requirement of certification and an increase of those who have had no regularly appointed opportunity for considering educational and teaching problems. In view of the degree of similarity—even of identity—of these problems in the last two years of the high school and the first two years of college, such a reduction could hardly fail to be looked upon as in the nature of a retrogression. There seems little occasion for the belief that the training of teachers for the last years of the high school should be essentially different either in this respect or in the matter of the extent of special preparation for the subjects taught. In the latter respect the later high-school years would profit by the more extended preparation essential for junior-college teaching.

II. INSTRUCTION OBSERVED

The method of comparison used. The right procedure to follow in any thoroughgoing comparison of instruction in junior colleges and on the junior-college level in standard colleges and universities would be the measurement of results by tests of achievement in each of the subjects represented. It is needless to point out that such a procedure is impossible. The impossibility arises from the fact that such tests are not yet available for use. Lacking tests of this sort in any considerable proportion of the courses to be found in junior-college years, recourse was taken to comparative judgments of instruction observable in junior colleges and in junior-college years of standard colleges and universities.

A total of one hundred and eleven class exercises were observed in junior colleges and forty-one in standard four-year colleges and universities—all but a score of them throughout the full period, and in the exceptions never less than three fourths of the full period. Thirty-nine junior colleges are represented, scattered from New England to California and from Minnesota to Louisiana. Three colleges and three universities (two state and one on a private foundation) were visited during the observation of the latter group. These six institutions are fully approved by the standardizing agencies in their respective sections, with their degrees generally acceptable at face value in all sections of the United States. On the other hand, several of the junior colleges were not accredited institutions, a fact which makes the comparison to follow in some degree unfair to the latter group of institutions. No effort was made in visits either to junior colleges or to other higher institutions to observe a selected group of teachers, the aim being to secure a random representation of junior-college instruction and of instruction on the same level in colleges and universities. The same person made all the observations here concerned.

The judgments of teachers and teaching were arrived at by the use of a modification of a method and score-card proposed by Rugg and described in the

Elementary School Journal.[1] This scale requires passing judgment on a basis strictly *comparative, a scale of teachers or class exercises* being made for each category under consideration, and each teacher observed being rated by comparison with the scale for each category. Although the judgments made covered a number of different categories, only the three most significant for present purposes will be reported upon; namely, *skill in teaching, scholarship of the instructor* as manifested during the class exercise, and the *level of class performance.*

Comparison of skill in teaching in junior colleges and in colleges and universities. The ranks assigned to the observed class exercises of colleges and universities on *skill in teaching* tend to be somewhat lower than for teachers in the junior colleges, but no large proportion of the teachers were ranked below "average," which has been given the rank of 3. A conservative interpretation of the data assembled would be that *classroom procedure* in junior colleges is assuredly on at least as high a plane as is instruction of freshmen in colleges and universities. The writer carries the conviction that such a conclusion is unfair to junior colleges, as he came away from his large amount

[1] H. O. Rugg, "Self-Improvement of Teachers through Self-Rating: A New Scale for Rating Teachers' Efficiency," in *Elementary School Journal*, Vol. XX, pp. 670–684 (May, 1920).

of classroom visitation in higher institutions with a distinct impression of the superiority of the junior colleges with respect to the item in question. There are, of course, very good and very poor teachers in both groups, but there is no doubt in the writer's mind that junior-college teachers as a group are superior in technique.

Scholarship of instructors. An examination, however, of the data on the *scholarship of instructors* will make clear that the relation of superiority of the junior-college group in skill in teaching is here reversed. The college and university group is notably better both as to percentage distribution and average of ranks assigned. This superiority may be illustrated by the fact that the college and university group includes almost as many ranked as "best" as does the junior-college group, although the latter includes almost three times the total number of cases. To be exact, fourteen of forty-one instructors in the colleges and universities were ranked as "best" in scholarship, whereas but fifteen of one hundred and eleven in the junior colleges were so ranked.

Level of class performance. The distributions of ranks assigned to the class exercises on the *level of class or student performance* show a difference in favor of the junior college. While this difference is not large, it at least encourages the belief that the level of student performance in junior colleges is no lower than in classes in the same subject in other higher institutions, which leads to the conclusion that in the results obtained from students a superior skill in teaching will in some measure compensate for a partial lack in scholarship of the instructor in the subject taught.

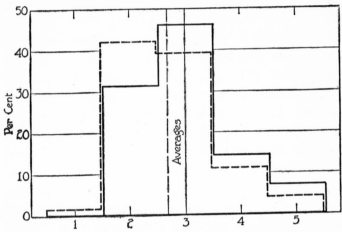

FIG. 13. Distributions of ranks assigned to junior-college and college and university teachers on skill in teaching. (Solid line, college and university; broken line, junior college)

Concurrence of the findings of this and the preceding section. The major conclusions of this comparative observation of classroom instruction in junior colleges and instruction on the same level in other higher institutions correspond closely with those drawn from the study of personnel presented in the section immediately preceding. In skill in teaching,

the group of junior-college instructors tend to be somewhat superior. This finding is in harmony with the
fact that most of them have had experience in an institution in which, because of the relative immaturity

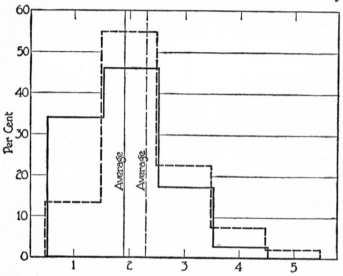

FIG. 14. Distributions of ranks assigned to scholarship of junior-
college and college and university instructors. (Solid line, college and
university; broken line, junior college)

of its students, methods of teaching tend to be matters
of greater concern than in higher institutions generally, a difference reflected in the much larger extent
of work in the special field of education reported by
them. In the matter of scholarship in the subjects
taught, on the other hand, the teachers in colleges and

universities are superior to those in junior colleges,—
a conclusion corresponding with the facts in the matter of differences in the amount of preparation, both
total and special. The findings of the two sections
agree again in the line of most desirable progress,

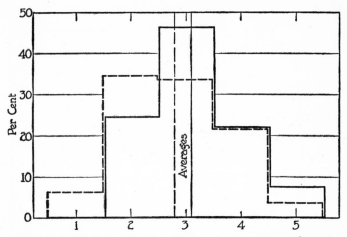

FIG. 15. Distributions of ranks assigned to level of class performance
in junior colleges and in colleges and universities. (Solid line, college
and university; broken line, junior college)

which is more extended preparation (than they now
have) of junior-college teachers for the subjects in
which they give instruction, this in turn involving
more extended periods of graduate training.

The implications also are the same as those drawn
from the materials on personnel. They are in the direction of (1) favoring large rather than small junior-

college units, so as to require larger teaching staffs, which in turn will encourage a higher degree of specialization in preparation and instruction; (2) encouraging instructional activity on both upper high-school and junior-college levels, not only for the sake of advantages like those accruing under (1) but also for the assurance that by such a distribution of instruction those who do junior-college teaching will have given some special consideration during their periods of training to problems of education and technique of teaching.

The tendency of the group of junior-college instructors toward superiority of skill in teaching as compared with those in other higher institutions should be accepted as assurance that the line of division between secondary and higher education would be more satisfactorily placed if the secondary rather than the higher institutions included the early college years. There can be little question that close association of the lower years with the upper years in colleges and universities leads to a confusion of criteria for judging teachers and teaching in freshman and sophomore years. The domination of teaching-groups by standards of research and other scholarly productivity—standards fully appropriate to upper and graduate years—must exercise a detrimental effect upon teaching-procedure in these lower years. The general establishment of junior colleges as parts of the secondary-school system would go far toward clarifying these confusing issues by achieving dissociation at a point where it is highly desirable. There seems no occasion, on the other hand, to fear that the improvement in scholarship of junior-college teachers, found in this and the foregoing section still to be desirable, while giving them ample appreciation of the importance of research and some acquaintance with its methods, cannot be achieved without developing them unduly in this respect.

A word may be addressed to those who are still disposed to wonder, after reading the last two sections, how junior-college teachers and teaching, when compared with teachers and teaching in colleges and universities, can be as satisfactory as they are, especially in view of the youth of the movement. After all, it is seldom that junior-college work is established in school districts in which work of a relatively satisfactory sort has not already been provided in the lower schools. One item of evidence to this effect is the better level of salaries of high-school teachers in communities with public junior colleges than that in communities in which junior-college work is not given. As a general thing such salaries attract to these high schools teachers who are somewhat superior to those to be found where salaries are lower. Junior-college teachers are usually chosen from the most professionally capable and ambitious of these selected high-school teachers. Such a tendency toward the sifting-out of high-school teachers could hardly fail to result in a condition as satisfactory as the one found, although it might still leave something to be desired in the way of further additions to the average extent of graduate training.

III. Success of Junior-College Graduates

The third method of comparison. Another possible method of passing judgment on the merit of instruction in junior colleges is that of comparing the scholastic success of graduates of these institutions who subsequently attend universities and colleges with that of students who have spent their first two years in these standard higher institutions and during that period have earned the right to junior standing. It may be judged that the making of such a comparison is hedged about by a great variety of difficulties, but the importance of obtaining some such measure of junior-college efficiency seemed to warrant the persistence necessary.

The names of junior-college graduates represented in this comparison and the universities and colleges to which they transferred after completion of the work in the lower unit were assembled during visits to junior colleges. Care was exercised to secure the names of *all* such graduates who went on from some

class finishing the junior-college course in each institution. Registrars of the institutions to which they
transferred were appealed to for the scholastic records
of the junior-college graduates during their first year
of subsequent attendance. Data of this sort were collected only for accredited junior colleges (that is,
accredited usually by the state university or occasionally by some other recognized standardizing agency).
The junior units in which these students did their first
two years of college work were nineteen in number and
include both public and private schools. More of the
former are represented and by a larger number of
students. The total number of junior-college graduates considered in the final comparison, ninety-five, is
divided almost equally between junior colleges of the
Middle West and California. Thirteen different universities and six colleges are represented in the data
supplied concerning the scholastic success of junior-
college graduates. With one exception the universities are all members of the Association of American
Universities. This institution and the six colleges are
all on the approved list of higher institutions prepared
by this association. The higher institutions reporting on considerable numbers of students are the universities of California, Illinois, Minnesota, Missouri,
Southern California, and Wisconsin, Stanford and
Washington universities, and Pomona College, with
smaller numbers of students registered in other insti-

tutions, such as the universities of Chicago, Iowa, Kansas, and Texas, and Columbia University.

The group of university students with which these junior-college graduates were compared were seventy-five who attended the University of Minnesota during three school years and who during the first two years earned the right, as determined by the number of credits and honor-points in their favor on the registrar's books, to unconditional admission to the senior college; that is, to full junior standing.

It may be desirable to repeat here that this standing is achieved by students who earn at least ninety credit-hours (the equivalent of sixty semester-hours) and ninety honor-points in the junior college of the College of Science, Literature, and the Arts. One honor-point is given for each hour of credit with the mark of C, two for each hour of credit with the mark of B, and three for each hour of credit with the mark of A. Marks below C do not bring honor-points. It is not to be understood that all the students in the University of Minnesota group had been admitted to senior-college standing. A small proportion may not have met the requirements as to courses and groups of subjects. All had, however, the requisite total of credits and honor-points. These seventy-five students were those of a group of more than three hundred typical students who entered the university at the same time, most of the remainder having been eliminated before the end of three school years or not having earned the credits and honor-points requisite for junior standing.

Limitations of space forbid presentation of further details of procedure, such as the method of equating and weighting marks etc., except to indicate that in order to assure comparability of the groups, only those junior-college graduates were considered who were granted sixty or more (seldom more) semester-hours of advanced standing in the institutions to which they transferred. To have introduced those who were granted less than this amount would have been unfair to the junior-college group.

The results of the comparison. While the percentages of average marks at identical points are seldom closely alike, the distributions as a whole are not sufficiently different to discredit either group in comparison with the other. If one group has a lower percentage than the other at any point, the difference tends to be compensated for at neighboring points on the same side of the median. The medians themselves are not far apart, the difference, although slight (the difference only between 79.8 and 80.6), being in favor of the junior-college graduates. Computing the average deviation (a simple measure of variability) for the two groups brings 5.6 for the junior-college graduates and 5.4 for the University of Minnesota group, which again emphasizes their similarity of success. The conclusion to be drawn seems to be that *there is no appreciable dif-*

*ference in the degrees of success in the work of the jun-
ior years of junior-college graduates and of those who
do their first two years of work in a standard university.*

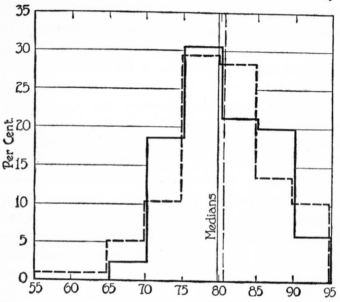

FIG. 16. Comparison of the percentage distributions of average marks
given to (1) junior-college graduates during the first year of subsequent
attendance in colleges and universities and (2) to students in the University of Minnesota during their third year of residence. (Solid line,
University of Minnesota; broken line, junior-college graduates)

Concluding comments. In view of what has been
presented in this and the foregoing chapters there is
little occasion for surprise at the approximate equality
of efficiency of the two groups of students represented

in the comparison. Certain portions of Chapter IV show the mental distributions of junior-college and state-university freshmen to be similar, arguing that the extent of selection for admission to college work is much the same in both. The curricular offerings during these years could not differ widely for the two groups of students; therefore, as far as the curriculum is a selective factor, it would operate with approximate equality on both groups. We have seen that although college and university teachers have better preparation in subject matter, this advantage is in part offset by a higher level of teaching-skill in the junior college. There is no reason to anticipate much difference in the subsequent records of junior-college graduates owing to these distinctions. All things considered, there should be occasion for surprise if conditions with such a large extent of similarity resulted in notable differences in the scholastic records during the third collegiate year.

IV. Recognition of Junior Colleges by Other Higher Institutions

Perhaps the final test of acceptability for advanced standing of work done in junior colleges is the extent of its actual acceptance by higher institutions. That a number of these are already recognizing the work done in accredited units is implicit in the material just reported in the foregoing section. Moreover, those in contact with the movement are aware that universities —at least those in the West and Middle West—are disposed to accept the work done in approved junior colleges and, even more, to look with favor on their rapid development. There has been some doubt on this score concerning separate four-year colleges, some of the authorities in charge of these institutions appearing to entertain misgivings as to the bearing of the movement upon the future of the separate college.

A simple form of inquiry blank directed to the registrars of a large number of randomly selected separate colleges brought returns which, so far as acceptance of junior-college work is concerned, should be reassuring to the friends of the new movement. Of one hundred and sixty-eight responses received (most of these from recognized, but some from unrecognized colleges), one hundred and eight (almost two thirds) report having received applications for advanced standing from junior-college students. All but four of these one hundred and eight institutions follow the practice of admitting such students to advanced standing, the two predominant types of recognition being "hour for hour" and "for courses only open to freshmen and sophomores" in the institution to which application is made. Ninety-one of the one hundred and four colleges follow these two types of recognition, forty-nine the former and forty-two the latter. A scattering of other types accounts for the remaining instances of recognition. Interestingly enough the proportions of approved and unapproved colleges reporting recognition differ hardly at all.

Thus not only does the junior-college offering give promise of meeting the needs of the situation in providing the first two years of work in colleges and universities, not only have the new units made excellent progress toward achieving an adequate instructional situation, and not only do graduates of accredited junior colleges compare favorably in scholarship with those who have done their work in a standard university, but the new unit is well on its way to a recognition by universities and colleges of work done by its students.

V

THE JUNIOR COLLEGE IN ITS DEMOCRATIZING FUNCTION

I. The Problems

Three at least of the claims often made on behalf of the junior college as reported in Chapter II have intimate meaning for its relationship to democratization of education on the level concerned. We refer to those special purposes which bear upon completing or "rounding out" the education of those who will not, cannot, or should not "go on"; to the provision of occupational training for semiprofessions; and to the popularization of higher education through lowering its cost and bringing it nearer the home of the student.

Three major problems of the whole task of democratizing education on the junior-college level will be canvassed in this chapter. (1) The first of these relates to the adaptation of work on this level to the rising tide of popular education which has brought and continues increasingly to bring into our higher institutions many students who, in contrast with those who met the requirements of the selective processes of a generation or two ago, are not as well qualified to continue their education into the levels beyond the junior-college years. This is the problem of mental democratization of higher education. (2) The second concerns the provision of lines of semiprofessional training for those who cannot or should not go on. Properly to democratize education for those who do not continue, we must, if this is at all possible, afford opportunities for training for occupations lying somewhere in the region between the trade levels and the more strictly professional levels. (3) The third problem bears upon the likelihood of increasing, through the establishment of junior-college units near the homes of students, the proportion of the population who will receive the benefits of higher education. In no small part this may be regarded as the problem of economic democratization of higher education through the junior college.

There is no intent to imply by separate treatment that these three problems have not intimate relationships each to the other. They are as much interinvolved as are the three conceptions of special purpose of the junior college which have given rise to the inquiry into the possibilities of educational democratization by means of this new unit in the system. No special discussion is accorded these important interrelationships, but some appreciation of them will be given the reader if he takes the pains to consider the way the three problems just named overlap one another.

II. The Junior College and Mental Democratization of Higher Education

A comparison of junior-college students with those enrolled in corresponding years of colleges and universities. The expectation, sometimes expressed and sometimes implied, of many whose statements have been incorporated in the analysis of purposes to which reference has just been made, is that popularization of education on the junior-college level will and should be accompanied by a wider range of mentality than is now represented in these years of our colleges and universities. The recent development of what are called mental tests makes it possible (1) to ascertain the extent to which this expectation is being realized and also (2) to canvass (at least partly) the question of whether our higher institutions are disposed to attempt to cope with as much of this type of popularization as has manifested itself without junior-college reorganization. Correspondingly this section will include (1) a comparison by means of mental tests of students in junior colleges and students in the same years of other higher institutions and (2) a study of a group of students in one such higher institution as to the relation of their mental-test scores to degree of success and subjects pursued during residence.

Distributions of scores in the army alpha test are not essentially different for junior colleges than for state universities. On the other hand, there is a marked contrast of distributions and a wide difference between the medians when the former are compared with distributions for institutions like Oberlin and Yale. The contrast for Yale is even more striking than that for Oberlin. In attempting to account for the larger difference for Yale, it should be kept in mind

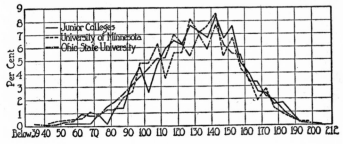

FIG. 17. Percentage distributions of army alpha scores of freshmen in ten public and Northern private junior colleges (581 students), in the College of Science, Literature, and the Arts of the University of Minnesota (463), and in Ohio State University (2545)

that Oberlin enrolls both men and women, and that men score about ten points higher than women in the army alpha test.

Significance for the junior-college movement. The most obvious point of significance in the comparisons thus afforded as to the mental character of junior-college students is that the authorities in higher institutions, more especially our state universities, have little or no ground for the fear that the junior college

[103]

in its present state of development brings into their upper years a flood of mentally incompetent students. The data make clear that junior-college students are in this respect about on a par with students of the same classification in most colleges and universities.

Those whose advocacy of the junior college rests on the hope that it will fulfill those special purposes,

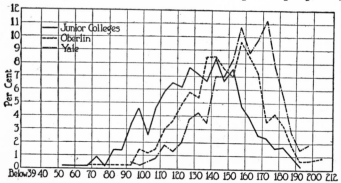

FIG. 18. Percentage distributions of army alpha scores of freshmen in ten public and Northern private junior colleges (581 students), in Oberlin College (330), and in Yale (400)

most intimately related to the popularization and democratization of higher education, to which reference was made at the opening of the chapter, will be inclined to deplore the fact that even in this early state of its development this new unit should not be enrolling a larger proportion of students in the lower ranges represented. They will not, of course, deplore the presence of a large number of superior minds among the student body, their regret being associated with the attenuation at the lower end of the distribution.

After all, it is not especially to be wondered at that the junior colleges have not yet fully achieved the type of popularization here alluded to. The movement is still in its youth. Being so, its full scope of function is not yet clear in the minds of all those connected with the examples of the institution now in existence. As was noted in Chapter II the primary purpose as seen by all groups concerned was the isthmian one of providing the first two years of work acceptable to colleges and universities, much as the conception of the function of the public secondary school a generation or two ago was preparation for college. In the junior college the earlier problem has merely been raised to a higher level in our system of education. Anyone who converses much with those connected as administrative heads or as teachers with these units, during the first few years of their existence, will soon become aware that "making good" with neighboring universities is a matter of compelling concern. And this is doubtless as it should be during these earliest stages.

This dominating conception of the chief function of the junior college during these early states of development is reflected in the scope of the work open to the prospective student, which, during the first years of the existence of a junior college, is not often more than colleges and universities prescribe during the first two years of a four-year period of training. Many high-school graduates mentally on a par with those in the lower portions of the mental distributions in junior colleges referred to have unquestionably considered continuation in the local junior college, have weighed the possibilities of succeeding in branches with which they have already had discouraging experiences in the high school (for example, foreign languages, mathematics, and the sciences), and have come to the decision that junior-college work was not for them. The writer could cite instances also where those in charge of junior colleges take the attitude of discouragement toward those of this group who show signs of wanting to essay junior-college work, doubtless either keeping in mind the necessity of safeguarding success in performing the isthmian function or—which amounts to the same thing—prompted by the feeling that those only should go on who can make a success of college work as traditionally administered.

Viewed from one significant standpoint the data referred to augur mental democratization of the level of work under consideration through the extension of the junior-college movement. This prophecy is to be found in the contrast of distributions in state universities with those in institutions on private foundations, such as Oberlin and Yale. The distributions of mental-test scores show that *the private institutions are not alone in having considerable proportions of students in the upper reaches of the army alpha test; the major difference is that the public institutions dip lower down.* By not being responsible to a public constituency the strong private higher institution has been in a position to draw a higher selective line. Hitherto this has been regarded as the right of a private individual or a corporation. On the other hand, the two institutions on state foundations are in more than one sense in the position (not rank) of the municipal junior college. In the first place they serve public constituencies, which insist in more or less definite ways on democratization, and in the second place they are both located in large centers of population which provide no small proportion of the student body. For instance 388, or 61.5 per cent of the first 631 freshmen in alphabetical arrangement entering the College of Science, Literature, and the Arts of the University of Minnesota in 1921, had their residence in the Twin Cities or in suburban communities near. It would be surprising, indeed, if there were not some among these who, if a mental measure were taken, would be found in the lower portions of the distribution and who, on account of the proximity of opportunities of higher education at low cost, are willing to essay this higher level of work when they would hesitate about doing so if they had to leave the home town to attend. This is perhaps even accentuated when the only academic passport for admission is a certificate indicating graduation from an accredited high school with a total of sixteen units, only six being prescribed and these being four units of English and two of mathematics. With the difference in distributions between these two types of institutions noted we are warranted in anticipating an even greater extent of mental democratization in junior colleges. It is likely to come much more rapidly after the more democratic purposes of the institution crystallize out of our current inexperience and after work more suited to the capacities under consideration is made available.

Relationship between army alpha scores and success in college work. An important consideration in any decision as to whether we are in need of an extension of the junior-college movement for the sake of democratizing higher education is the degree of success of colleges and universities in providing opportunities for collegiate education to students in the lower portions of the mental distributions. The giving of the army tests to large numbers of students in colleges and universities after the termination of hostilities in the late war has afforded the occasion for making studies which inquire into the relationship between the scores on the test and the degree of success of students when measured by their length of stay in school, average marks received, etc. Portions of the conclusions from such a study are reported here, the group of students concerned being those who were freshmen in the College of Science, Literature, and the Arts of the University of Minnesota during the year 1918–1919. The scores used were obtained by Professor Van Wagenen of that institution in January, 1919. Among those taking the test were an unselected group of 463 freshmen in the college named, 192 of these being men and 271 being women. For various reasons which are not given here on account of limitations of space, the number of students concerned in the tabulations from which conclusions are drawn was 344, of whom 123 were men and 221 were women. By a statistical procedure involving probable error distances they were divided into three groups, to be designated here as the "low," "middle," and "high" groups, the division being determined by mental-test scores. The number of students in each group and the score range of the group for men, women, and both sexes are as follows:

Group	Men		Women		Total	
	Number	Range	Number	Range	Number	Range
Low . . .	26	61 – 102	32	62 – 102	58	61 – 102
Middle . .	88	103 – 157	158	103 – 157	246	103 – 157
High . . .	9	159 – 194	31	153[1] – 184	40	153[1] – 194

[1] Through error a single case of a score of 153 was misplaced in the high group; that is, five points above its proper location throughout the tabulations made. Except for this case the range of the high group of women is 158 to 184 and of the total high group 158 to 194. This displacement of a single case can have scarcely more than an inappreciable effect upon the findings to be presented.

Since earlier studies have shown conclusively that there is a marked relationship between mental-test scores and length of stay in higher institutions,[1] space will be spared by omitting presentation of such findings in the investigation reported here. Suffice it to say that much larger percentages of those in the low group were eliminated than in either of the other two groups.

Facts concerning elimination constitute only a partial account of the situation. More appears when a study is made of the relation between the mental level of the student and the likelihood of his accumulating any large number of honor-points during a period of residence of a year or two.

These honor-points are obtained in the University of Minnesota by receiving marks higher than D, which is the lowest passing grade. Each hour of credit for which a student receives a mark of C gives him 1 honor-point; each hour of credit with mark B, 2 honor-points; each with A, 3 honor-points. If he receives marks of C in all his work in a quarter during which he carries fifteen hours, he receives 15 honor-points;

---

[1] For example, Colvin said: "The tendency to eliminate the less intelligent students is indicated when we inspect the record of the class of 1922 (at Brown University). In this class 334 men took the Brown tests. Of these, 115 had left college by the end of their sophomore year. Of those leaving 14 per cent stood high in their psychological tests, 41 per cent received average scores, and 45 per cent low scores."—S. S. COLVIN, "The Use of Intelligence Tests," in *Educational Review*, Vol. LXII, pp. 134-135 (September, 1921)

if B, 30 honor-points; if A, 45 honor-points. No honor-points are assigned to marks lower than C. Advancement from the junior to the senior college in the College of Science, Literature, and the Arts is conditioned upon the student's earning 90 credits and 90 honor-points. In effect, then, to be advanced to the upper unit the student must receive an average mark of C (not merely a passing mark of D) in an average of 15 credits per quarter for six quarters.

The findings of the present study make clear that the student in the low group has practically no chance of advancement to the upper unit in the colleges, as 84.5 per cent of the men and 84.2 per cent of the women in this group received marks in all their work which placed their averages below the honor-point level. Moreover, this plan seems not to be suited to the needs of the great middle group constituting the bulk of the student body, since more than half— 53.6 per cent—of these do not attain an average mark that brings honor-points with it.

A further description of the honor-point situation is provided in another statistical approach, the computation of the percentages of each of the three groups who earned ten honor-points or less during each quarter of residence. The main findings of this approach lead to the same conclusion as those arising out of the proportions receiving average marks below the honor-point level: that *the plan looks toward the selection*

[111]

of students of superior quality for work on the upper level, rather than toward training the student in terms of his capacity on the level in which he is enrolled.

The work taken by eliminated students. That the university functions primarily for those who can go

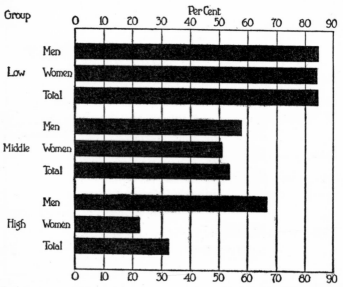

FIG. 19. Percentages of students in low, middle, and high groups with averages of marks below the honor-point level

on and not for the group less well fitted or less inclined to proceed with work on the senior-college level is made manifest in data concerning the subject-groups represented in the work taken by the thirty-two men and sixty-one women (of this total of three hundred and forty-four students) who left sometime between the end of their second quarter of residence and the beginning of what would have been their third year in the university—a total of ninety-three students who did not remain beyond what we regard as the

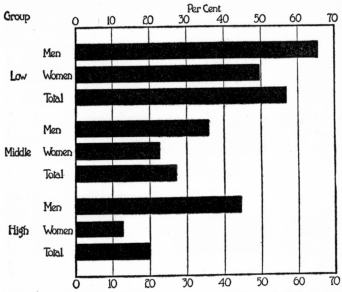

FIG. 20. Percentages of students in low, middle, and high groups earning less than ten honor-points per quarter of residence

junior-college period. While some of these materials may doubtless be looked upon as appropriate for the education of students not going on, others are of little value for terminal training. Such would be the work in foreign language, usually French or Spanish of an elementary sort, or mathematics. The former was taken in greater or less amount by almost all those who dropped out—by 85 per cent of the total number, in fact. Mathematics was taken by two thirds of the men, but by a smaller proportion of the women. The taking of work in both the subject-groups, especially the particular courses pursued by the students under consideration, assumes subsequent work in the same or closely dependent lines. They are in effect, when taken by a student who does not proceed as is assumed, lower portions of a truncated curriculum, not the culminal portions of a shorter period of education better suited to the needs of those eliminated. This is remote from "rounding out" the education of students not going on.

It is perhaps gratuitous to restate in this connection that there are among these eliminated students some whose army-test scores were in the middle and high groups as here classified. The proportions are, however, much smaller than for the low group. Notwithstanding their superiority the inappositeness of the materials of a truncated curriculum is hardly less conspicuous.

These facts would not have been presented were there any misgiving that they are not more or less representative of stronger colleges and universities generally. The sifting process may differ in detail, but elimination and discouragement of those in the lower mental ranges who gain admission would in any wide study be found to be practically universal.

College freshmen and the literate white draft compared. Having revealed something (1) of the range and distribution of mentality represented in higher institutions and (2) of the relationships of the level

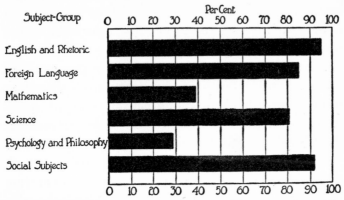

FIG. 21. Percentages of eliminated students taking courses in certain subject-groups

of mentality to degree of success, it is now pertinent at least to suggest the magnitude of the task higher education has yet before it if it is to provide opportunities of training for anything like *all* those who, according to our democratic assumptions, are entitled to it and can be expected to profit by it. It is not impossible to accomplish this in brief space, especially as the alpha test was first put in use by the United States army on large numbers of the draft in operation during the late war. The means used is a comparison of the distribution of scores obtained by the 344 freshmen used in the study just reported with that of 51,620 men in the white draft, who are all those men from the 100,000 native-born "who took alpha only or alpha and beta only, alpha and an individual examination or alpha, beta, and an individual examination."[1] In other words, all took the alpha test, and so we know that all were literate. The distribution does not adequately represent all the literate white native-born men of the nation, because many of the most intelligent of those men had already entered the army as officers or as officer-candidates. This fact can detract little from the significance of the comparison.

The two distributions display a striking contrast. They show that college students are drawn almost exclusively from the upper reaches of the total distribution. Put in approximate numerical terms, the comparison shows that more than nine tenths of the college freshmen come from the upper fifth of the literate white native-born. On the other hand, less than a tenth come from all the remaining four fifths.

If it is conceded on "practical" grounds that—not to say more—those in the total population who now have *some* representation in the college group have a

[1] "Memoirs of the National Academy of Sciences," Vol. XV (1921), p. 750. The percentage distribution is taken from page 764. Further description is provided on pages 553–559.

right to education of some kind to some extent above the high-school level, it can be demonstrated that the task of providing this higher education has been barely begun. Thus, of the low group of freshmen in the University of Minnesota upon whom attention has been centered in this portion of the chapter, those with

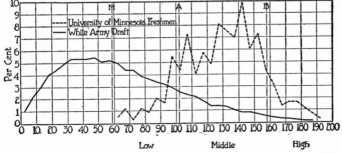

Fig. 22. Percentage distributions of army alpha scores of 344 freshmen in the College of Science, Literature, and the Arts of the University of Minnesota and of 51,620 men in the literate-white army draft. (The lines A and B separate the freshman distribution into the low, middle, and high groups; the line M locates the median of the literate white draft)

scores ranging from 61 to 102 constitute but 16.9 per cent of the whole group of 344 students, whereas this range of scores includes approximately a third of the army distribution. It should be noted, also, that all the individuals in this low group are well above the median score of the white draft, which is 58.9.

The last contrast of figures is, of course, far from the same thing as stating that 16.9 per cent of all the

[117]

30 per cent, let us say, of our white literate population of appropriate ages are enjoying the opportunities of higher education to some extent. A dependable estimate along these lines would be difficult to make. But when it is remembered that few if any of the students of this range of mentality obtain entrance to some of our stronger institutions, and that in most of the others to which they are admitted they are soon discouraged by a sifting process well-nigh universal, educational opportunities for them—except as provided in the high schools, which many of them have completed and in increasing proportions will complete —may be judged to be almost totally absent. In the face of the rising tide of education the present facilities for this type of student in standard colleges and universities strike one as distressingly ineffectual.

The solution of the problem. In this situation neither the American ideal of democratic education nor the scholastic ideals of standard colleges and universities seem likely soon to give way. It would require some gigantic force now indiscernible to wrench from us our conviction that we must attain both mental and economic democratization of educational opportunities to a much larger extent than now obtains. In consequence the tide is certain to continue to rise and the opportunities to reach down increasingly to the mental levels we have seen to be now relatively untouched.

On the other hand, the sifting process seems almost inherent in our present college and university system and is not without important considerations to recommend it. These institutions whose training is offered in periods of four or more years have it in their nature to administer requirements in terms of the full duration of these periods, whether the requirements are of particular courses prescribed or of quantity and quality of work to be done. A host of their traditions have grown out of the contemplation of the completion of a full four-year curriculum or more. Pressed with this flood of "inferior" candidates for higher education—many of whom, although deserving of some extent of opportunity beyond the present high-school level, are not warranted in aspiring to a full traditional college or university course—they have proceeded to protect the longer course by one or another process of selection. Many of the private and some of the public institutions have set up barriers at entrance; for example, the plan of accepting only candidates whose high-school averages place them in the upper two thirds of their classes, the requirement of passing a rigid entrance examination, or the prescription for admission of large numbers of units in subjects of high selective value, such as ancient languages and mathematics.

These have often been justified by the absence of facilities for taking care of larger numbers of students.

Other institutions, more of them subject to public than to private control, not being in a position to bar such students at entrance, have set up more or less elaborate but effective devices of sifting to which the students are subjected after entrance. Still other institutions operate two types of selection, one prior to admission, the other subsequent to it.

. Viewed from this standpoint of success in curricula four or more years in length, these plans of exclusion and selection are not open to unqualified condemnation. It is when attention centers round the broader service which must be rendered those who are now being excluded or abused after they have been admitted that the unendurableness of such plans becomes conspicuous. However, their universality and their compatibility with long-course traditions assure us that they are almost as unlikely soon to disappear as is our general acceptance of the concept of a democratic higher education. In consequence, without reorganization it must be long indeed before mental democratization can be achieved. The hope must rest *not in readjustments within colleges and universities of the current type, but in institutions in which the first two college years under consideration are terminal grades.* That is to say, it rests in the utilization of the junior-college idea. Our assurance that the interests of those who will not or should not go beyond the first and second college years will be better conserved in such an institution is grounded in the fact that the lower schools with which this work should be associated have already made propitious beginnings toward differentiating work for those who can and should continue their education and for those who cannot or should not continue it.

III. The Junior College and Training for Semiprofessions

The problem and the method of inquiry. As has been noted, one of the aspirations designated as a special purpose of the new unit is the provision of occupational training of junior-college grade, this aspiration being entertained by approximately half of all the sources examined in the search for the claims made for the junior college.

The authors of the statements analyzed have in mind here preparation for occupations the training for which is to be concluded during the junior-college period, and which are, from the standpoint of the period of training involved, *semiprofessions*. Such occupations are to be distinguished on the one hand from *trades*, the training for which is concluded during the conventional secondary-school period, and on the other from *professions*, adequate preparation for which requires four or more years of training beyond the high school.

[121]

Those who advocate culminal occupational training on this level make mention of large groups like commerce, industry, agriculture, and home economics. They seldom, however, specify particular occupations. In fact, although frequent brief references to the problem are to be found in literature dealing with occupational training, one looks in vain for anything like an adequate treatment. With all the other aspects of the junior-college problem into which it was necessary to inquire in this investigation, it was manifestly impossible to include a comprehensive study of this particular aspect. Moreover, our present want of experience with semiprofessions must prevent our arriving at anything like finalities, except in the matter of the desirability and feasibility of development along these lines.

The study of this aspect of the junior-college problem followed two main directions: (1) The first was a canvass of present educational facilities to note any outcroppings of opportunities for semiprofessional training. This phase of the inquiry included examination of current junior-college offerings, two-year curricula in other higher institutions, courses for high-school graduates in business colleges, extension departments in universities, a group of miscellaneous institutions advertising training along a wide variety of lines, and private correspondence schools. (2) The second was that of ascertaining the opinions of a large number of deans (and heads of departments) of engineering, commerce, and agriculture as to the proper level of terminal training for a number of occupations in or related to their special fields. Mention of minor supplementary inquiries is deferred to the points at which they are presented.

1. That some *junior colleges* include occupational materials in their offerings was made apparent in Chapter III. The proportion of the total offering assigned to such courses in junior colleges was there seen to be much larger than in the junior-college years of separate colleges of liberal arts or of colleges connected with universities. An examination of the distribution of original courses from which this conclusion is drawn would show that some of them will be of service to the student with professional ambitions, others to the student desirous of securing some extent of occupational training on the semiprofessional level, and still others will be useful to either type of student.

The writer's examination of catalogues of junior colleges and his conversations with junior-college heads and instructors lead him to believe that without doubt offerings of the sort referred to have in some instances been introduced for the primary purpose of providing terminal occupational training on this level. On the other hand, this intent is not as general as may be desired, a majority of the institutions seeming to have an eye single to meeting the demands of higher institutions to which junior-college graduates will be likely to transfer, an attitude not altogether unreasonable in the earliest stages of development of an educational institution.

Among the instances of obvious intent to provide in junior colleges culminal occupational training the following may be cited. One of the best examples in agriculture is that of Chaffey Junior College at Ontario, California. In this institution courses valuable both for culminal and preprofessional purposes are offered. The unit maintained in the State Normal School at Oshkosh, Wisconsin, features a curriculum "organized to meet the needs of students who desire to become technical chemists after two years of study." A number of students who have completed this work and who did not continue their education are employed in lines for which the curriculum was intended to prepare them. A state junior college in the South offers an automobile-mechanics curriculum terminating in the second college year, but at the time of the writer's visit only a few high-school graduates were enrolled in it. Those who were taking the special work of the curriculum were for the most part not high-school graduates. While undoubtedly valuable occupational training was being given, the students were not receiving it as semiprofessional preparation in the sense in which this term is here used. In much the same situation is a curriculum in oil-production offered in a junior college of Southern California. There is in operation in connection with the Riverside, California, Junior College a half-time coöperative plan of semi-professional training along industrial and commercial lines that gives promise of great usefulness. In conjunction with the junior colleges at Kansas City, Missouri, and Grand Rapids, Michigan, are given the theoretical portions of the curriculum for nurses in training. In the same units is provided work along secretarial and other commercial lines that may be looked upon as in the nature of semiprofessional training. Here also should be included some of the work in home economics available in a number of junior colleges, public and private.

The relatively large amount of work in the field of education available in junior colleges, especially in private units, is in harmony with what is in essence by far the most prevalent semiprofessional training function of the junior colleges—preparation for teaching. This is especially characteristic of private junior colleges in Missouri and the Southern states, but is also to be found elsewhere to some extent. It is the claim to the performance of this function exclusively which makes the catalogues of private junior colleges yield as large a proportionate recognition of the claim under consideration as the other types of literature examined, as stated in Chapter II. As illustrations we may quote a statement typical of the catalogues of junior colleges in Missouri, that "the State Department of Education will grant to all graduates of the college who have completed the prescribed courses in education a three years' state certificate permitting the holder to teach in the public schools of towns and cities of Missouri"; and another, characteristic of those in Texas, that classification "by the State Department of Education as a Junior College of first class . . . signifies that the student completing five courses in our first college year, one of which is Education, will be granted a first-grade state certificate for four years without examination." Although elementary-school teaching (into which most of the holders of these certificates go) is, from the standpoint of the period of training typical of its participants, still a semiprofession, it may well be asked whether it should remain so, or, if it must, whether one or two years of regular collegiate work is the proper sort of training for it. State normal schools should be in a position to give better training for elementary-school teaching than are institutions stressing the first two years of work in colleges of liberal arts. The only excuse for approving the practice is the dearth of teachers with anything like adequate preparation for the work. Certainly, for high-school teaching, into which a considerable proportion of junior-college students go upon graduation, the semiprofessional level is far too low.

The offerings described seem at least to be the beginnings of a constructive tendency toward endeavoring to provide something in the way of semiprofessional training for those who are not going on. Although they are totally absent from most units and not always wide in scope where offered, we have in these beginnings an earnest of generous future development, especially in view of the recency of the junior-college movement.

A letter of inquiry was sent to deans or directors of all *colleges of engineering and agriculture* with the request that they should give information concerning all two-year curricula offered in their institutions, stating the character of any such curricula as collegiate or noncollegiate and also stating the enrollment in each during 1920–1921. To the one hundred and twenty-eight letters sent to heads of standard engineering colleges, as listed in the educational directory issued by the Bureau of Education, one hundred and three replies were received. Of that number six institutions reported one-year, two-year, or three-year curricula of college grade in engineering or allied industrial activities. The numbers of students enrolled were stated by only one institution. The dean of another college of engineering said of the two-year curriculum in highway engineering, "We have had a number of men enroll for this course, but in every instance they have remained and completed the full course required for the degree of C.E." The dean in still another college said of their two-year technical curricula that there are usually only two or three students each year in them, that the men generally find they want the four-year curriculum, and that they are enabled to transfer without much loss of time.

In agriculture forty-seven letters were sent out, and forty replies were received. Six institutions reported that they were giving two-year collegiate curricula. Examination of catalogue descriptions showed, as might be expected, that the foundational work in sciences and cultural subjects given with the four-year curriculum was pared down or condensed and that most of the student's time was given to the applied subjects.

From the results of this inquiry we must conclude that our professional schools tend to hold rather closely to their professional standards, and that they are doing little in a direct way to train people for occupations on the semiprofessional level. The usual small enrollments in the shorter curricula, and the tendency of students to shift to the longer fully professional offerings, are not likely to influence the authorities in such institutions to introduce more of the shorter. At the same time it may be seriously doubted if, with the stigma which attaches to attendance upon a shorter curriculum where the longer is the more honorific, these semiprofessional curricula in standard professional schools can ever make much headway in colleges and universities.

2. A third source examined were the bulletins of twenty-eight *extension divisions* of universities, twenty-one being state institutions and the remainder municipal and private institutions. It was found that the extension work of about twelve state institutions and two private institutions is largely or entirely straight liberal-arts-college material, and it may safely be said of the majority of the twenty-eight that the work is planned primarily for people who will eventually be graduated from one of the university colleges and enter a profession, as contrasted with a semi-profession. This situation is not difficult to explain. The easiest courses to offer in extension classes or by correspondence are those already planned and taught in the university proper; and the university aims to give professional training.

Constituting exceptions to the conclusion that extension divisions are not concerned with semiprofessions are the following items: Three university-extension departments have definitely outlined curricula in the field of business requiring two or three years to complete through evening courses only. Practice varies as to allowing regular university credit for these courses, some of which are accounting, money and banking, commercial law, corporation finance, real estate, insurance, etc. One of the three institutions offers evening curricula three years in length in architecture and in civil, electrical, and mechanical engineering. Still another institution, a state university, offers a large number of courses in business and engineering, for a majority of which credit toward regular university degrees is not given. Though not arranged in definite curricula, the nature of the courses seems to be somewhat along the line of a recognition of semi-professional occupations.

3. The study of *business colleges* was made from the catalogues of twenty-two representative schools. Seventeen of these are giving only courses to fit people for clerical work, such as bookkeeping, stenography, typing, which is clearly on no higher level than the work done by the commercial departments of our high schools. The other five institutions are giving the same sort of training, but, in addition, offer a few courses only for high-school graduates who have had an ordinary business-college course or a secondary-school business course. These courses are in higher accounting and secretarial service. One secretarial course is advertised as being from four to eight months in length, another from six to eight months in length. From this we must conclude that they are too shallow to turn out a secretary who is many notches above a stenographer. It is also doubtful if the courses in accounting could turn out an accountant very superior to a bookkeeper, although there is nothing definite in

the description of the course upon which such an opinion could be based. To sum up, it may be said that the business colleges have assumed that their most important function is to train people for clerical occupations, but they are doing a little along semi-professional lines.

4. Another group of schools, designated as *miscellaneous*, were listed in the United States Bureau of Education directory[1] as institutions of higher rank than secondary schools, but not regarded as universities, colleges, or normal schools. All were approached for publications descriptive of the work offered, and these came in from a total of twenty-nine institutions, three of them supported publicly and twenty-six privately. There are five schools or departments of schools giving training for engineering and allied activities, seven for business activities, five for home economics, and twenty-two for art, music, expression, and special training. All these schools are giving training on what may be presumed to be (at least approximately) the semiprofessional level, and all but a few confine their activities to one of the four fields mentioned.

Schools of the engineering type offer two-year and three-year curricula above the high school. Some idea of their scope may be had by noting the names of curricula in one school: industrial mechanical, in-

[1] *United States Bureau of Education Bulletin No. 33* (1920), pp. 14-44.

dustrial electrical, industrial chemistry, industrial teacher-training, electrical construction, and architectural drawing and design. The business schools, while conducting some work on the semiprofessional level, also give courses clearly clerical in nature. Most of the five schools specializing in home economics offer two-year curricula calculated to fit students to be dietitians, costume designers, institution managers, home-makers, and teachers of home economics.

By far the largest division of this group is made up of schools of art, music, and expression, of which only two are publicly supported. The catalogues of this group stress the cultural as well as the occupational aspects of the work they offer.

5. The last group of catalogue studies were those of *privately operated correspondence schools*. Only a small group of seven schools advertising rather extensively were requested to send materials descriptive of their offerings. Some of them list courses covering a wide range including elementary, secondary, and university work, and accordingly they have no standards for admission. Although comparison of a school's courses with those of another such school, or with those of a high school or a university, is possible only in a vague way, the attempt was made to take account of work of a professional or semiprofessional nature.

The main divisions into which these courses fall relate to engineering and allied activities and business, with two schools giving just a little attention to commercial illustration and design. Some idea of the magnitude of the work that these schools do, or that they claim to do, is conveyed by a survey of the catalogue of one of the largest, which shows the field of engineering and allied activities to be separated into twenty-one divisions, in each of which there is offered an average of eighteen courses. The work of a school stressing business courses covers the following range: business administration, higher accounting, law (toward the degree of LL.B., and also commercial law for business men), interstate commerce and railway traffic, banking and finance, business letter-writing, industrial-management efficiency, commercial Spanish, and coaching for certified public accountant.

This examination of the offerings of somewhat more than three hundred institutions or organizations for evidences of training of semiprofessional sorts, although not discovering a full array of systematized and standardized curricula, shows at least an appreciable beginning and a partial awareness of the large need represented. An occasional junior college has sensed this need and is providing preparation along semiprofessional lines. Recognition of the function concerned has in a small proportion of instances found its way as two-year or three-year curricula into the offerings of colleges of engineering and agriculture. Registration in these curricula has not usually been large and is not likely to become so on account of the presence of dominating curricula of standard length. University-extension divisions in several instances, through establishing courses and curricula of an occupational sort on this level, seem to be increasingly appreciative of the value of this type of service. Business colleges, although engrossed primarily with the task of preparing for occupations on the clerical level, have in a few instances taken steps in this direction through making special provision for high-school graduates. The educational offerings of groups of miscellaneous institutions and correspondence schools also contain evidences of a corroboratory character.

If the outcroppings discovered are any indication, proper lines of development of semiprofessions and semiprofessional training are the fields of business, engineering and allied activities, applied arts, agriculture, and home economics. Despite the difficulties of establishing lines of distinction between trades on the one hand and semiprofessions on the other, and again between semiprofessions and professions, we seem to have in these evidences some support of a belief that there are and should be occupations on the intermediate level, and that they should be legitimized by the provisions of ample standardized curricula in preparation for them. That most of the outcroppings are found in connection with the less formal agencies of education should not be regarded as discrediting the necessity for the development, inasmuch as many educational innovations of merit have first made a place for themselves in a supplementary and external capacity, later to be incorporated as regular features of our school system.

Expert opinion on semiprofessions. For the purpose of determining specifically what occupations might be classified as semiprofessions on the basis of the amount of education and other preparation required, a list was made of all occupations for which in the opinion of some authority preparation should be made in a course of training approximately two years in length, with a high-school education or its equivalent as a prerequisite. An examination of the list showed that there were, in addition to many important and unimportant occupations in widely scattered fields, three main classes; namely, commerce, engineering, and agriculture. To secure a collective opinion of the training levels in which occupations in these three main fields were located, check sheets were sent to deans or directors of schools in the three fields represented, the number of check sheets returned being approximately one hundred and fifty. The method of the inquiry was to request those whose expert opinion was sought to indicate each of the occupations listed as *trade* or *clerical* (occupations "in order to enter upon which one should be trained in a high school, trade school, commercial school, or other institution which pre-supposes a knowledge of the common-school subjects and gives education on a level of less than college grade"), *semiprofessional* (occupations "in order to enter upon which one should prepare himself with a course of training approximately two years in length with a high-school education or its equivalent as a prerequisite"), and *professional* (occupations "for which the training should be that given by an in-stitution requiring for entrance at least graduation from an accredited secondary school and offering a course of college grade no less than four years in length and culminating in an appropriate and rec-ognized degree").

Many of those who coöperated wrote letters ex-pressing belief in the fundamental importance of such a study and volunteering comments on the difficul-ties they had found in thus classifying occupations.

Space can be spared for only the briefest treat-ment of the results of the balloting by the experts. Fifty per cent or more of the deans of colleges and heads of departments of *commerce* agreed that fourteen of the fifty-seven occupations in the list submitted are appropriately semiprofessions, these occupations being commercial, loan and stock brokers, city department-store buyers, chief clerks, credit men, commercial designers, insurance agents and ad-justers, jobbing and wholesale merchants, statistical clerks, and shipping-department heads and store-keepers with large concerns. A third to a half placed in this list of semiprofessions twenty-one more of the list, among them merchants, agents, and salesmen of various sorts, private secretaries, general accountants, and traffic managers. The remaining twenty-two occupations were placed, by a majority of those venturing opinions, either among the professions or the clerical positions, by far the largest number (nineteen, to be exact) being classified with the former. Among these are cost and certified public accountants, auditors, comptrollers, credit managers, employment managers, sales managers, and general managers, bond salesmen, and statisticians.

Among the *engineering and related occupations* which were placed in the list of semiprofessions by a half or more of the deans of colleges of engineering are cement testers, chemical-laboratory workers, general contractors in building-trades, draftsmen of various sorts (for example, mechanical, structural, architectural, sheet-metal, topographical, etc.), electricians, inspectors, superintendents, and surveyors. The full number includes forty-three of a total list of one hundred and four occupations submitted for judgment. To them would be added, if a third to a half of the deans had their way, twenty-two more occupations, leaving but thirty-nine in the strictly professional and trade lists, all but ten of these being very commonly designated by these officers as unquestioned professions.

The results of balloting by deans of colleges of *agriculture* (including forestry) are in harmony with those of the two preceding groups of experts. Just a fourth of the forty-eight occupations in the list submitted to this group are looked upon as semiprofessions by a half or more of the deans consulted, among these occupations being those of florists, foremen on truck farms, managers of butter and cheese factories, makers of butter, cheese, or ice cream, testers for cow-test associations, poultrymen, lumber salesmen, forest rangers, woods superintendents, etc. A group of twenty-five are placed among the semiprofessions by a third to a half of the deans, leaving only eleven of the original list in the professions and trades.

If the results of the balloting may be assumed to have anything of determinative value—and it may be questioned whether more competent groups of judges can be found than these leaders in their respective fields of training—we have undoubted evidence of the desirability of providing training for semiprofessions, and that, too, for a large number of them.

A special request was also made that the deans and department heads should specify in the lists of occupations any that have been indicated as appropriately semiprofessions for which their institutions gave "essential preparation by approximately two years' training." Returns to this request show that a considerable proportion of these officers have confidence that the present content of courses offered in their schools is suited to the needs of some of these semiprofessional occupations. While this type of information will help to answer the question whether the necessary content is at hand, it has little pertinence for the question whether as traditionally administered it can serve the purpose under consideration. Further light would be thrown on this question by the facts concerning the proportion of special occupational work prescribed during the first two years of professional curricula as presented in Chapter III. The relatively small proportions of such work in many lines and institutions means that if the student endeavored to secure the requisite preparation for a semiprofession (assuming that he had decided on his occupational goal and knew the relation of the courses to its attainment), he would need to get administrative approval for his deviation from regular curricular channels. Add to this the student's almost certain distaste for entering upon an irregular and shortened program in an institution which in its nature emphasizes curricula at least four years in length, and you have a situation which affords little or no hope of doing much toward training for these semiprofessions in standard colleges and universities.

On the other hand these opinions indicate that at least *some* of the materials in the first two years of professional and preprofessional curricula are pertinent for semiprofessional training. Certain other materials now typically in more advanced years could, through abbreviation and partial simplification, be lowered to the under-classman level and, if introduced as culminal training in junior colleges, would serve to train for occupations on this intermediate level. If strong junior-college units offer these special occupational materials of the early professional or the preprofessional years, and the shortened and depressed courses referred to, there is little occasion for doubting that most essential semiprofessional training will be afforded, and with proper guidance both the individual student and society will thereby be more effectively served.

Other possible lines for semiprofessions. The canvass referred to in an earlier portion of this section found some justification for regarding certain additional occupations as future semiprofessions. Since those in any single line were few in number it was not practicable to secure a composite picture of expert opinion, as was done in commerce, engineering, and agriculture. Here might be placed managers of commercial, institutional, and industrial cafeterias, and dietitians; professional shoppers; designers, cutters, and painters in art-glass works; decorative modelers; costume, commercial, jewelry, and stage designers; jewelry engravers; lithographic and photo engravers; commercial and interior decorators; veterinarians; masseurs, nurses, pharmacists, welfare supervisors, etc.

Since courses in *home economics* of a more or less terminal character are often proposed for junior-college years, a word should be said concerning them and the desirability of regarding home-making as a semiprofession. Without doubt this occupation, for which most women are destined, is one of those for which training on the strictly professional level as here defined is none too much. In this sense, as well as in the sense also which admits that the period of training involved is only one element (though an important one) in raising one's life work to a level where it is professionally conceived and accomplished, home-making may be made as much of a profession as any that can be named. From the standpoint, however, of the most extended period of training which is practicable for many, it is desirable to administer courses in this field for a large proportion of young women on the assumption that this occupation is to be for them a semiprofession; that is, to give these courses as culminal training in junior-college years. Fortunately this is one of the fields in which junior colleges have already made a good beginning. But the importance of the field justifies much greater recognition.

This may be achieved in a manner much like that suggested for the three fields more extensively dealt with in this section (namely, commerce, engineering and allied activities, and agriculture), which is to utilize all that is valuable as culminal training of those professional and preprofessional materials which commonly find a place in the first two years above the high school, and to depress and abbreviate certain of the courses more frequently finding place in the upper years of four-year curricula.

The major inferences from this study of semi-professions. The first large portion of the current section discloses outcroppings of provisions for training on the semiprofessional level. These provisions, although relatively infrequent and predominantly afforded as supplementary and external agencies of education, are sufficiently extensive to assure us of a need not adequately met by the more formal agencies. It is significant that a consciousness of this need should be expressed by actual offerings of a semiprofessional sort even in these early stages of junior-college development while most junior colleges are directing efforts primarily at doing effectively the first two years of college and university work. The second large portion gives substantial corroboration to the major finding of the first and indicates more specifically some of the lines of occupational service for which training on the semiprofessional level should and can be given.

DEMOCRATIZATION

The implications of the evidence do not seem to support the early and vigorous development of opportunities for semiprofessional training in standard four-year colleges and universities. While institutions affording professional education have been in existence for a long period, few made efforts of the sort here being considered. It seems to be in the nature of institutions with curricula four or more years in length to have in mind exclusively those who contemplate completion of the full range of work provided. Moreover, even if faculties in charge of these standard colleges could as a whole be brought to see the desirability of offering semiprofessional curricula, it may be doubted whether students could be induced to enroll in them. To students there would always be something in the nature of a stigma attached to aspiring to less than the highest available in an institution.

The logical place for the development of semiprofessional curricula seems to be the educational unit where the years in which the training is to be given are *terminal* years. This is the junior college. The authorities in charge will be more disposed to regard as a legitimate rôle of the new unit the provision of curricula concluding with the years of training for which they are responsible. To the student there will be less of what may seem a surrender of caste to enter upon a curriculum of an occupational sort if this terminates at the same point as those of other students

[143]

who plan to transfer to higher institutions. Although something still remains to be done in high schools to elevate the commercial and other vocational curricula to the same honorific status in the mind of the student as that enjoyed by the college preparatory curriculum, there has in recent years been much improvement in this regard. By analogy we are justified in anticipating a similar growth in esteem of semiprofessional curricula, a growth much more rapid than in the professional schools with curricula four or more years in length.

Providing this training for semiprofessions in junior colleges has the support also of the most significant considerations drawn from the materials presented in the preceding section of this chapter and in its concluding section, which deal respectively with the problems of mental and economic democratization through the establishment of this new unit. Culminal occupational training in these years will comport well with the needs of those who, because of moderate mental equipment or because of financial limitations, or for other reasons, should not or cannot continue their training on the higher level.

There are many unsolved problems in this field of semiprofessional training; for example, as to the lines of training which will be found feasible in junior colleges generally or in particular communities, the securing of suitable teachers, the financial responsibilities involved, etc. These will tend to retard development along right lines even in junior colleges; but the needs of individuals for the training under consideration and of society for the types of services to be rendered by those receiving it may be accepted as an earnest of the enduring merit of the proposal, as well as of the ultimate place of the opportunities for semiprofessional training in the junior college.

IV. THE JUNIOR COLLEGE AND ECONOMIC DEMOCRATIZATION OF HIGHER EDUCATION

How the claim was scrutinized. Notwithstanding the strong presumption in favor of the claim that establishing junior colleges will, through the influence of lowered costs and sheer proximity of opportunities for the first two years of curricula of higher schools, popularize higher education, it is desirable to scrutinize the claim in order (1) the more certainly to establish or to disestablish it, (2) to note the degree of its validity, (3) to evaluate the two most common types of junior colleges on this basis, and (4) to lay a partial basis for policies to be pursued in junior-college development of the future.

The lines of inquiry upon which report is to be made in this concluding section of the chapter are (1) the parents' justification of the movement, in order to see what consideration in support of the junior college looms most prominently in their minds, (2) the proportion to which students living at home while in attendance acknowledge themselves able to attend elsewhere, (3) the annual cost of attendance in the several types of higher institution both for students living at home and for those living away from home, (4) the extent of popularization through propinquity of opportunities for higher education, and (5) the occupational distribution of fathers of students in secondary and higher institutions, including junior colleges.

Parents' justification of the movement. One body of material assembled for the investigation of the junior-college movement which has some relevancy to the problem in hand came from parents of junior-college students in response to a question put to them. The question was simply why the son or daughter concerned was attending the local junior college rather than a college or university elsewhere. A total of 199 blanks on which this question was printed were returned answered to the writer, coming from parents of students in four junior colleges in Minnesota, one in Michigan, one in Texas, and three in California. On these responses were given in all 423 reasons.

An analysis of the reasons finds four given with much greater frequency than others. Two of these— *home influences extended* and *more attention to the individual student*—have no relevancy to the immediate problem and further reference to them will be deferred to the next chapter.

The reason offered more frequently than any other, *attendance at junior college less expensive*, may be judged to have intimate meaning for the problem of

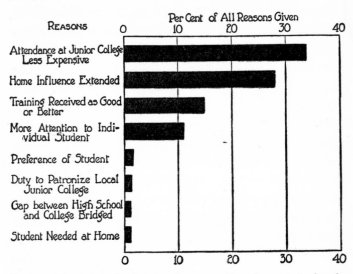

FIG. 23. Percentage frequency of reasons given by parents for the attendance of sons and daughters at local junior colleges

economic democratization of higher education. It was given in a total of 143 of the responses, which is more than a third of all the 423 reasons given and means that it appeared in almost three fourths of all the 199 responses made. A large proportion—a fourth of all answering the question—whose answers were grouped under this head state frankly that they "cannot afford" to send a son or daughter elsewhere. The proportion would doubtless have been even greater if all those who meant this when they reported "less expensive" had said so.

In so far as parents referred to the equality of instruction in junior colleges with instruction elsewhere —which was their almost universal practice in the remaining responses—some additional reason is implied. This surely must in some instances involve the most common reason given, attendance in junior college less expensive, although it must also involve others.

Ability to go elsewhere of students living at home while in attendance. One source of the information assembled for this volume was a blank filled out by the students themselves. Many of the data supplied constitute the basis of subsequent portions of this section. A question which only students who were living at home were asked to answer was, Could you go to college if you had to live away from home while in attendance? This question was put to students in public junior colleges, private junior colleges, institutions of the separate-college type, and a state university.

A total of 1016 students living at home answered the question by responses equivalent to "Yes," "No," or "Doubtful." For practical purposes the "noes" and "doubtfuls" may be considered as a single group.

These include 364, or 35.8 per cent, of all students responding. The percentages for all three groups—that is, public junior colleges, private junior colleges, and other higher institutions—run high, none dropping below a third of those answering the question.

There can be no doubt that the chief deterrent factor to attendance elsewhere for these students, if no collegiate opportunities were at hand, would be the financial outlay involved. Only occasionally could it be some other influence not directly traceable to economic considerations.

Annual cost of attendance. Information concerning the cost of attendance was secured from the students themselves on the blanks referred to in the foregoing section. They were requested to report for a full school year on each item listed; namely, board, room, tuition and fees, textbooks and school supplies, laundry, traveling expenses to and from school, and incidentals. An estimate of the total annual cost was also asked for. A first point of inquiry, the answers to which were used throughout the comparisons to follow, was, Do you live at home while attending?

Estimates were provided by more than 2000 students—957 in sixteen public junior colleges, 729 in eight private junior colleges, and 348 in three Mid-Western colleges and a state university. Median costs on each item have been computed. Two sets of median totals were also obtained, one emanating from the estimated totals of the students themselves, the other from the sums of the respective medians for each of the items. Of the two totals the second probably supplied a better estimate of the cost of the bare essentials of a year of college work, although some merit must attach to the first, since the students probably have in mind other items of cost than those listed to account for the differences between the two sets of totals.

1. One notable tendency to difference in the measures of totals is naturally that between the costs for students living at home and those living away from home while in attendance. For public junior colleges the difference between the medians of the first totals is that between $126 and $400; for private junior colleges, that between $262 and $917; and for institutions of the conventional type, that between $286 and $623. For the medians of the second totals the differences are approximately equal to those of the first, except for the private junior-college group, for which it is reduced by somewhat more than $200.

2. A second notable tendency to difference in both totals is that between the figures for public junior colleges when they are contrasted with the two remaining groups of institutions. For example, the medians in the first totals for students at home are less than half as large for public junior colleges as for the other two types of institutions, and the medians

DEMOCRATIZATION

in the second totals show even greater proportionate differences. The costs for students not living at
home while in attendance likewise show significant

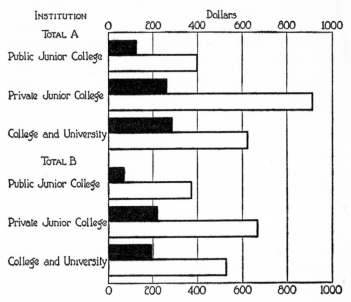

FIG. 24. Median total annual costs of attendance for students at home
and for students away from home in public junior colleges, in private
junior colleges, and in other higher institutions. (Black, at home; in
outline, away from home)

differences in favor of public junior colleges, although
these differences are not proportionately as large.

3. A third tendency to difference is that between
the totals for private junior colleges as compared with
institutions of the third group, the colleges and the

[151]

state university. This is usually in favor of institutions of the latter group.

The difference between the total cost of attendance when a student attending a public junior college lives at home and when he lives away from home is accounted for almost entirely by the cost of board and room. This does not mean that the cost of food during nine months for a student living at home is negligible. A careful estimate of the cost of food for young adults living at home (leaving out of account the item of labor) places it at $135 for a period of nine months. To make a fair comparison with costs for students away from home it is necessary to add this item of probable cost of food to the total annual expenses. Such addition would not be called for in the case of the cost of room, since provision for the member of the family will usually be available whether he attends while living at home or elsewhere. In other words, there would seldom be additional outlay from the family income for rooming accommodations for a student who lives at home while attending a local institution.

The items that account for the differences between the public junior colleges on the one hand and the two remaining types on the other are primarily tuition and incidentals; but laundry, texts, and travel are partly contributory. Since many public junior colleges make no tuition charge or make a charge only for nonresidents, the median cost on this item is very low for this group. It is considerably higher for private junior colleges than for other higher institutions, the difference having its explanation primarily in two facts: (1) the lower tuition charge in the state-university group, which furnished almost a third of the students in the colleges and universities who supplied estimates of cost on these items, and (2) the fact that some of the students in the private junior colleges were taking work in special departments like music and art, for which additional tuition charges are made.

Since the data presented concern types of units rather than particular schools, they must hide differences in yearly costs among the institutions of any single type. Differences in total costs among public junior colleges are primarily determined by differences in tuition, which range from no cost to the student to a maximum of $100 in a single school. The median of students' estimates of total costs (for students away from home) in a low-cost private junior college was found to be $526, and in a high-cost institution in the same group, $1346. The range of medians in the standard higher institutions represented was $524 to $700.

The outstanding findings of this study of the estimates of expenditures by more than two thousand students in twenty-eight different institutions are that attendance while living at home is much cheaper than attendance away from home, and that, since public junior colleges serve local constituencies primarily, the argument of popularization through lowered cost —and it is a powerful argument—applies more particularly to this type of unit rather than to the other types. Another conclusion of some moment is that for students away from home the standard higher institution tends to be somewhat less expensive than the private junior college, although there is sufficient variation from unit to unit to afford exceptions to the rule. The cost of attendance in public junior colleges for students away from home is lower than in either of the other types, but it is likely to rise somewhat as the numbers of such students increase to the point of reducing the proportionate frequency of living accommodations for students in the communities in which such units are located.

Popularization through propinquity of opportunities for higher education. In Chapter X, where an effort is made to locate the size of community and of high-school enrollment in which the establishment of junior-college units of desirable minimum size would be feasible, certain facts are presented which have meaning also for the present problem. At one point reference is made to the proportion of the population (that is, the number in each 1000 of the total) represented by those of its high-school graduates who in a particular school year were enrolled in either of the first two years of work in higher institutions. As some of these communities contain local higher institutions —usually colleges—it has been possible to compare the proportions in communities with such higher schools and those without them. For the latter these proportions average 5.6 per 1000 of the population; for the former, 10.9. This is the same thing as saying that the presence of a higher institution in the community almost doubles the proportion of its population who secure the benefits of the first two years of college education.

Reference is made at another point in the same chapter to the percentages which those graduates from the high schools who are in the first two years of higher institutions constitute of the total enrollment of the high schools. Here again, high schools in communities with and without local higher institutions are compared. The respective average percentages are 11.8 and 17.3, showing a difference of 5.5 per cent. This difference represents an increase in the proportion of almost a half—a difference in favor of high schools in communities with local higher institutions. Both of these comparisons demonstrate that propinquity of higher institutions affects the proportions favorably—tends to popularize higher education. The fact that there are those who take up their residence in communities with colleges in order the more easily to provide the opportunities of higher education

for their sons and daughters adds to, rather than subtracts from, the inference drawn as to the large extent
of popularization—or of economic democratization
—of higher education.

*Occupational distribution of the fathers of students
in secondary and higher institutions.* Still another
test of whether the junior college is designed to foster
the economic democratization of higher education is
made possible through a canvass of the occupational
distribution of fathers as reported by the students who
were appealed to for the information used in this section. The form and methods of inquiry adhered as
closely as possible to those used by G. S. Counts[1] in his
report of a recent investigation of the social composition of the student-body in secondary schools. The
single exception as to the form of inquiry used is that
for Harvard freshmen. The data used for this group
were taken from the admission books of the institution; these supply, among other items of information,
the "business or profession" of the father.

The total number of students included in this study
is 2744. Their distribution to the several groups under which they are studied are public junior-college
freshmen and sophomores, 1062; private junior-
college freshmen and sophomores, 705; college and

---

[1] "The Selective Character of American Secondary Education." Supplementary Educational Monographs, No. 19, May, 1922. The University of
Chicago, Chicago, Illinois.

state-university sophomores, 346; Harvard freshmen, 631. The sophomores of the public junior-college group, 281 in number, are also given separate consideration at one point. Of the sixteen public junior colleges represented three are located in California, one in Illinois, two in Iowa, one in Kansas, one in Michigan, four in Minnesota, two in Missouri, one in Texas, and one in Wisconsin. With the exception of the one in Wisconsin, which is a unit in a normal school, all are in city or high-school districts. One of the seven private junior colleges is in Iowa, five are in Missouri, and one is in Virginia. One of each of the three colleges is in Illinois, Minnesota, and Wisconsin, and the state institution is the University of Minnesota. Data borrowed from Counts's study concern 17,265 students in the public high schools of Bridgeport, Connecticut; Mount Vernon, New York; St. Louis, Missouri; and Seattle, Washington; and 619 students in Phillips-Exeter Academy and the University of Chicago High School.

The basis of classification of fathers' occupations was that used by Counts. The order of grouping is roughly, but not accurately, that of the economic status of the occupational divisions represented, from the highest, proprietors, to the lowest, common labor. Counts states that the aim was "to get classes of reasonable homogeneity from the standpoint of social status, position in the economic order, and intellectual

TABLE III. PERCENTAGE DISTRIBUTION BY OCCUPATIONAL GROUPS OF THE FATHERS OF STUDENTS IN PUBLIC HIGH SCHOOLS, PUBLIC JUNIOR COLLEGES, PRIVATE JUNIOR COLLEGES, OTHER HIGHER INSTITUTIONS, AND PRIVATE SECONDARY SCHOOLS

PARENTAL OCCUPATION	PUBLIC HIGH SCHOOLS[1]	PUBLIC JUNIOR COLLEGES	PUBLIC JUNIOR COLLEGES (SOPHOMORES ONLY)	PRIVATE JUNIOR COLLEGES	SOPHOMORES IN COLLEGES AND STATE UNIVERSITY	FRESHMEN IN A LARGE EASTERN UNIVERSITY	TWO PRIVATE SECONDARY SCHOOLS[1]
1. Proprietors	19.8	19.1	17.8	29.5	25.1	35.7	42.7
2. Professional service	9.4	14.0	15.3	15.3	20.8	30.3	31.0
3. Managerial service .	16.5	16.3	17.8	9.4	7.8	5.4	11.5
4. Commercial service	9.5	9.3	9.6	6.9	8.7	8.6	9.0
5. Clerical service . . .	5.8	3.8	2.8	1.1	3.5	2.4	2.1
6. Agricultural service	2.4	14.2	11.7	26.9	22.5	1.4	0.7
7. Artisan-proprietors .	4.2	2.8	3.2	1.7	2.6	0.3	1.3
8. Manual labor	29.1	15.6	18.3	6.7	7.1	6.5	0.3
9. Unknown	3.3	4.9	3.6	2.4	2.0	9.4	1.4
Total	100.0	100.0	100.1	99.9	100.1	100.0	100.0

outlook."[2] The procedure in tabulation revealed no difficulties not already made clear in his report; the single exception was in the use of the data for Harvard freshmen, especially because they did not contain responses to such questions as, Where or for whom does he [the father] work? or Is he owner or part owner of the business in which he works? making it impossible to locate as definitely as in the other groups a small proportion of the parents con-

[1] G. S. Counts, The Selective Character of American Secondary Education, p. 138.
[2] Ibid. chap. iv.

cerned. In order to avoid all unfairness as regards the distribution for this institution, these doubtful cases were placed in the lower of the two or three levels on which they might be classified. With the method safeguarded in this way it may be concluded that the distribution to the lower levels is at least as large as, if not larger than, it would have been had answer to the questions quoted been available, as was the case in the remaining groups.

A comparison of the percentage distributions for students in public high schools and public junior colleges shows more tendencies to similarity than to difference. However, there is a larger percentage in professional service and there are smaller percentages in clerical service, artisan-proprietors, and manual labor, indicating that the public junior college is to some extent more economically selective than is the public high school. The differences are in kind (but not degree) somewhat like those shown by Counts[1] for points lower down in the school system. A larger percentage in agricultural service is explained by the smaller size of some of the cities in which the public junior colleges are located and their proximity to farming territory. It is hardly to be assumed that this particular larger percentage represents a greater extent of economic democratization of education on this level, as the fathers of those whose responses fall in

[1] "The Selective Character of American Secondary Education," chap. vi.

this group are all but exclusively farm-owners. The same statement is applicable to the large percentages for this group for public junior-college sophomores, private junior colleges, and sophomores in colleges and the state university.

The percentage distribution for sophomores in public junior colleges is very similar to that for all students in this type of unit, but it shows a slightly greater extent of economic democratization. This is probably explained by a partial tendency of the sons and daughters of the more well-to-do to transfer to higher institutions elsewhere at the opening of the second college year, whereas those on lower economic levels are under greater compulsion to continue to avail themselves of opportunities at lower cost nearer home.

The distributions for private junior colleges and for other higher institutions are sufficiently similar to be considered simultaneously. The totals of the first two classes of occupations, proprietors and professional service, are almost equal, being, respectively, 44.8 and 45.9 per cent. The latter exceeds the former in the percentages of those in managerial and clerical service and artisan-proprietors, but the former in turn exceeds the latter in the proportion in agricultural service. The percentages of manual laborers are almost equal.

When compared with the figures for public junior colleges, however, the percentages for these two groups show some interesting contrasts. The larger percentages of those who are proprietors and in professional service are notable, as are also the much smaller percentages in manual labor, and the tendency to smaller percentages in the middle groups of occupations. For Harvard freshmen and students in the two private secondary schools the differences just mentioned are even somewhat more accentuated, being especially marked for the last-named group.

A final check on the degree of economic democratization achieved in each of the types of higher institutions represented in this section is afforded by the ratios between the fathers in each occupational group as shown and the percentages of the total male population forty-five years of age and over in the corresponding groups. The reasons for using figures pertaining to men of forty-five and over are presented by Counts and need not be repeated here. Two distributions have been obtained: one for Minnesota and Missouri combined, the other for Massachusetts. Data for the two Mid-Western states were used because they represent fairly well the distribution in most of the states in which the junior colleges, the colleges, and the state university are located. For an analogous reason data for Massachusetts were used in the computation of the ratios for Harvard.

The significance of the ratios may be the more readily sensed if one bears in mind that, assuming families to be of equal size in all the occupational levels, equal representation of all occupational groups in the higher institutions would result in ratios approximating unity. The significant fact is that the several groups are far from equally represented. None of the types of institution included in the comparison has achieved an extent of economic and social democratization in which its authorities are warranted in taking great pride. Nevertheless the public junior college, as shown by the smaller percentages in the upper levels of occupations, is farther along the way than any of the remaining types. At certain points the private junior college compares favorably with other colleges in the Mid-West and with Harvard, but at others the comparison is not as favorable to it. The ratios for agricultural service are not particularly significant, for reasons already given. All things considered, the upshot of the comparison on the basis of occupational distribution of fathers is a conclusion in confirmation of the public junior-college movement.

Conclusions concerning economic democratization. Each of the lines of inquiry pursued for the content of this section lends support to the claim that the public junior college fosters the economic democratization of higher education. This is shown in the fact that lowered cost is the most frequently recurring reason given by parents for attendance of their sons and daughters in local junior colleges rather than in higher

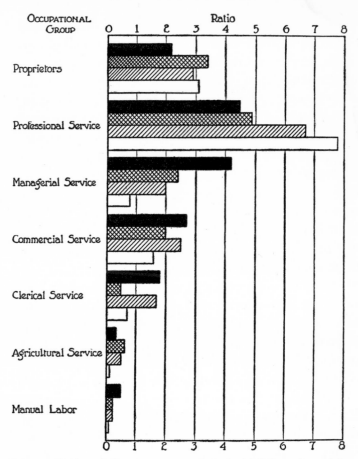

FIG. 25. Ratios of the percentages of students' fathers in certain groups of occupations to the percentages of males of forty-five and over engaged in the same groups. (Black, public junior colleges; cross-hatching, private junior colleges; single-hatching, Mid-Western colleges and a state university; in outline, Eastern university)

institutions elsewhere, but it is shown more especially in the large proportions of these parents who admit frankly that they could not afford to send their sons and daughters to institutions away from home. It is shown in the large proportions of students in all types of higher institutions, junior colleges included, living at home while in attendance who acknowledge that they would be certain or likely to be deprived of the opportunities for higher education if they were required to attend away from home. It is emphatically demonstrated in the lowered costs for students living at home while in attendance, the argument applying particularly to students in public junior colleges. It was shown again in the increased ratio of those enrolled in higher institutions to the populations of communities, and to the high-school enrollments in these communities, in cases where opportunities for higher education are immediately accessible. The bulk of this increase must be attributed to the reduction in costs to those who can attend while living at or near home. Most significant of all, perhaps, is the democratization shown in the increased proportions in public junior colleges of the sons and daughters of fathers in the lower levels of occupational groups, levels less frequently represented in other types of higher institution. Without doubt we have in the public junior college an important influence for the economic and social democratization of educational opportunity.

The claim is not as apposite to the private junior college, although it should not be impossible to make it so.

It will be essential to keep this important argument of economic democratization in the foreground of attention throughout the consideration of the type of junior-college unit to foster. At other points in this volume data appear which emphasize the necessity of encouraging the establishment of sizable units rather than small units. In order to have the argument of economic democratization apply, it will be imperative to establish the institution primarily in communities of good size; otherwise inordinately large proportions of students must leave home to attend, thereby removing an important justification for the movement.

It remains to be said that through making the first two years of higher education available at lower cost, the junior college will often operate to popularize the *upper years* of collegiate and university education by reducing the cost of the full course to approximately that of the years away from home. To many parents and desirable prospective students the cost of four full years away from home must seem prohibitive, whereas the cost of two years will seem a much less insurmountable obstruction. Add to this relief the increased maturity of the junior-college graduate, his advance of two years toward a status of self-help, and we are making more feasible for many the completion of a full college or professional curriculum.

VI

THE JUNIOR COLLEGE IN ITS CONSERVING AND SOCIALIZING INFLUENCES

I. The Junior College and Home Influences during Immaturity

The expectations. Reference to the list of claims made for the junior college by its friends, as presented in Chapter II, shows three which although not identical in significance have elements in common that warrant their scrutiny in proximity to each other. Two of these were mentioned with notable frequency. They concern *continuing home influences during immaturity* and *affording attention to the individual student* in the junior colleges in ways not possible in other higher institutions. The third, proposed by a few only of the friends of the private junior college, refers to *offering better opportunities for training in leadership* than can be afforded in four-year colleges and universities.

Those who put forward the first of these three claims have in mind primarily the conservation of the moral interests of the student during the earlier portions of the college period, when he is often still too young and too much in need of guidance to be thrust into what is sometimes regarded as the disorganizing social environment of the large college or university. They would urge that the student, although scholastically prepared for college work, still requires the stabilizing influence of frequent contact with the home. The local junior college, they contend, provides a solution of this serious problem.

There is no intent here to enter upon an extended discussion of the problem, nor upon a justification of the misgivings many friends and patrons of higher education entertain with reference to the moral dangers to the young student in his first years in college or university away from home. It will be assumed that the dangers are present to some extent, especially where large numbers of students attend institutions inadequately staffed for purposes of social and moral guidance. Probably very few will be inclined to scout the presence in such situations of at least some measure of moral hazard. The chief item of concern here need not be the presentation of evidence to prove or to deny the hazard as much as to show whether or not those whose sons and daughters attend higher institutions believe it exists and what effect that belief has upon college attendance.

Statements of parents with children in public junior colleges. A pertinent fact which does not require establishment is that students are entering college long before social and moral maturity may be presumed to have arrived. For instance, the middle 50 per cent enter Minnesota above the age of seventeen years nine months and below that of nineteen years six months. A fourth of the freshmen range in age from fifteen years to seventeen years nine months. It would be surprising, indeed, if discerning parents with sons and daughters of these ages ready for college work should not hesitate to remove them from domestic influences.

In the third and concluding section of Chapter V, dealing with the problem of economic democratization of higher education by means of the junior college, there was presented a digest of the responses of parents to a simple question designed to ascertain why their sons or daughters attended local public junior colleges rather than colleges or universities elsewhere. At that point, because of its pertinence to the problems under consideration, attention was directed in particular to the reason most frequently given for such attendance—the financial one. It is now appropriate to refer to the reason furnished by the second largest proportion of all the parents: in actual figures by 118, or 27.8 per cent of all the reasons given, and by approximately three fifths of the total of 199 parents making some sort of response. This reason is the *opportunity afforded by the local public junior college to extend the period of home influence over the early years of college attendance.*

CONSERVATION AND SOCIALIZATION

The junior college actually serves in this way. By means of a comparison of the ages of freshmen in public junior colleges with those of freshmen in the University of Minnesota it has been possible to ascertain whether or not the former type of unit is, after the manner suggested, serving to extend home influences during attendance upon college work. The group of students concerned were freshmen entering the College of Science, Literature, and the Arts of the university in the fall of 1921, the first 631 in alphabetical arrangement. It appeared that 388 of these freshmen, 212 men and 176 women, came from Minneapolis, St. Paul, and suburban communities near enough to make possible daily trips to attend regular day sessions. This does not mean that they actually commuted, but merely that residence was near enough to make commutation possible. Those reporting residence in the suburban communities constituted an inconsequential proportion of the 388. The remaining 243 students, 167 men and 76 women, came from beyond commutable distances; that is, they would all need to be away from home during attendance at the university. The grouping here made is intended to disclose the difference in ages, if any, between the group whom the University of Minnesota was serving as would a local junior college, in making possible the continuation of the influence of the home, and the group who must leave home to attend.

There are significant differences in ages between the two groups, both by sex and by totals. For example, the median difference between men from outside the Twin Cities and those from inside is eight months—two thirds of a calendar year. There is the same difference for women, and therefore about the same for the sexes combined. The ranges of the middle 50 per cent show similar or even greater differences. It is clear that attendance away from home is undertaken at a later age than attendance where frequent contact with home is possible.

What is noteworthy in the ages of freshmen in sixteen public junior colleges is that they are almost identical with those for freshmen in the University of Minnesota whose residences are in the Twin Cities. This approach to identity takes on real significance for the question under consideration when it is called to mind that students in the public junior colleges come, almost exclusively, from homes in the immediate vicinity. It leads to the conclusion that the public junior college tends to prevent delay in entering upon college work.

The question may be raised by the inquiring reader as to the qualifying effect upon our conclusions of any difference that may exist between the ages of high-school students in large cities and of those in smaller communities which would account for the difference between the ages of freshmen in the University of

Minnesota from within the Twin Cities and of those from without. If there is a corresponding difference in the ages of high-school seniors, the facts presented would be without meaning for the present problem.

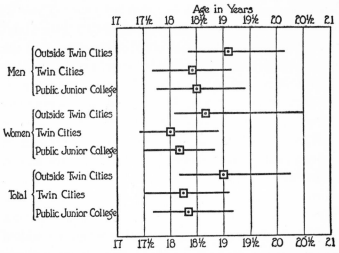

FIG. 26. Ranges in age of the middle 50 per cent and median ages (1) of freshmen in the University of Minnesota from outside the Twin Cities and suburbs and from the Twin Cities and suburbs and (2) of freshmen in public junior colleges. (The length of line represents the range of the middle 50 per cent; the square locates the median)

In order to answer this question a supplementary comparison was made similar to that just reported, but of seniors (1) in high schools of Minnesota outside the Twin Cities[1] and (2) in Central High School,

[1] The data from which these measures were computed were made available by Professor W. S. Miller of the University of Minnesota.

St. Paul. The respective medians for the two groups show a close correspondence, being seventeen years seven months and seventeen years six months. There is no difference in ages found in these data that will explain away the differences between freshmen inside the Twin Cities and those from outside.

Conclusion. The main findings of this section are (1) that large proportions of freshmen are so young as to justify discerning parents in their feeling of insecurity about the moral welfare of their sons and daughters in large colleges and universities inadequately staffed for social and moral guidance, (2) that large proportions of parents of students in junior colleges indorse the new unit because it does make possible the continuance of home influences during the first years of college work, and (3) that this attitude is sufficiently general to influence markedly the age at which young people of both sexes enter college. Moreover, (4) the presence in the local community of opportunities of higher education tends to lower the age at entrance as much as from six to nine months, or, conversely, the absence of such opportunities tends to delay it by that long.

Not all this unfortunate loss of time is imputable to immaturity alone. Without question some of the delay is attributable to financial causes, as when a student remains out for a year to work and lay aside funds against the expense of subsequent attendance. There must even be other occasional causes for postponement of entrance upon college work. But there can be no reasonable doubt that immaturity and parents' fears of its consequences are a potent factor, if not the predominant one. In so far as this is so, the junior college will operate to remove the obstruction and will make it possible for the home to exercise its conserving influences over a larger proportion of the period of social immaturity.

II. The Junior College and the Individual Student

The claim made. The second of the claims made in this chapter is that the junior-college unit is better designed to afford attention to the individual student than are the larger institutions. The assertion is made in the light of the fact that, enrollments being smaller, classes are not so large, and the individual student is therefore not so likely to be lost sight of as he is in educational units with larger class registrations.

It is shown in the third section of Chapter V that this is one of the four reasons most frequently given by parents for sending their sons and daughters to local junior colleges rather than to higher institutions elsewhere. This explanation was found to include 47 of the total of 423 reasons volunteered. As there were 199 parents responding, this means that it was a prominent influence in the minds of almost a fourth of all answering the question.

Facts as to the size of class sections in higher institutions, including junior colleges. The method of scrutiny of this claim was simply that of tabulating the size of classes on the junior-college level as reported by instructors appealed to in public and private junior colleges and in four-year colleges and universities. A total of 43 institutions are represented in the findings here reported. Of these, 27 are junior colleges (20 public and 7 private), 14 are standard four-year colleges, and 2 are universities. To save space the names of the junior colleges represented will not be given, but it may be said that the public institutions are located in eight different states, and the private institutions in three different states. The four-year colleges are Agnes Scott, Alma, Amherst, Bates, Cornell, DePauw, Hillsdale, Lawrence, Park, Pomona, Puget Sound, Wellesley, Whitman, Willamette. They are located in eleven different states. The two universities are Stanford University and the University of Wisconsin, both of them, as are most of the colleges, wrestling with the problem of rapidly mounting enrollments. In these universities, only the departments of English, mathematics, chemistry, and history were appealed to for information, on the assumption that data from these would adequately represent the situation for the first two years of university work. A total of 430 different instructors are represented in the data utilized—138 in public junior colleges and 60 in private junior colleges, 123 in four-year colleges, and 109 in universities. This means that 198 were teachers in junior colleges and that 232 were teachers in colleges and universities. Information was secured in such a way as to assure that the findings should be representative of all these groups.

Percentages of large classes in junior colleges, four-year colleges, and universities. One mode of comparing the size of class sections in junior colleges and universities is by their percentages of classes in excess of thirty students. Of such classes the junior colleges have only 11.6 per cent, the remainder being classes of thirty students and less. In contrast it was found that the other types of higher institution had 32.7 per cent, or almost three times the proportion.

Between public and private junior colleges there is little difference, the former having 10.7 per cent of large classes, the latter 13.5 per cent. The four-year colleges and the universities likewise differ only slightly in their percentages, which are, respectively, 33.1 and 31.9. A closer scrutiny, however, of these large classes in these two older types of higher institution shows a tendency to somewhat larger instructional units for the universities; for of the 126 classes in excess of 30 in the colleges the median is only slightly in excess of 40, whereas for the 69 university classes of this size the median is approximately 60, or 20 students larger than for the colleges.

Another comparison of the size of class sections. A second mode of comparing the instructional units is by the median size of the class and the range of the middle 50 per cent of the classes when they are arranged in the order from least to greatest. This method, again, shows little difference between the two types of junior colleges or between the two older types of higher institution, although it does corroborate the conclusion in respect to the difference found between junior colleges on the one hand and colleges and universities on the other.

Size of classes in small, medium, and large junior colleges. Since, as was seen in Chapter I, junior colleges differ widely in total enrollments, and since the magnitude of these enrollments must have much influence on the size of class in any unit, special inquiry has been made on this point in order to note the size of enrollment in junior colleges at which the argument of small size of class ceases to apply. For this purpose the twenty public junior colleges so far represented in this chapter were distributed into three groups including eleven "small," seven "medium," and two "large" units. The small junior colleges here include those enrolling a total of 100 students or less; the medium, those enrolling from 100 to 200; the large, those enrolling over 200. Unfortunately the

[176]

distribution of institutions is not even over the full range of size. The disability applies especially to the middle group, most of which enroll nearer 100 students than 200. This makes the middle group not unlike the group of small units, and this similarity is

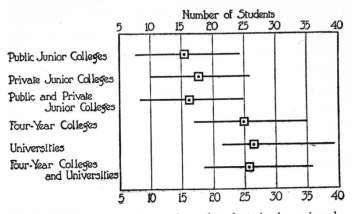

FIG. 27. Median and quartile numbers of students in classes in public junior colleges, private junior colleges, public and private junior colleges, four-year colleges, universities, and four-year colleges and universities. (The length of line represents the interquartile range—that is, the range of the middle 50 per cent; the square locates the median)

reflected in the measures of size of class presented. However, as will be seen, this special inquiry has much meaning for the validity of the claim under consideration—the larger extent of individual attention possible in junior colleges.

The measures of tendency show no large difference between the size of classes in small and medium junior colleges. The real increase appears where large junior colleges are concerned. In these the classes seem to approximate the size of those in colleges and universities, although there is some difference in favor of the junior-college units at the upper limit of the range of the middle 50 per cent in the total distribution.

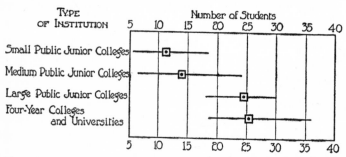

FIG. 28. Median and quartile numbers of students in classes in small, medium, and large public junior colleges and in four-year colleges and universities. (The length of line represents the interquartile range—that is, the range of the middle 50 per cent; the square locates the median)

The evidence presented at other points in this volume—more especially in Chapter X, but elsewhere also—favors the establishment of only sizable junior colleges rather than small junior colleges. It is there recommended that the type to be fostered should have an enrollment of 200 or more students. The meaning for the claim now being considered is apparent: if recommendations of this sort are to be put in operation in the establishment of junior colleges, a good portion of the argument of a larger extent of individual attention because of smaller classes is removed. Certainly it cannot be accepted in the unqualified form in which it applies to the less desirable units enrolling fewer than 200 students. On the other hand, even in units of good size there would be some validity to the claim. There could, moreover, be no such large classes as are sometimes found in colleges and universities.

The influence of large institutional registrations. The problem of attention to the individual student is not, however, solely a problem of the size of the classes to which he is assigned, however important this factor may be. It is in part a problem of sheer magnitude of the total enrollment of an institution. Even were all classes kept to teachable size, there must be a tendency toward loss of sight of the individual when enrollments mount as they have during the last third of a century. For example, in the University of Minnesota the enrollment of freshmen increased from 254 in 1889–1890 to 3053 during the autumn quarter of 1919–1920. And for most of our higher institutions there have been similar, when not equivalent, increments. Despite efforts to have these large entering classes distributed to units of manageable size, which has not always been possible, there must almost certainly follow the process designated by McConn[1] as

[1] Max McConn, "The Freshman Flood," in *Survey*, Vol. XLVIII, pp. 299–305 (May 27, 1922).

the "depersonalization" of the process of higher education. Such a superfluity of students for facilities available must almost inevitably result in a temptation to prodigality in dealing with them, to a disparagement of the individual when the loss of a considerable number of students cannot affect appreciably the total number still remaining. Since there is no prospect of early abatement in the growth of registrations, the elevation of the individual to a place where he is likely to have anything like adequate consideration, especially during the earlier years of the college course when this is still essential, seems to wait upon a reorganization of higher education which distributes the student-body to smaller groups than is now the practice. The general establishment of junior colleges would make this possible.

Epitome. The evidence presented concerning the size of classes in junior colleges and in four-year colleges and universities is to the effect that institutions of the former type have at present a distinct advantage. If, however, sizable junior-college units only are fostered, the pertinence of the argument of more attention to the individual student because of smaller classes in junior colleges will be reduced, since we have found that the sizes of classes in units of good size approach those in higher institutions, even if they do not equal them. The argument, however, will doubtless always be in some part applicable.

But size of class itself does not comprehend all the problem of attention to the individual student. The junior college, even if it is fostered only in sizable units, by merely reducing the total number of students in a single institution will place a check on the process of depersonalization in higher education,—a process which is encouraged by the mere fact of a large total registration,—and it will do so during those college years when attention to the individual student is most imperative.

III. THE JUNIOR COLLEGE AND TRAINING IN LEADERSHIP

Extra-curricular organizations in junior colleges. It has already been indicated that among the aspirations entertained for the junior college is the hope that it will afford better opportunities for experiences which constitute "laboratory work" in leadership than do larger institutions like universities. It will be the concern of this section to inquire into the extent of justification for the aspiration, first, by ascertaining the scope of extra-curricular activities; second, by reporting the extent of student participation in them as compared with that in other higher institutions; and, third, by comparing the frequency with which students in junior colleges and other higher institutions are officeholders in student organizations.

The variety of extra-curricular organizations found in operation in junior colleges is wide. The large divisions under which they may be grouped are athletic, literary, musical, and social and religious. Under these have been listed the particular interests represented by the organizations. Under what may be designated as athletic activities were found basket-ball teams, football teams, baseball teams, track teams, swimming teams, etc., hiking clubs, tennis clubs, and athletic associations; under literary activities were literary societies, debate, dramatics, oratory, the school paper and other publications, and clubs for language, history, science, English, reading, and the like; the musical organizations included choral societies, glee clubs, orchestras, and bands; and the social and religious groupings comprehended the Christian associations, other religious organizations, students' councils, etc.

While from considerations of limitations of space and of monotony to the reader it is deemed inadvisable to report the number of times each of these many kinds of student activities was met with, it is not out of place to give some notion of their average frequency in all the junior colleges visited by the writer. For twenty-six public junior colleges in which personal inquiry was made on this point there were an average of 11.2 extra-curricular organizations. For sixteen private junior colleges the average was slightly higher, being 11.9.

The expectation that junior colleges with the larger enrollments will maintain larger numbers of organizations is borne out by further examination of the data assembled. For the purpose here in mind the public junior colleges were divided into three groups: six junior colleges with enrollments of less than 50 students, eleven with enrollments of 50 to 149, and nine with enrollments of 150 or more. Each of the four divisions of activities—athletic, literary, musical, and social and religious—shows an increase from the smallest to the largest junior colleges, an increase reflected in the average total numbers. These averages are, respectively, 8.5, 10.0, and 14.4. These figures show a much larger increase between the second and third groups than between the first and second. From the standpoint of those who have confidence in the educational efficacy of well-conducted extra-curricular organizations, this fact urges the establishment of junior colleges of good size, rather than small units with few such interests and with small numbers of students participating.

The reader perhaps hardly needs to be admonished that the figures cited cover all degrees of effectiveness of functioning, from organizations with scarcely a spark of vitality to those at the other extreme, conducted with vigor and operating as important instruments of student self-education, social and otherwise.

A study of the distribution of memberships held in extra-curricular organizations was made, involving four groups of students as follows: 995 in fifteen public junior colleges, 680 in seven private junior colleges, 227 in three standard four-year colleges, and 116 in a state university. The data for junior colleges concern both freshmen and sophomores, predominantly the former; those for the remaining higher institutions concern sophomores exclusively. This difference in classification of students would be likely, if it influences the results at all, to be unfavorable to the distribution in junior-college groups.

The largest percentage of students holding no memberships is in the university group, where it attains almost a third. For the public junior-college group the proportion is between a fifth and a fourth of all. It is almost equal in the two remaining groups, dropping as low as 7.9 and 7.0 per cent, respectively, for private junior colleges and four-year colleges, the similarity perhaps having its explanation in the fact that almost all the private junior colleges were formerly institutions claiming to do full college work and have in consequence carried over similar tendencies with respect to extra-curricular activities. The average numbers of memberships held per student were as follows: in public junior colleges, 2.2; in private junior colleges, 3.4; in four-year colleges, 3.2; in state university, 2.0.

Comparison of officeholding by sophomores. Since laboratory training in leadership is afforded in directing these student affairs more than through mere membership in them, a better criterion by which to compare the institutions in the respect concerned is the extent to which students on the junior-college level in the four groups hold office in these organizations. A portion of such a comparison is provided in the following percentages of sophomores reporting no offices held: public junior colleges, 78.6; private junior colleges, 58.8; four-year colleges, 85.1; state university, 91.5. The average numbers of offices held are roughly in harmony with these, being, respectively, 0.3, 0.7, 0.2, and 0.1. The contrast to be found here between junior colleges on the one hand and other higher institutions on the other has its explanation in the absence in junior colleges of upper-classmen, who, in the other institutions, are naturally elected to the positions of leadership, leaving few offices available for under-classmen. There are differences in each pair of types of institutions: for the junior colleges the differences are in favor of the private group; in the two remaining, in favor of the separate college.

Conclusions. Inquiry into the extent to which extra-curricular organizations are in operation in junior colleges shows a wide range of interest already represented, with a somewhat greater numerical frequency in private institutions than in public institutions.

[185]

Larger units naturally provide greater possibilities in this direction than can those with small student registrations. In so far as these activities are to be regarded as legitimate instruments of training, this constitutes an added objection to the very small institutions, of which a number are in existence.

The extent of student membership in these organizations reaches its highest point in (1) private junior colleges, the three remaining types of institution ranking in the order of (2) separate four-year colleges, (3) public junior colleges, and (4) a state university. As this comparison did not distinguish between freshmen and sophomores in the junior-college units, although only sophomores were represented in the other institutions, one which did so would find these units in even a more favorable position than has been shown.

In the more critical comparison of officeholding by sophomores both types of junior colleges outdo the other types of higher institution, the contrast being attributable to the absence in the former of upperclassmen, to whom the positions of responsibility would otherwise go.

There is no assumption by the writer that in their present state of development and supervision all types of extra-curricular organization are uniformly valuable means of training, either in leadership or otherwise. Without an acquaintance with what goes forward under many of the names reported, mere numerical frequency can easily result in an exaggerated notion of their present value, both in junior colleges and in colleges and universities. Moreover, it is probable that with their longer standing and greater magnitude the activities in the older types of institution are more frequently estimable instruments of education in leadership than those in the smaller, newer units. The numerical data, nevertheless, assure us that as these activities come to be administered with a view to their educational possibilities, which is almost certain to happen in all types of institution, the junior college will not lag behind its older sisters in the educational family. In fact, the larger proportionate extent of officeholding in junior colleges, owing to the absence of upper-classmen, assures us that as we attain the desired level of efficiency, students in the junior college will have much more satisfactory conditions for laboratory work in leadership than will freshmen and sophomores in institutions in which upper-classmen naturally fall heir to the positions of responsibility in extra-curricular activities.

Each of the three contentions of the advocates of the junior college which have been scrutinized in this chapter has been found to have the corroboration of the facts presented. Establishment of junior-college units actually operates to prevent delay in the local student's entrance upon college work, giving assurance that parents look upon the junior college as a means of extending home influences during immaturity. In these days of large and mounting enrollments in colleges and universities, with the accompanying increase in hazard for the socially immature in attendance, it is imperative that some adequate agency of conservation be instituted. The exercise of this influence will be further enhanced by such enrollments in junior colleges as permit a larger regard for the individual student both in and out of the classroom, counteracting the tendencies to depersonalization now too marked in the earlier years at least of our typical higher institutions. If to these forces is added the expansion of opportunities for self-education in leadership made possible by the absence of upper-classmen in the junior colleges, it may be seen that this new institution has potentialities of conservation and socialization during these two school years not possessed by present-day colleges and universities.

VII

THE TREND OF REORGANIZATION IN HIGHER EDUCATION

I. SPECIAL PURPOSES OF THE JUNIOR COLLEGE ON REORGANIZATION OF HIGHER EDUCATION

In the list of current conceptions of the special purposes of the junior college as presented in Chapter II are several having more or less intimate bearing on the organization of secondary and higher education. Among these, to name only a few, are *placing in the secondary school all work appropriate to it* (purpose 10), *fostering the evolution of the system of education* (11), *economizing time and expense by avoiding duplication* (13), and *making possible real university functioning* (16). The implications of such claims are so far-reaching that no study of the junior-college movement making any pretensions to comprehensiveness could escape criticism if it neglected to inquire into their validity. This phase of the junior-college problem is discussed in this chapter and in Chapter VIII, the latter dealing exclusively with the problem of overlapping in high school and college, the former being devoted to a discovery of the evidences of the reorganization which is destined to assign to the junior college a logical place in the school system. These evidences are presented as pertaining to the problem of reorganization as a whole rather than to the validity of each particular claim as given in Chapter II.

The far-reaching reorganization disclosed in this chapter has come upon our secondary and higher schools so gradually and imperceptibly that there is little general consciousness of its profound character and extended ramifications. Indeed, some who are presumed to be leaders in the field seem still to be totally unaware of it; or, if they see it, they are unappreciative of its forces, and, like King Canute, endeavor to command its tides to recede. They appear by their attitudes to assert that the American college is today what it has always been, and that it is foreordained to remain immutable in the future. The facts presented render such assumptions untenable, but they do much more in throwing light on the justifiability of the claims of the friends of the junior college as to its place in reorganized secondary and higher education.

II. The Advancing Age of the College Entrant

Ages of freshmen a hundred years ago and today. An important consideration in evaluating the assumption that the American college has undergone little or no change since its establishment in the colonial period and remains today essentially what it has always been, is the age of the student. Although it is not a matter of common knowledge, some information has been available to indicate that during the later decades of the nineteenth century students entered college at more advanced ages than during the first third of the century. Even as late as 1851 a writer in the *North American Review*[1] speaks of boys entering college at fifteen or sixteen and of their need of parental discipline while in attendance. The marked advance in age is shown in the following quotation from an earlier president of Harvard:

In the four consecutive years beginning with 1762, the average age of the students on entering college was sixteen years and two months, . . . while in the four consecutive years beginning with 1860 it was seventeen years and eight months. . . . In the first of the above-mentioned groups of classes, nearly a third were under fifteen when they entered. . . . On the other hand, in the . . , last group . . . there was but one under fifteen and only eighteen under sixteen.[2]

Desirous of securing a more nearly complete description of this advance in age of college freshmen by a standard method of computing ages, in order that all results of comparisons would be valid, the writer ob-

[1] Vol. LXXII, p. 82.
[2] *Massachusetts Teacher*, Vol. XIX (1866), pp. 342 ff.

tained access to the records of admission to Harvard College for a point near the opening of the nineteenth century and at points two or three decades apart up to 1916. In the half-century beginning about 1830 and ending with 1880 the median age for this institution advanced from sixteen years and three months to eighteen years and seven months, an increase of two and a third years. From 1880 until 1916 there was a slight decline, but not sufficient to warrant anticipation of any significant change in this respect for some time to come. The typical Harvard freshman of a century ago was fully two years younger than the freshman of the more recent period.

The conditions as to ages of freshmen at other older colleges in the earlier part of the nineteenth century have one essential element in common with that just described for Harvard. This is the fact that all the distributions show large numbers of students entering at eleven or twelve to sixteen and a half years of age. Thus, almost a fifth of Amherst's freshmen during the years 1827–1831 were fifteen and a half years old and younger, and almost a third were sixteen and a half and younger; almost a third of Bowdoin's freshmen during 1810–1817 were fifteen and a half and younger, and between two fifths and a half were sixteen and a half and younger; even in Dartmouth, where freshmen during 1800–1804 were on the average somewhat more mature than in other colleges, a sixth were fifteen and a half and younger, and more than a fourth were sixteen and a half and younger.

The marked contrast of these ages with those of our modern higher institutions can be illustrated for

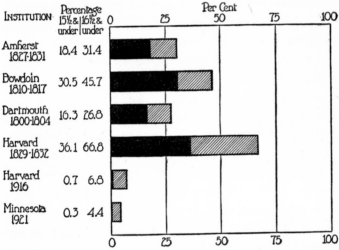

FIG. 29. Percentages of freshmen in Amherst (1827–1831), Bowdoin (1810–1817), Dartmouth (1800–1804), Harvard (1829–1832 and 1916), and the University of Minnesota (1921) fifteen and a half and sixteen and a half years of age and under. (Black, percentages fifteen and a half and under; black and shaded combined, sixteen and a half and under)

Harvard and for the University of Minnesota. For the Eastern private institution the percentage of those entering at fifteen and a half years of age and younger in 1916 was practically negligible, being only seven tenths of 1 per cent, and those sixteen and a half and younger constituted only 6.8 per cent of the whole group. For the Mid-Western state university the corresponding percentages were very similar, being, respectively, three tenths of 1 per cent and 4.4 per cent. Scarcely any freshmen enter college today at the immature ages at which they were admitted a century ago.

What these facts must mean. Thus we find that these early distributions of ages of entering freshmen have at least one characteristic in common : they show large proportions of students beginning what was a hundred years ago regarded as college work at an age much below that of college and university freshmen at the present time. At least in respect to the age of the student-body there is an outstanding difference between the college of the past and that of the present. It would be surprising indeed if this advancing age were not accompanied by far-reaching changes in the college along other vital lines. For example, the materials of instruction must have been of such a nature that children of the tender years between eleven and sixteen could and did accomplish the work.

Biographers of our earlier poets are accustomed to point out, sometimes as though it were an indication of extraordinary precocity, the youthful ages at which they entered college. Emerson and Lowell, it is reported, entered Harvard as freshmen when they were fourteen and fifteen respectively. Bryant and Longfellow were admitted as sophomores when they were fifteen, the former at Williams, and the latter at Bowdoin. These ages, while not quite typical for their generation, have been shown to be sufficiently common to detract measurably from the feeling of awe which they inspire in the minds of those unacquainted with the facts.

III. The Widening Scope of Entrance Requirements and the Downward Shift of the College Curriculum

The widening scope of the requirements for admission. It would be surprising indeed if the advancing age of the college entrant, discussed in the foregoing section, were not accompanied by an increasing amount of educational content required for admission. Such a tendency is just what strikes one's attention with most emphasis when he attempts a summary of the changes which have taken place in the requirements for admission to college during the last hundred years. The nature of the changes must, as in the case of the study of the ages of college entrants, be shown by reference to Eastern institutions which have maintained continuous existence throughout at least a century. They will be illustrated for Amherst and Yale, which, on account of the great similarity of the New England colleges in this respect, may be looked upon as typical.

Throughout most of the nineteenth century the requirements for admission in the classical languages, although experiencing some change, were characterized by relative stability. Preparation in both Latin and Greek was prescribed in the twenties and thirties. In fact, the only prescriptions for entrance outside these fields were, as will be pointed out again, in such subjects as are now typically found only in the elementary school; namely, arithmetic, English grammar, and geography. Near the end of the first third of the century the content in which examinations for entrance were set was Latin grammar, Sallust or four books of Cæsar's Commentaries, the orations of Cicero, Virgil, and Latin prosody. By the end of the century Sallust had given way entirely to Cæsar, and Yale had prescribed Ovid's Metamorphoses. During this period the *amount* of material read had diminished to some extent; for instance, in the number of Cicero's orations and the range of content selected from the Æneid, the Bucolics, and the Georgics, but there seems to have been no marked change in this respect.

In Greek the prescription in grammar was, of course, persistent throughout the period, but the particular content read shifted considerably from the religious to the secular, as is shown in the change in the requirements from the Greek Testament to the Anabasis and the Iliad.

TABLE IV. THE HISTORY OF REQUIREMENTS FOR ADMISSION IN SUBJECTS OTHER THAN THE CLASSICAL LANGUAGES

[Amherst (A) and Yale (Y)]

MATERIALS PRESCRIBED	ISSUE OF CATALOGUE								
	Y, 1822	A, 1835 / Y, 1834	A, 1841 / Y, 1842	A, 1850 / Y, 1850	A, 1858 / Y, 1850	A, 1871 / Y, 1870	A, 1879 / Y, 1880	A, 1890 / Y, 1890	Y, 1900
Arithmetic	Y	A, Y	A, Y	A, Y[1]	A, Y[1]	A, Y[1]	A, Y[1]	A, Y[1]	
English grammar		A, Y	A, Y	A, Y	A, Y	A, Y	A, Y		
Geography		A, Y	Y	Y	Y	A[2], Y	A[2], Y		
Algebra to quadratics				A, Y	A, Y	A, Y	A		
Algebra through quadratics							Y	Y	Y
Euclid (first two books) or plane geometry					Y	A, Y	A, Y	A, Y	Y
Ancient (classical) geography						A	A	Y	
Roman history							Y	Y	Y
Greek history								Y	Y
Roman antiquities							A		
Ancient history								A	
French (elementary grammar)							A		
French or German[3]								A, Y	Y
English literature								A	Y

[1] Higher arithmetic.   [2] Modern geography.   [3] So far as to translate at sight easy prose.

A careful estimate of the prescriptions in these languages in terms of present-day counters places their total at something like seven or eight units—not far from half of the total amount of current requirements of admission to college.

The real changes in requirements for admission during the period considered were outside the field of the classics. The only subject prescribed by Yale in 1822, in addition to the classical materials, was arithmetic. By the middle of the next decade two more present-day elementary-school subjects, English grammar and geography, were added to the entrance examinations. These persisted as requirements until near the close of the century. The first subject now typically of high-school grade to make its appearance, in addition to the work in ancient languages, is what we now refer to as elementary algebra, and this prescription was imposed during the forties. In the passage of three decades more the prescription in this subject had been extended to include essentially what we now designate as "higher" algebra. Before this extension was made, plane geometry (Euclid) had been prescribed, so that by the end of the nineteenth century the equivalent of two and a half units of supra-arithmetical mathematics were required where none had been prescribed at the opening of the period under consideration. Upon the heels of algebra and geometry came subject after subject, until by the end of the century there were, in addition to the prescriptions in the classics, those in algebra through quadratics, plane geometry, ancient history, French or German, and English literature.

These changes, put in quantitative terms and considering only work now regarded as appropriately of secondary-school grade, constitute an increase from seven or eight units to fourteen or fifteen—now typically fifteen or sixteen. In other words, the amount of work prescribed for admission to college was at least doubled during the period of a century : at least two more years of liberal education is being required for admission to college now than formerly. This conclusion is in harmony with the advancing age of the college entrant already demonstrated, but does not do justice to the expansion of typical general education preliminary to college training afforded in the rapid expansion of the elementary school during the same period.

The downward shift of the materials of the college curriculum. Intimately related in turn to the widening scope of entrance requirements is the downward shift of most of the subjects which have found place in the standard college curriculum during the last hundred years. This downward tendency becomes evident during even a cursory examination of the curriculum of any one of our older colleges as set forth in the catalogues issued during any considerable period of years extending from the early decades of the nineteenth century as a starting-point.

A systematic inquiry concerning this depression of courses from upper to lower college levels was made for three of our oldest and most estimable institutions, Amherst, Williams, and Yale, from which only illustrative extractions are made for our present purpose. The ancient languages and literatures are the only fields in which there was no consistent downward shift. The history of the year-place of beginning courses in modern language presents a marked decline. Being usually sophomore and junior offerings in the thirties and forties, these dropped to typically freshman levels by the opening of the twentieth century. The first course in the history of English literature changed from a junior and senior offering of the sixties and seventies to a dominantly freshman course in recent years. Trigonometry, which was a standard sophomore course in 1825, is now curricular material for first-year students, and all other courses in mathematics have shifted downward, those preceding trigonometry continuing their downward course into the secondary school. The sciences, too, joined this downward trend, courses like physics ("natural philosophy") and general chemistry having been junior and senior work in the twenties and thirties to become available to freshmen in the later period. Even philosophy, ethics, logic, and economics (political economy) joined the downward movement, but did not drop as far typically as the sciences. Many courses dropped even farther in universities, especially those on state foundations, for the reason that they are needed as preprofessional work, which is a matter of greater concern in these than in institutions like separate colleges; some of these last adhere to the hope of providing only liberal training throughout the four-year period.

It is already obvious that the shift being described could not and did not stop at the freshman college year. The sequel, the depression of course materials into secondary-school offerings, has already been foreshadowed in illustrating the widening scope of college-entrance requirements. The subjects seen to have been added to prescriptions for entrance—English grammar, geography, arithmetic, algebra through quadratics, plane geometry, ancient history, French and German, and English literature—were all inheritances from college curricula. The first three continued their downward career until they reached the elementary grades; most of the others have found a place in the first two years of our four-year high school.

Nor does this complete the narrative of the downward progress of courses formerly peculiar to the college. Many other courses, some less often honored by a place with those prescribed for admission, either accompanied those named or followed them in due time, among them rhetoric and composition; such courses in mathematics as solid geometry, trigonometry, and occasionally college algebra and analytic geometry; many courses in science, such as physics, chemistry, and those in biology; economics, sociology (as "social problems"); and several of the courses in history, such as American, English, European, etc. What a sound basis they have who refer to the high school as the "people's college"!

The textbooks of yesterday and today. In order the better to compare the courses in the college of a century or less ago with their counterparts in colleges and high schools of today, a careful examination was made of textbooks in use then and now. Some of the comparisons were with present-day college texts, more often they were with present-day high-school texts, and not infrequently they were with both. The comparisons essayed were in the history of English literature, rhetoric and composition, plane geometry, physics, chemistry, general history, American history, and economics, with briefer studies in a few other subjects. Only the general conclusion from the comparison is here stated; each of the comparisons tells essentially the same story, that the subjects and courses during the process of depression to lower years in the system have experienced no apparent dilution. On the contrary, among the group of courses considered there are some, such as plane geometry and American history, which have been notably extended as to content and even intensified as to difficulty during the period of downward trend. All of them, of course, are much enriched as to nature of content and improved as instruments of education; that is, in their pedagogical make-up.

To those prompted to direct attention to the fact that textbooks do not always limit the content of courses and that, in consequence, valid conclusions as to courses cannot be drawn from a comparison of textbooks only, it may be said that the farther back into the preceding century one goes the less use of supplementary volumes will one find. Even as late as the year 1849 the catalogue of Williams College supplied the following information: "The College Library is open to the Senior and Junior classes the first Friday of the term and every Wednesday. To the Sophomore and Freshman classes every Saturday."

Some of the extensive depression together with undiminished or even increased thoroughness was inevitable as a result of development within each field; for instance, from the findings of research in science or history. With the enlargement of the content by these investigations, advanced differentiations and specializations were bound to make their appearance. Then came the desire to secure a recognition of these differentiations as advanced courses in the college curriculum; for example, qualitative, quantitative, and organic chemistry. Before their introduction was feasible it was necessary to lower the general or preliminary course far enough to make a place for the advanced differentiation. After making all allowances for this development, the fact remains that the advancing age of the student for any given college year and the increasing extent of his training before arriving at that point made the downward shift of the materials in undiluted and even in enhanced form practicable as well as desirable.

IV. The Changing Organization of the College Curriculum and the Function of the Major Subject

The changing organization of the college curriculum. As there seemed to be ground for the conjecture that there might be some relationship between the organization of curricula and the advancing age of the college student, an effort was made to note any changes in this respect during the last hundred years. A canvass of the catalogues of several New England colleges at year-points a decade apart through the period 1825–1915 disclosed far-reaching modifications of which the following characterizations in summary for Amherst and Williams are illustrative:

	AMHERST	WILLIAMS
1825	Fully prescribed	Fully prescribed
1835	Fully prescribed	Slightly optional in sophomore and junior years
1845	Fully prescribed	Slightly optional in junior year
1855	Slightly optional in sophomore, junior, and senior years	Slightly optional in junior year
1865	Slightly optional in junior and senior years	Slightly optional in junior year
1875	Slightly optional in junior and senior years	Slightly optional in junior year
1885	Much election in last three years	Partly elective in senior year
1895	Largely elective in last three years	Largely elective in last three years
1905	Largely elective in last three years	Largely elective with major system
1915	Largely elective with major system	Largely elective with major system

Curricula for both colleges at the opening of the period begin as "fully prescribed," proceed in the course of a decade or more to being "slightly optional" in one or more years of the full course, become increasingly elective as the decades pass, and wind up by being "largely elective with the major system." In other words, they moved step by step from the complete prescription of a restricted secondary school, through gradually increasing freedom comporting with the increasing age of the student, to an elective pro-

[205]

gram which assumes sufficient maturity on the part of the student to assure wise selection of subjects and courses, and which opens up the opportunity for specialization. Out of the curricular chaos that reigned during the operation of the largely elective plan emerged the major system, which *requires the student to specialize.*

This major system is at the present time well-nigh the universal practice, as is shown by an examination of the catalogues issued for 1920–1921 or 1921–1922 by one hundred and fourteen colleges; ninety-four, or 82.5 per cent, require the completion of a major for graduation. As intimated, this is the equivalent of saying that at least this proportion of the colleges require specialization of the student.

The function of the major. Whatever may be the intent of the college authorities in prescribing the major, it is important to know its actual function in practice. This has been ascertained for something less than two hundred alumni of one estimable separate college in the Mid-West by (1) inquiring of them the basis upon which they selected their majors and (2) studying possible relationships between these majors and subsequent occupational activity.

Three recurring influences appear in the selection of undergraduate majors; namely, occupational preparation, interest in the subject, and esteem for the instructor. The overwhelmingly predominant motive in selection is the first named, which is reported by more than four fifths of all the graduates responding; interest is operative with almost two thirds; whereas esteem for the instructor induced only 6.6 per cent of the graduates to pursue the major reported.

The proportion of men who made actual occupational use of the major subject subsequently to graduation was just a half of the total number, that for women was 71.6 per cent, and that for all persons responding was 61.3 per cent, or a full three fifths of the total.

There is no escape from the inference that for this group of college graduates the occupational function of the major was the paramount one. This function appears both at the time of selecting it and in the use made of it subsequently to the completion of the college course. Thus the system which emerged from the curricular chaos of a quarter of a century ago is not merely a recognition of the need for specialization: to the student it is preëminently an opportunity for *occupational* specialization, or at least the beginning of such an opportunity. This occupational function is also in line with the greater maturity of college students in these later years as compared with the students a century ago.

V. The Occupational Destination of College Graduates

The nature of the inquiry. Since the data just discussed touching the basis of selection and the function of the major now almost universally required indicate a large occupational bearing, it is pertinent next to present information about the occupational destinations of college graduates. As the question is particularly apposite to the graduates of separate colleges of liberal arts (that is, those unconnected with large universities where opportunities for professional training are afforded), this section has to do with graduates of such schools only. The colleges represented in the study are nineteen in number and are to be found in many sections of the country. Almost a thousand graduates—988, to be exact—are represented in the occupational distribution to be presented, 438 men and 550 women. For reasons that will become apparent they are divided as to being "one year out" and "ten years out," the numbers in these two groups being, respectively, 574 and 414.

Salient facts of the occupational distributions. Scrutiny of the numerical and percentage distributions discloses the following significant facts:

1. For those who have been out but a single year the predominant occupation is of an educational sort, and for most of these it is teaching of one kind or an-

other. *This group includes more than three fifths of all the graduates—almost half the men and three fourths of the women.* In terms of these first years of service of their graduates *these colleges must be looked upon primarily as teacher-training institutions.*

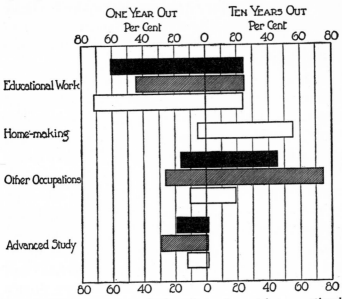

Fig. 30. Percentages of college graduates in certain occupational groups one year and ten years out of college. (Black, all graduates; shaded, men; in outline, women)

2. At ten years out, the proportions of those who are still in educational work, both of men and of women, have been materially reduced, but *the group still includes approximately a fourth of all the gradu-*

ates, the percentages of men and women being almost identical by this time.

3. The percentage of women who are home-makers by the end of the first year out is not large, but it experiences huge accretions during the passage of nine years more. By this time *those engaged in home-making include from one half to three fifths of the total number of women graduates.*

4. The "other occupations" begin with a moderate percentage of the total number of men and women— about a sixth of the whole—but increase to nearly half by the end of the first decade.

5. Advanced study—graduate or professional—in the first years after graduation engages the interests of about a fifth of the whole, but disappears as an interest during the passage of ten years.

6. The shifts during the intervening period seem to be (1), for men, from education and advanced study into other occupations; (2) for women, from teaching into home-making. Graduates of both sexes appear to some extent to use educational work as a stepping-stone.

7. Many men entering upon educational work shift from teaching to administrative positions such as superintendencies and principalships.

8. In the "other occupations" group, among the men one year out, the largest single number are in "business." If to these are added those in banks,

there are a total of 13.9 per cent in the business group broadly defined. The next largest group are in the ministry. Each of these groups is considerably augmented by the end of a decade, business (with banking) including 22.4 per cent. The ministry by this time gives occupation to a full fifth.

9. The only appreciable proportion in "other occupations" of women graduates who have been out one year is to be found in clerical and secretarial employments, this classification holding its own after the passage of nine more years; a few other occupations come into partial prominence as appropriate for college women, namely, library work, medicine, and social service.

These facts, joined with those bearing on the advancing age of the college student and the adjustment in the direction of specialization growing out of this and the downward shift of the materials of general education, seem to urge that the college give serious consideration to a larger extent of occupationalization in its upper years than has been characteristic of it to date. Data of the sort presented here are testimony that the pace toward professionalization demands quickening. Touching educational work, which is an occupation common to both sexes and the predominant one into which these graduates go, colleges should either face their obligation squarely or retire from the field. Their present attitude is now too much one of assuming teacher-training as a by-product, a function incidental to the process of liberal education. With the rapidly accumulating developments in the technical aspects of education it becomes increasingly imperative to make them a part of the professional equipment of the teacher previously to his entrance upon the work. To do this with the usual staff and facilities to be found in many of these colleges is quite impossible. The field of education with which high-school teachers in training must be brought in contact is too wide for one man or a part of one man, himself often untrained in the field, to be able to present effectively. Moreover, these institutions are frequently without facilities for practice-teaching, the recent demise of their preparatory schools leaving them to the mercy of a critical public in the communities where they are located. In these obstructions of attitude and inadequacy of facilities there are grounds for scouting the expectation that many of them will ever be able to assume the obligation we have seen to rest upon them. While some colleges are doubtless making rapid strides in the right direction, for most of them reforms will be required that to the usual faculty group in control will seem too revolutionary to be permissible.

If obstructing attitudes of college authorities can be overcome, professional training in other predominant lines seems more nearly feasible. This would be true of the business field and of home-making, and also of the preprofessional portions of training for those occupations which are to be entered only after more protracted periods in higher institutions; namely, law, medicine, and the ministry. It should not be impossible, furthermore, for colleges to develop professional specialties along some of the lines less frequently found in the distributions, such as library training, social service, journalism, etc.

The shift of women from teaching to home-making must receive serious consideration in planning training for them. Here we are face to face with the problem perennially recurring in discussing education for women: their preparation for two lines of professional service, one likely to be temporary, the other permanent. In the face of this double responsibility the typical postponement of all professional work for women during the full period of collegiate education seems decidedly out of place. The facts cited indicate that the college could not go far wrong in giving the majority of young women occupational training both for home-making and for teaching. It would be more reasonable, however, to open up opportunities for professional training in wider variety for the field which is to be the temporary one. And this double responsibility urges that the beginning of professionalization of women's training be not postponed long after the opening of the senior-college period. In fact, there is little or nothing in the materials just presented, nor in any of the other portions of the chapter, to warrant us in delaying occupationalization of training more than is now characteristic of the senior-college period.

VI. READJUSTMENTS WITHIN PRESENT-DAY HIGHER INSTITUTIONS

Accommodations within the separate college. The major system is not the only evidence we have of inroads upon our former four-year period of liberal education. One who examines any considerable number of recent catalogues of separate four-year colleges and compares them with those issued during an earlier period will find another frequent difference in the accommodations by which they provide a compromise on the length of the liberal curriculum, the word "liberal" here being used in the sense of intentionally nonoccupational. The character and frequency of these accommodations will be shown by summarizing the results of an examination of the recent catalogues of two hundred and twenty-seven randomly selected institutions of the "small college" type.

The accommodations are classified under six main heads, with a seventh group having something in common with the movement, but sufficiently distinct and conservative to raise the question of the appropriateness of including it. These classes are as follows:

1. *Affiliation with universities to give combination arts-professional curricula, with the first three years in attendance at the college.* Announcements of this sort are found in thirty-one different catalogues, a total of 66 curricula appearing, of which the most frequently recurring are arts-agriculture, 11; arts-engineering, 16; arts-law, 12; and arts-medicine, 20. Here are almost 14 per cent of the colleges prepared to concede a full year on the four-year liberal-arts period, not to mention the proportion of the three preceding years assigned to courses of occupational bent.

2. *Arrangements to give bachelors' degrees when later portions of the four-year period are spent in professional or technical schools elsewhere.* Closely allied with the first type are the arrangements for giving a degree for two or three years of residence in a college under consideration and (1) the fourth year taken in a professional or technical school or (2) the completion of a professional or technical curriculum elsewhere. Forty-eight different institutions, or 21 per cent, follow practices classed under this head.

3. *Preprofessional curricula two or three years in length, without announced affiliation.* The 123 preprofessional curricula offered in seventy-four of the colleges, or almost a third of the whole number, are distributed as follows: agriculture, 8; business, 5; dentistry, 3; engineering, 24; law, 13; medicine, 63; nursing, 2; miscellaneous (journalism, forestry, the-

ology, etc.), 5. Almost three fourths of these curricula are two years in length.

4. *Four-year professional curricula.* Some of these, such as business administration, aim to give complete professional training; others, such as medicine and law, give only partial professional preparation. Sixty-one colleges, or 27 per cent of the total number, offered 79 such curricula, with 20, the largest number, in business administration, 14 in engineering, 33 in home economics, and a scattering distribution to agriculture, forestry, the applied arts, secretarial training, journalism, industrial mechanics, law, medicine, and public health.

5. *Professional names in titles of departments.* A total of 190 departments bearing professional names were found in one hundred and thirty-one catalogues, or almost three fifths of the whole number, the following being among the most frequent: agriculture, business administration or commerce, secretarial training, journalism, engineering, home economics, and law. Departments of education were omitted from consideration, although there are valid grounds for including them. The amount of actual occupational content offered in the departments listed varies widely, some containing only a few courses of an applied sort, others including extended offerings. However, all instances warrant the conclusion that here are accommodations to the desire and need of students

for a period of nonoccupational collegiate education less than four years in length.

6. *Professional courses in departments bearing liberal-arts titles.* Thirty such courses were found in twenty-five different catalogues.

7. *Recognition without substantial accommodation.* Under this head were tallied all outlines or suggestions of four-year preprofessional curricula having in them practically no genuinely professional material. While this type of evidence constitutes no concession on the part of the college, and is therefore not included in the total of accommodations, the reason most commonly expressed for placing this guidance in the thirty-nine catalogues represented was that proper election of fundamental studies would shorten the time required to complete the curriculum of the professional school.

The first six of the seven types of modification were made by a total of 163, or almost three fourths of the 227 colleges. The total frequency of the accommodations was 539, which is an average of almost two and a half per institution when all the colleges are included in the computation, and approximately three and a third when the 163 making them are included.

While these accommodations to the pressure for abbreviated periods of unspecialized training have been distributed to six types, they may be roughly divided into two major groups: first, the tendency to show the student how he may complete his liberal training in two or three years and then transfer to a professional school, and second, the introduction of professional studies into the upper end of the four-year period of college training.

Moreover, the movement to make concessions is not a scattered one, but is so general as to be almost typical. There are, of course, colleges that still maintain a stubborn resistance to what they look upon as the illegitimate encroachments of utilitarian motives, but they have been seen to be even now a dwindling minority. This is in striking contrast with the college curriculum of two or three generations ago, which was liberal in intent throughout, being fully or almost fully prescribed and being without the slightest opportunity for specialization by the student. The changes here described, as in the case of the change in the type of curriculum offered, are in harmony with what has been shown to be the greater maturity of the college student and the increased extent of his training by the time he has arrived at any point in the present college curriculum.

It is desirable to suggest that there is no intent here to characterize the materials of professional or other occupational training as not possessing liberalizing qualities. The aim has been merely to make clear the shift from the former unapplied curricula to the partly occupationalized curricula of the present day.

THE TREND OF REORGANIZATION

The junior-college line of cleavage in universities. It is appropriate at this point to summarize briefly the chief characteristics of the movement to introduce a line of cleavage between the two lowest years of our universities and the remaining years. This does not refer to the presence in these institutions of an increasing number of two-year preprofessional curricula, nor to the group requirements for under-classmen and the major system prescribed for upper-classmen in the liberal-arts units connected with universities, although there is something in common between these and the division being effected. Attention is directed only to the instances of the junior-college line of cleavage.

At the present time there are six large universities of the West and Middle West operating under the plan: the universities of California, Chicago, Washington, Minnesota, Leland Stanford Junior University, and the University of Nebraska, the reorganizations having been effected in the order given. The first two were introduced near the end of the last century, the others much more recently. Responses to special inquiries of other universities show that the step is being seriously considered and may soon be taken in at least a few more institutions.

The name given the lower unit has so far taken three forms. It is called the "lower division" in three universities, the "junior college" in two, and the "junior division" in one.

THE JUNIOR–COLLEGE MOVEMENT

In only two of these six universities does the lower unit comprehend all lines of work offered to students in these two years. In one of these, The University of Chicago, the problem of such inclusion is simplified by the absence of engineering schools. In Stanford University, however, the engineering departments have been incorporated in the plan, but not without making "certain exceptions to the general rules of the lower division."[1] In the four remaining institutions it is either solely or mainly the liberal-arts group to which the line of cleavage is applied, except that the junior division serves in a preprofessional way all schools beginning with the third college year.

Three of the official bulletins in which descriptions of the lower unit are provided seem to have aimed at stating its *purpose* in some way other than merely to say that it includes the first two years of the college. Each of these three stresses at least one function in common, although this is differently expressed in each instance. In Stanford University, it is "to introduce the student to fundamental fields of human interest"; in the University of California, "it is expected that the student . . . will make an effort to establish a basis for that breadth of culture which will give him a realization of the methods and results of some of the more important types of intellectual endeavor, and a mental

[1] Annual Report of the President for 1919–1920. Supplement to the *Stanford Illustrated Review*, Vol. XXII, No. 5 (February, 1921), pp. 10-11.

perspective that will aid him in reaching sound judgment"; and in the University of Washington, "to con-
tribute to a broad general training in preparation for
the advanced work of the upper division." The only
important additional purpose posted in these bulletins
is given for the lower division in the institution last
named, "to supplement the work of the high school."
"The object" [of the requirements in the lower unit],
says the catalogue, "is to secure for the student a
knowledge of a wide range of subjects, to distribute his
knowledge over the fundamental fields. To this end
the high school and college are viewed as essentially
a unit."

Other evidences that a distinction of function between the lower and upper divisions is seen are to be
found in the provisions for *advice*, the recognition by
certificate of the termination of the lower division, the
administrative *separation of courses* for the two units,
and the point set for the *beginning of specialization*.
A final function of the lower division in three institutions is that of *selection* of students for work on the
higher levels. In the University of Chicago the student is advanced to the senior college when he has
met, among others, a requirement of the completion
of "18 majors of work with at least 32 grade points."
Similar to this quali-quantitative requirement is the
one in the University of Minnesota which insists upon
the completion for promotion of "90 credits and 90

honor points." Somewhat different, but of the same general import, is the requirement in the University of Nebraska which says, "If the sixty hours of work required for completion of the lower division is not completed in the first five semesters of attendance, the student is automatically dropped from the university unless extension of time be granted by the Senate Scholarship Committee." All these regulations seem to be intended to operate as scholastic hurdles which must be taken for advancement to the upper unit.

The major impression resulting from this examination of the junior-college movement within the university is that where it appears, it seems founded upon a conviction that the functions of the lower years of the university—more especially of the college of liberal arts—are to be distinguished in considerable part from those of the upper years. The upper years are assumed to be the proper place for specialization, whereas the lower years are still years of general education. This characteristic of the lower division, coupled with the emphasis upon the desirability of having the work in this division continuous with that of the high school, not to mention other administrative provisions, such as that pertaining to guidance, argues that the higher institutions are proceeding as if the first two years were really a part of the full period of general or secondary education, and that higher education proper begins in the upper unit.

[222]

VII. THE TREND OF ENROLLMENT IN HIGHER INSTITUTIONS

The questions raised. Probably few readers have followed the presentation of the materials of the foregoing sections without wondering whether the tendencies shown have been reflected to any extent within the fact of growth of higher education. Of the recent rapid growth of higher institutions as a whole all are aware, but curiosity in this instance attaches to more detailed aspects of the general situation. Some will be disposed to ask, What is the trend of growth of the several types of higher institutions represented—universities, separate colleges, and professional schools? Are they developing at the same rate, or has there been a tendency from the standpoint of numbers for one or another to dominate the field? Is there any difference among the several types as to the trend of enrollment in the lower and upper years? Is professionalization of curricula in universities increasing or decreasing, and how does this affect the proportionate distribution of students in liberal-arts and professional curricula? Is the proportionate enrollment of lower-classmen and of upper-classmen in the liberal-arts unit of these institutions gaining or losing, and are there differences between the sexes in this respect? The materials of this section are devoted to answering these and related questions.

[223]

The trend of enrollment in the several types of higher institutions. The rates of growth of the several

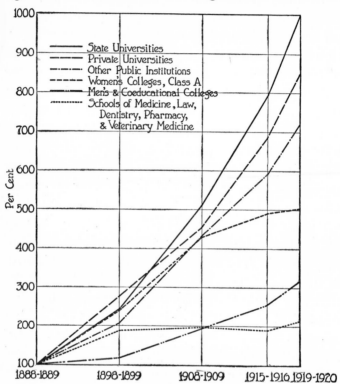

FIG. 31. Percentages of enrollments for 1888–1889 represented by enrollments in later periods in each of several types of higher institutions

types of higher institution differ. State universities show the most rapid rate, reaching by 1919–1920 a total little short of 900 per cent over their enrollment

[224]

in 1888–1889. Private universities and other public institutions (state colleges of agriculture and mechanic arts, other separate publicly supported technical schools, and municipal universities) follow rather closely with increases of 621.3 and 747.1 per cent respectively. The remaining types are ranked in the following order, but at some distance from the first three groups named: women's colleges (Class A[1]), 404.7 per cent; men's colleges and coeducational colleges, 216.9 per cent; schools of medicine, law, dentistry, pharmacy, and veterinary medicine, 112.0 per cent. The rates of growth in the professional schools (the majority of which are now associated with universities) as a whole have been considerably reduced by the fluctuations in medicine, one of the predominant groups. The actual decline in the rate of growth in this group, as is well known, is explained by the standardization in the field, a movement which has resulted in closing the doors of many of the weaker schools. The most marked gains are seen to be in the universities and other institutions of polytechnic type, rather than in the college groups.

The shift in the position of dominance. These differing rates of growth during the period of three decades or more which the data cover inevitably resulted

[1] Women's colleges of Class B, normal schools, schools of theology, and higher institutions for colored students were not included in the study because of the relative uncertainty of the requirements for admission to many of them.

in a shift in the proportional predominance of the types of institution considered. From something more than a fourth of the total enrollment in the groups of institutions considered, the proportion in state and private universities and other institutions of poly-technic type mounted to well over a half; whereas the proportions for women's colleges of Class A and men's colleges and coeducational colleges combined dropped sharply during the first decade from more than two fifths of the whole to less than a third. When the percentages for the schools of medicine, law, dentistry, pharmacy, and veterinary medicine are added to the former group, its position of dominance during the last twenty or more years becomes even more appar-ent. This fact of numerical dominance may have had something to do with the degree to which separate colleges have in recent years introduced the curricular modifications described in a preceding section.

The proportions of students in lower and upper college years. A study of the proportions of students enrolled in the under-classman (first and second) and upper-classman (third and fourth) years in large rep-resentative samples of the several types of higher institutions concerned in this part of the chapter dis-closes certain significant related tendencies to change. If an increase in the percentage which those enrolled in the third and fourth years are of the total—or, conversely, a decrease in the proportion in the first

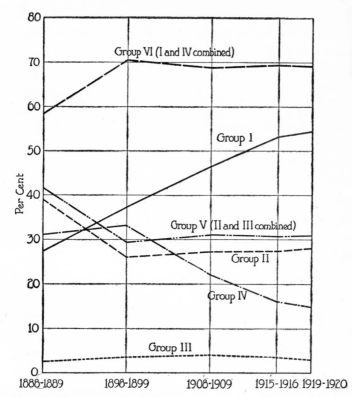

FIG. 32. Percentage distribution of students in each type of higher institution and each group of types in 1888–1889, 1898–1899, 1908–1909, 1915–1916, and 1919–1920. (Group I, state universities, other public institutions, and private universities; Group II, men's and co-educational colleges; Group III, women's colleges, Class A; Group IV, schools of medicine, law, dentistry, pharmacy, and veterinary medicine; Group V, II and III combined; Group VI, I and IV combined)

and second years—be taken as an indication of increasing efficiency, women's colleges of Class A have by far the best record. They show a decrease in the

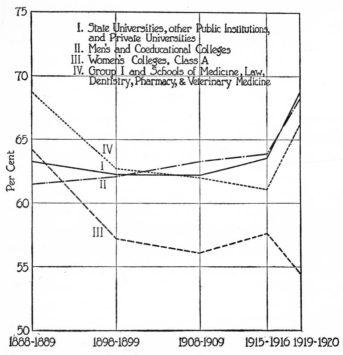

FIG. 33. Enrollment in the first two collegiate years as percentages of total enrollment in the first four collegiate years of several types of higher institutions

proportion enrolled in freshman and sophomore years from almost two thirds in 1888–1889 to 54.5 per cent in 1919–1920. They even experienced a decline between 1915–1916 and 1919–1920, whereas other types showed a marked increase owing to the large influx of deferred registrations for 1919–1920. This "backwash" for 1919–1920 makes it inadvisable to give serious consideration to conclusions from a comparison of percentages for the remaining groups for the period from 1915–1916 to 1919–1920, although no serious question can be raised against the predictive value of the percentages during the preceding periods. The group made up of state universities, other public institutions of polytechnic type, and private universities show no conspicuous change: they seem to have been holding their own. However, when they are combined with schools of medicine, law, dentistry, pharmacy, and veterinary medicine, they show marked progress toward smaller proportions in the lower years. On the other hand, the men's colleges and coeducational colleges lost ground almost consistently. This trend is not striking, but it is unmistakable and, in contrast with the situation in institutions with acknowledged opportunities for occupational training, should give pause to the friends of the separate liberal-arts college.

Elimination and transfer from separate colleges. A study of retention and elimination in separate colleges and of the destination of transfers from these colleges affords findings of significance in this connection. The first of these is that for thirteen estimable Mid-

[229]

Western colleges the percentage of students who remain for their third year is 49.0. This is another way of saying that for a majority of the entering students, the separate college serves as a junior college. The facts just presented lead to the expectation that this will be increasingly true. The second finding concerns that special group of those eliminated who transfer to other institutions before completing the four-year curriculum. It was possible to ascertain the institution of destination of 219 such transferees, 86 from eight Eastern colleges and 132 from thirteen Mid-Western colleges, of whom a *total of 182, or 83.1 per cent, shifted to universities or other institutions where professional training is available.*

The increase of opportunities for professional education in universities. A count was taken of all professional schools in eighteen large universities of the country for each half-decade for the twenty-five years beginning with 1894–1895 and ending with 1919–1920. The average numbers of professional schools per university (not including colleges of liberal arts and graduate schools) were respectively 4.2, 4.9, 5.2, 5.9, 6.5, and 7.3. These figures indicate a steady growth. There is little need of mentioning the particular schools that were added, except to state that the earlier additions were in the older professions, such as medicine and law, whereas in later years the more frequent additions were in commerce and education.

The shift of enrollment within the university. The same group of universities—six Eastern and twelve Mid-Western, Western, and Southern—were studied as to proportionate enrollments as follows: (1) the percentages of the total enrollment in colleges of liberal arts, in junior-college years, and in senior-college years of colleges of liberal arts; (2) the percentages of the total liberal-arts enrollment in junior-college years and in senior-college years; (3) the division of junior-college and senior-college liberal-arts enrollments as to men and women; etc. From these computations may be drawn several conclusions highly pertinent to the problem of organization in higher education. For the Eastern universities the most notable change shown is the steady decline of the numbers enrolled in the last two years of the liberal-arts unit, compared with the total liberal-arts enrollment. The downward trend is not rapid, but is so consistent as to be unmistakable, dropping by small steps from 45.9 to 40.6 per cent. Correspondingly, the percentage of junior-college liberal-arts students to the entire student-body shows a tendency to increase. The decline of the senior-college group for the Mid-Western, Western, and Southern universities is not so consistent, but is nevertheless apparent. Other tendencies in harmony with these are to be noted, but the most important is the shrinkage in the proportion of men in the senior-college years of the liberal-arts unit from 60.1 in

1894–1895 to approximately two thirds of this proportion in the later periods of the quarter-century, at the same time that men were much more nearly holding their own in junior-college years.

The decline of students, especially of men, in the senior-college years of nonoccupational curricula would without doubt appear to be even greater if account could have been taken of those registered in special occupational programs announced in the catalogues but administered by the liberal-arts unit. Such curricula are not offered in all colleges of liberal arts in universities, but they are sufficiently numerous to warrant the statement made. In the arts college of one state university whose catalogue was examined reference was made to ten such curricula, for example journalism, business administration (five differentiations), chemistry, etc.; in another there were five, such as home economics, economic entomology, and chemistry. It may be seen from these illustrations that some of the lines represented, as commerce and journalism, have in other institutions been erected into professional schools.

Professionalization of training for women is lagging behind that for men, as may be judged from the increasing proportion of women in senior-college years of the liberal-arts unit. If recent movements affecting the social status and occupational life of women may be taken as an earnest of developments of tomorrow,

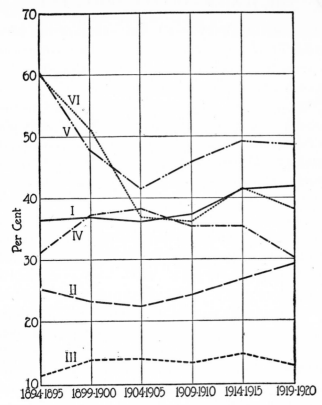

FIG. 34. Percentage distribution of students to certain divisions of twelve Mid-Western and Western universities. (I, percentage of liberal-arts enrollment in total university enrollment; II, percentage of junior-college liberal-arts enrollment in total university enrollment; III, percentage of senior-college liberal-arts enrollment in total university enrollment; IV, percentage of senior-college liberal-arts enrollment in total liberal-arts enrollment; V, percentage of junior-college men in total number of junior-college students in liberal arts; VI, percentage of senior-college men in total number of senior-college students in the liberal-arts unit)

the shift that has taken place for men will also soon follow for women. The erection of departments of education into schools, which has been taking place of late, is one step in this direction.

Significance for the problem of reorganization. The trend of enrollment in higher institutions is in accord with other evidences of the forces of reorganization so far presented in this chapter. This is true of the rapid growth which has resulted in the numerical dominance of institutions of the university and polytechnic type, in the slow but unmistakable decline of the proportion of students in the upper years of separate colleges, and in the declining proportion of men in senior-college years of the liberal-arts unit of universities, a decline unaccompanied by an equivalent reduction in the proportion of men in the junior-college years of the same unit. It harmonizes with the advancing age of the college entrant in that it shows an increasing tendency to terminate the period of general education somewhere near the middle of the college course. It comports with the changing organization of curricula of liberal colleges, which now almost universally require specialization in senior-college years. This specialization, whatever may be the intent of the college authorities in prescribing the major system, is entered upon by students with confidence in its occupational significance. It is in line with the modifications within separate colleges, which are in the nature of accommodations to the desire of students for an abbreviated period of nonoccupational training, as well as with the appearance of the junior college as an administrative unit in some of our larger universities.

VIII. THE EUROPEAN ANALOGY

The junior college prefigured. The conception of the junior college as the culmination of the American secondary school and as the feature of reorganization of our school system which would usher in the real university is not one of recent origin. It has its beginnings at least as far back as the middle of the nineteenth century. Distinctions between the conception in its earliest form and that which now characterizes it are that it was not then designated by the name it has come to carry in our own time, and that it was not as often thought of as a separate two-year unit superimposed upon the unit below or connected in some way with other schools in the system. In its first stages it seems to have been conceived of more nearly as an upward extension of the secondary school without a line of demarcation between the two levels of training.

The idea of upward extension took its root in a comparison of European (more especially the German and the French) school systems with the American system, a comparison which seemed to some of the educational leaders of the period to put the latter in an unfavorable light. Among the defects of our system most frequently mentioned were the shorter period of secondary education here and the consequent responsibilities of the higher schools for much of general education left uncompleted by the lower units.

One of the first, if not the first, of the American leaders in higher education to call attention to the differences referred to and to urge reorganization somewhat along the lines of the European plans was Henry Phillips Tappan. Even as early as 1851, the year before he assumed the responsibilities of the presidency of the University of Michigan, he wrote a volume dealing with university education.[1] He made recommendations looking to the establishment of real universities at the point where preliminary education should leave off. To him education had two states— the preparatory and the executive.

After a right worthy discipline of the man, by this preparatory course, we next proceed to the executive part of . . . education. Under this denomination we embrace professional studies, as Law, Medicine, Theology, or the studies relating to any course of life for which the individual may design himself.[2]

[1] Henry P. Tappan, University Education. G. P. Putnam's Sons, New York, 1851.　　　　　　　　　　　[2] Ibid. p. 12.

His convictions as to the nature and organization of universities he found embodied in those of Germany, for he said:

We have spoken of the German Universities as model institutions. Their excellence consists of two things: first, they are purely Universities, without any admixture of collegial tuition. Secondly, they are complete as Universities, providing libraries and all other materials of learning, and have professors of eminence to lecture on theology, law, and medicine, . . . in fine, upon every branch of human knowledge.[1]

Another educational leader who early sensed the desirability of development along somewhat similar lines was William Watts Folwell, now president emeritus of the University of Minnesota. In his inaugural address, delivered in 1869, he urged relegating to the secondary schools

those studies which now form the body of work for the first two years in our ordinary American Colleges. It is a clear case that such a transposition must by and by be made. . . . How immense the gain . . . if a youth could remain at the high school or academy, residing in his home, until he had reached a point, say somewhere near the end of the sophomore year, there to go over all those studies which as a boy he ought to study, under tutors and governors! Then let the boy, grown up to be a man, emigrate to the university, there to enter upon the work of a man. . . .[2]

[1] Ibid. pp. 44–45.
[2] W. W. Folwell, University Addresses, pp. 37–38. H. W. Wilson Co., Minneapolis, 1909.

In a note accompanying the address as published, Dr. Folwell suggests the origin of his idea:

Away back in the 50's when the speaker was a schoolboy he enjoyed the friendship of Professor Charles A. Joy of Columbia College, who had taken up his life work after a long period of study in German Universities. From him came the knowledge of the Gymnasium, the splendid secondary school, fitting German boys for the work of men in the university.

Insistence upon the relevancy of the European organization to the American system continued with increasing frequency toward the end of the century and later. It will probably be conceded without argument that of the more recent advocates of the type of reorganization referred to, the most persistent and influential was President William Rainey Harper. Among others in university circles who have done much to popularize the junior-college idea are Edmund J. James, Alexis Lange, and David Starr Jordan. Harper seems to have inspired the establishment of the first junior colleges. It is not to be assumed, of course, that either he or any other leader of the period relied solely or even primarily on the argument of European analogy: it is indicated merely that, as is implicit in the quotations from President Folwell, European analogy entered as an important element into the thinking which urged reorganization. On account of its frequency of recurrence it seems desirable to scrutinize with some care the pertinence of the analogy by attempting a comparison of French and German secondary schools on the one hand with those of the United States on the other.

Ages of students compared. Assuming that the German boy begins the work of the *Vorschule* when he is six years of age, and is promoted regularly, he would be nine when he entered the *Sexta*, the first year of the Gymnasium, the predominant type of German secondary school. Assuming a continuance of regular promotion during his progress through the institution, he would be seventeen when he entered the *Oberprima*, its ninth and highest class, and nearly eighteen on completing its work and equipped for admission to the university. If these assumptions were borne out by the facts, the German student in the last year of his secondary school would be at approximately the same age as the American student in the senior year in high school, which is typically seventeen and a half years.

Certain students of the German secondary school, however, have made clear that the rate of promotion is such as to delay the student's arrival in the *Oberprima* and, consequently, in the university. Bolton says that during his visits he "was surprised to find in the upper classes pupils who were no longer boys in appearance, but full-grown men, many of them with mustaches. They appeared to be fully as old as freshmen and sophomores in American colleges." He cites figures supplied by Dr. Juling, reporting on Prussian

Gymnasia, showing that for the year 1890 only 19 per cent of the graduates were under nineteen years, the percentages for the years nineteen, twenty, twenty-one and over being, respectively, 26, 26, and 28 per cent.[1] Referring to the ages of students in the Royal Gymnasium in Leipzig, Bolton says that the average age of pupils who had just entered the lowest class (*Sexta*) was ten years ten months and sixteen days, which, from what has already been said, indicates an average retardation at this point of somewhat less than two years. "The average of the class just finishing was nineteen years ten months." This seems to mean that owing to delayed progress, although there are twelve years in each of the two systems compared, students in the German school were approximately a year and a half older on the completion of their secondary education than are American high-school seniors when they receive their diplomas. On account of possible differences in definition of age it is safer to say that they were from one to two years older. At another point Bolton shows the average ages of students in the last three classes of several German secondary schools, mostly Gymnasia, to have been 17.6, 18.7, and 20.1 years respectively.[2] The first of these figures is not far from that for the ages of seniors in American high schools, and this fact, with the ages for the last two

---

[1] Frederick E. Bolton, The Secondary-School System of Germany, pp. 12–13. D. Appleton and Company, New York, 1900. [2] Ibid. p. 16.

years of the Gymnasium, leads us to conclude that there is an even greater difference in ages on the completion of the respective secondary schools than that drawn from the situation in the Royal Gymnasium in Leipzig. Russell, citing data of Thomas Alexander, shows that in 1913 the average age of students in the *Oberprima* in the Friedrich-Wilhelm Real-Gymnasium at Stettin was 19.0 years,[1] which is again approximately a year and a half in advance of the age of seniors in American high schools.

The upshot of all this, as well as can be judged from the data referred to, is that the student of the Gymnasium at the time of graduation is about as old as is the student in American colleges when he is near the end of his freshman year or well started on his sophomore year.

It is relevant to point out that the retardation noted obtains despite the long school year, which extends over two hundred and forty days. Schools are in session from forty to forty-two weeks of six days each. This is approximately a third in excess of the typical length of the school year in the United States.

The French lycée for boys extends over what is assumed to be seven years of work, divided into two cycles—one of four years, the other of three years. The work of its first year is entered upon after the boy has completed a primary-school curriculum covering

[1] William F. Russell, Economy in Secondary Education, p. 5. Houghton Mifflin Company, Boston, 1916.

four years, this in turn being preceded by a year in the infant class, which he normally begins at the age of six years. The full curriculum being twelve years in length, the French boy presumably arrives in the last form of the lycée when he is sixteen years of age and completes it when he is about seventeen, or a few months before the American high-school student enters upon his last year of work in the secondary school. Although no data on age distributions for the French schools were available to the writer, there is little occasion to believe that there is not some extent of retardation in the lycée as there is in the Gymnasium. Promotions are by form and not by subject, as is the practice in American high schools, and a failure in two major subjects is very likely to result in the student's repeating the work of a form. It is seldom indeed that a boy spends less than a full year in a form. It is not unlikely that there is as much retardation relatively as there is in the Gymnasium, although it may be that completion of the work of the lycée finds the student somewhat younger than the German youth at the end of the gymnasial curriculum.

Curricula compared. A number of obstructions present themselves as soon as an attempt is made to compare curricula of American schools with those of German and French secondary schools. The difficulty in comparison is contributed to in no small part by distinct differences in the subjects emphasized. In the Gymnasium the emphasis is largely on traditional materials, such as ancient languages and mathematics, but in the first years of the American college it is on work in the mother tongue, modern foreign languages, science, and social subjects. Differences so marked as these thwart effective comparison in particular subjects. Another obstructing difference is in the maintenance in Germany of different schools for students with different intentions toward higher education, and of segregated education for boys and girls in both Germany and France. Couple with this the contrast of the European secondary school as a distinctly selective institution and the American aspiration toward universal education on this level, and there results a situation which demands, with us, much more in the way of elective programs. Another complicating circumstance is the differing lengths of secondary-school periods. As our organization cuts across the European periods of secondary education, this interferes with satisfactory comparison, since with their longer periods both French and German schools can introduce the more characteristically secondary-school subjects earlier than our schools and can extend their study over longer periods.

A single subject, Latin, will be used in the curricular comparison, which must be all too brief. The study of Latin is begun in the lowest gymnasial class, the *Sexta*, and is continued throughout the nine-year period. In

the Prussian Gymnasium of the nineties a total of
sixty-two hours, or a shade less than an average of
seven hours per week for each year, were devoted to it.
Ignoring the differences in the length of the school
year, if the student in the typical American high school
carries the full course of study in Latin, he will have
a total of only fifteen hours, or less than a fourth of
the work in this subject prescribed in the German secondary school. Manifestly the German student should
be able to cover vastly more ground during his progress through his institution, and he should also be
much farther advanced at any age-point in the course.
We ought not to be surprised therefore that the lad in
Untertertia (the fourth class in order from the beginning) who, according to Bolton's figures, averages
14.5 years of age is reading Cæsar's "Gallic War,"
whereas the American boy does not undertake it until
the year following. Nor is there cause for wonder if
more than a single author is read during any one
year. Among the materials read in this subject in
Obersecunda, when the boy averages 17.6 years of
age—practically the average age of the American
high-school senior—is Livy, Book XXI. American
college catalogues picked up at random show that this
is standard content for freshman courses. Again, the
student in *Oberprima* (the last year) reads Tacitus,
which is typically material for our sophomore college
courses. Once again, there should be no cause for sur-

prise in these last contrasts in view of the longer period of Latin study in the Gymnasium and the fact that the average *Oberprimaner* is not much younger than the American college sophomore.[1]

The study of Latin is likewise begun in the first year of the lycée, the total number of class hours throughout the seven years being much more than twice the amount that would be devoted to the subject by an American high-school student during four full years. The "Gallic War" is also undertaken earlier. Mention of other classics read would indicate that students in the last year are reading materials to be found in the freshman and sophomore courses in the American college.[2]

Further curricular comparison of European and American systems seems to warrant another inference, one which touches the total amount of ground covered in the subjects represented as affected by the type of organization of education in use. Our typical organization of an eight-year elementary school, a four-year high school, and a four-year college appears to cut across the German secondary-school period, if not also the French, at two points. We thereby distribute to

[1] Interpretations are based on curricular descriptions not only in Bolton's "The Secondary-School System of Germany" but also in James E. Russell's "German Higher Schools," chaps. ii and xvi. Longmans, Green & Co., New York, 1913.

[2] Interpretations are based on F. E. Farrington's "French Secondary Schools," pp. 192–199. Longmans, Green & Co., New York, 1910.

three different agencies the responsibility for training during the period of years concerned. Each of these agencies acts in ways to some extent independent of the others and without full knowledge of what they are attempting. There must in such a situation be some overlapping in the work covered—an overlapping that wastes time and prevents covering as much total ground as would otherwise be possible. It is therefore to be anticipated that bringing more of these school years into a single institution will operate to bring our students farther on in the same period of years.

The point of termination of general education. One characteristic common to the Gymnasium and lycée is not a feature of the traditional American four-year high school, and this is the fact that they terminate the general education of the student who is going on. The university to which the German and the French student are advanced on the completion of the work in the lower school is for them a place of specialization. On the other hand, in the majority of instances the American student who continues his education after his high-school course, moves on to an extension of his period of general education, an extension which, in terms of the organization of college curricula, is two years in length. Partial exceptions are students who pursue curricula in engineering, agriculture, etc. For most students the work of these two years is made general by prescriptions that assure contact with each of the main fields of learning. At the close of the two-year period the student is required to select a major subject, which, as we have seen, he looks upon as occupational specialization and which, in a majority of cases, subsequently serves him occupationally. This interpretation of the end of the first two college years as the typical American termination of general education for those intent on specialized training has the support also of the foregoing sections showing the extent to which colleges have made provision for meeting the desire of students for a shortened period of unapplied education, the appearance of the junior-college division in universities, and the trend of enrollment in higher institutions which shows diminishing proportions of students in the last two years of colleges of liberal arts, whether these are separate institutions or parts of universities.

The congruity of the analogy. The major conclusion from these comparisons is that while the analogy of French and German organization of secondary and higher education with that proposed by those who urge the upward extension of our own high school by the addition of junior-college years is far from complete, there are significant points of similarity.

On account of the retardation in the German secondary school seen to obtain at the time that the analogous relationship was frequently emphasized, the average age of the graduate did not fall far below that of our present college sophomores. There is no reason to believe that this situation for the lycée is essentially different. Although the comparison of respective curricula is beset with difficulties, there is sufficient evidence to indicate that the analogy does not entirely break down here, despite the obviously more democratic function of the American high school and college. In Latin both the lycée and the Gymnasium carry the student through the materials covered by such of our college sophomores as continue this subject; and the like, although not demonstrated here, is approximately true for mathematics. These facts are especially significant in view of the approach to equivalence of the ages of students in the last two years of the Gymnasium and of the first two years of the American college. Perhaps the most relevant element of the analogy is to be found in the fact that the first two years of American collegiate education as now administered are distinctly a part of general education and that the years beyond this are now and are increasingly becoming the period of specialization. The college and university with us seem to be standing astride the line of division between general and special education. The appropriateness of this element of the analogy impresses one especially when he recalls the approach to equality of the ages of gymnasial graduates and college sophomores.

It is not unreasonable to suppose that the somewhat shorter period of general education in these European systems, even after allowances are made, as has been done for retardation, is in part attributable to economies resulting from their longer periods of secondary education. As has been stated, our organization cuts across the period of German and French secondary education at two points. To distribute the work of this period to three distinct units, as we do, is to invite wasteful duplication, and this must result in a longer period of years to cover the same ground or the covering of less ground in a given period. It seems probable, therefore, that should we effect reorganization by introducing the junior-college years as an upward extension of our secondary school, we should be taking steps simultaneously toward shortening the typical period of general education and toward making room for an enlarged and enriched content during the same period, or in both these directions at once.

IX. Aims of the Secondary School, the College, and the University

Reason for and nature of the canvass of aims and functions. It is not impossible that the reader, as he has surveyed the results of the forces of reorganization in higher education presented in all but the last of the foregoing sections of the chapter, has from time to time wondered to what extent these momentous changes are paralleled in the best thought of the day. It was speculation such as this that prompted the making of the canvass and comparison of the aims and functions of the secondary school, the college, and the university.

The materials used were, with few exceptions, addresses, articles, or parts of volumes dealing to a greater or less extent with the purposes of the educational units under consideration. With few exceptions, again, these writings are from the pens of leaders in their respective fields and made their appearance in recent years (that is, since 1910). Since the method of analysis and tabulation was very similar to that given in Chapter II, which deals with the current conceptions of special purposes of the junior college, its description will not be detailed again here.

General impressions from the comparison. The first brief glance at Fig. 35, which shows the comparison of the results, yields the general impression that there is a *much greater approach to unanimity in the conceptions of purposes for high schools than for either of the other two units concerned.* This impression is given by the more frequent appearance of the heavier shadings in the secondary-school column. The second general impression is that *secondary-school and college aims have much more in common than do college and university aims.* This impression is given by shading for the same purposes in the secondary-school and college columns. Thus, for only two purposes recognized in the former column is there no recognition in the latter, and, vice versa, for only two purposes in the latter is there no recognition in the former. Otherwise there is common recognition of aims in both columns, although, of course, not often to the same extent.

On the other hand, there are ten purposes recognized in the college column which are unrecognized among university purposes. So striking is this difference that one gains a rather distinct impression of discontinuity between the college and university columns. This impression is emphasized by the recognition on behalf of the university (in the lowest portions of the figure) of four purposes unmentioned by those positing the aims of secondary schools and colleges.

The similarity of secondary-school and college aims and the dissimilarity of these and university aims may be shown in another way; namely, by saying that of the sixteen purposes at all frequently recognized (that is, by more than 20 per cent of the authors) in the secondary-school column, fifteen are found to be recognized in the college column and only five in the university column. Conversely, of the seven aims receiving frequent recognition in the university column, only three are recognized in the secondary-school and college columns.

Specific similarities and differences. With certain exceptions these general impressions are further supported by a comparison of recognition of each purpose listed. While the authors of the statements concerning secondary schools and colleges rather commonly contend that a chief aim of these schools is general or liberal training (aim 1), those proposing the purposes of the university posit it with only half the collegiate frequency. The author of no university statement proposes training for the general needs of life (2). The purposes touching civic-social responsibility (3), morality and character (4), religion (5), and domestic responsibility (6) either do not appear or scarcely appear in the statements of purposes of the university, although they are all proposed to a greater or less extent for the two lower schools. In the university statements the differences seem to reflect an assumption of previous performance of the purposes proposed for the college: they are prior aims and functions, not often to be regarded as concomitant. The same may be said of training for the proper use of leisure (8); physical efficiency (10); the achievement of a democratic school system (13); the recognition of individual differences (14); preliminary training (17), which comprehends college preparation in the high school and preprofessional training in the college; and training in the fundamental processes (19); except that for a larger proportion of these than of the fore-

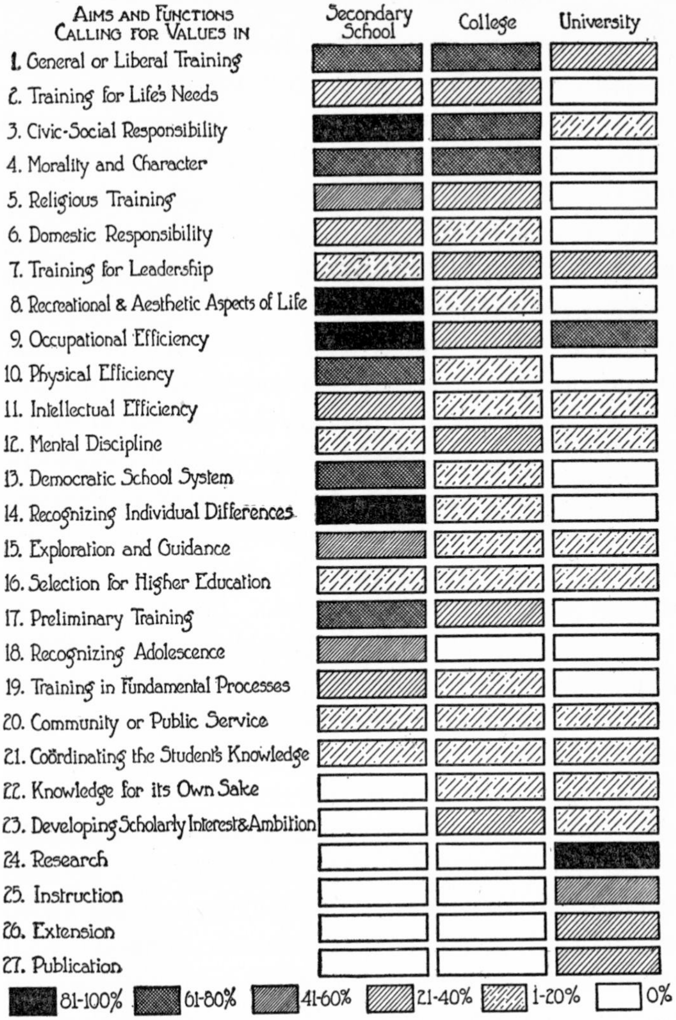

Aims and Functions Calling for Values in	Secondary School	College	University
1. General or Liberal Training			
2. Training for Life's Needs			
3. Civic-Social Responsibility			
4. Morality and Character			
5. Religious Training			
6. Domestic Responsibility			
7. Training for Leadership			
8. Recreational & Aesthetic Aspects of Life			
9. Occupational Efficiency			
10. Physical Efficiency			
11. Intellectual Efficiency			
12. Mental Discipline			
13. Democratic School System			
14. Recognizing Individual Differences			
15. Exploration and Guidance			
16. Selection for Higher Education			
17. Preliminary Training			
18. Recognizing Adolescence			
19. Training in Fundamental Processes			
20. Community or Public Service			
21. Coördinating the Student's Knowledge			
22. Knowledge for its Own Sake			
23. Developing Scholarly Interest & Ambition			
24. Research			
25. Instruction			
26. Extension			
27. Publication			

Legend: ■ 81-100% ▨ 61-80% ▤ 41-60% ▥ 21-40% ▨ 1-20% □ 0%

FIG. 35. Extent of recognition of each aim and function for secondary schools, colleges, and universities

going group the recognition for colleges of liberal arts is slighter than for secondary schools.

Exceptions to this general tendency are to be found in purposes 7, 9, 11, 12, 15, 16, and 21. Of these the last two are infrequently proposed for any of the three institutions. Despite the apparent equality of recognition of training for leadership (7) for the college and for the university, the *kind* of recognition differs widely for the two units. For the college the leadership contemplated is of a general civic or social type; for the university it is always the leadership of the specialist, a fact apparent in the original statements only. Purpose 9 presents a somewhat anomalous situation. It appears that recognition of occupational interests is very commonly proposed for both the secondary school and the university, but not nearly as frequently for the college. The high school is urged to give training for vocations; the university, for professions; but only about a fourth of those proposing the college aims insist that this unit be concerned with either. Exploration and guidance (15) persists throughout, but is appropriately more characteristic of the secondary school than of the collegiate and university concepts of purpose. There is a growing conviction that guidance is primarily the function of the secondary-school period when this is understood to cover the full period of secondary education from the seventh grade through the fourteenth.

Research, instruction (as handmaiden to research and professional training), extension, and publication (24, 25, 26, 27) are proposed for the university only.

Summary. The findings of the comparison may be epitomized as follows: If the statements of the aims of the three units are to be accepted, those of the secondary school and of the college have much more in common than have those of the college and the university. In fact, if a clear line of demarcation in function among the institutions were to be made on the basis of these statements of leaders in their respective fields, it would fall much more naturally at the close of the college period than at its beginning. If the training appropriate for the two lower units followed the lines recommended in the present analysis, it would be general or liberal and would for the most part be constituted of those elements necessary for all irrespective of the line of specialization. Training for the professions and other advanced specializations would be delayed to the university period, although elementary specializations such as the "vocations" would be provided in the lowest of the three units. In addition to providing opportunities for professional training, the university would foster research, would offer advanced instruction as handmaiden to research and professional training, would carry on extension activities, and would be an agency of publication.

Beyond these findings it appears that the friends of the college whose statements have been used in this study are generally far from agreement on what should be the purposes of that institution—much less so than the secondary-school group and somewhat less so than those speaking for the university. The approximation to unanimity of the secondary-school group has been noted. If the statements of leaders in this field are at all prophetic, the high schools of the country will soon have common aims. The larger number of blank spaces in the university column indicates a somewhat nearer approach to unanimity for this institution than for the college. The extent of agreement would have been even greater if some of those proposing aims for the university unit were not thinking primarily in terms of the college of liberal arts in aspiring but undeveloped universities. The college has much farther to go than its sister institutions before it finds its real and generally accepted functions. In this respect it is the most nondescript unit in our system of education, which should be a matter of grave concern to its friends, especially as it is the oldest of the units in the American system.

Rôle of the junior college in clarifying college aims. In this situation, as may be judged not only from what has been reported in this section but also in all the preceding sections of this chapter, the more general acceptance of the junior college and the adaptation of the older units to it would make for a pronounced elimination of the nondescript character of college purposes and an allocation of purpose that would be certain to bring order out of the current chaos and interference of function in higher education.

With the acknowledged period of secondary education extended to include two more years and our line of demarcation placed neither at the beginning nor at the termination of our present period of collegiate education but at its mid-point instead, allocation of purpose to each unit and differentiation among them should take care of themselves with something of automaticity. Most of the aims and functions found to be largely recognized in the secondary-school group would at once rise to the new level and give to the first two years of what is now college work a new and real significance. If these two years were made terminal grades in an extended period of secondary education, thought with reference to them would move toward clarification, and practice would become functional. With this elevation of secondary-school aims would come the partial recognition in junior-college years of the occupational aim now almost denied entrance in corresponding years of the four-year college, a recognition that would foster the location of the semiprofessions referred to in Chapter V. At the same time the purposes held to be appropriate for the period of university education would naturally apply to the last two years of college—the proper point for the beginning of specialization for one's professional destination and for the type of training appropriate to that period of life at which the student has ordinarily arrived by the time he is a college junior.

This readjustment has the advantage of being in full agreement with the results of the irresistible forces of reorganization which have been uncovered in the preceding parts of the chapter; namely, the advancing age of the college entrant, the increasing extent of preparation required, the downward shift of the materials of instruction, the changing organization of the college curriculum, the vocational bearing of the major, the occupational destination of college graduates, and the accommodations which are in the nature of concessions to the demand for earlier professionalization, not to mention others fully as significant.

Abatement of the college-entrance controversy. Finally, the two-year upward extension of the period of secondary education which the acceptance of the junior-college plan implies, bringing with it the completion of the student's general education before his advance to the higher institution, should go far toward removing from the region of controversy the problem of college preparation. Probably nothing can ever put an end fully to the disagreement on this question between the representatives of the lower and of the higher schools, but some abatement is much to be desired. It will hardly come while the two institutions concerned overlap on each other's functions as much as do the high schools on the one hand and the colleges and universities on the other. As long as both bear the responsibilities of general education the authorities representing each will feel that they are in a position to know and to determine wisely what shall constitute that general training, and herein lies perennial conflict.

Given an organization of education which acknowledges that professional or academic specialization is to begin at the opening of the junior year, and we change the question of college preparation from what is necessary for a continuation of general education to what is an essential foundation for a course of training in a specialty. *The requirements in the way of preliminary training for professional or other special curricula are much more unequivocally definable than those for a mere extension of general training to higher levels.* The same may be said of mental capacities and other personal equipment desirable. Although putting an end to controversy is not the highest form of function to be performed by an educational institution, such an achievement is doubly welcome when it is an accompaniment of a differentiation of purpose of institutions that is itself logical and commendable.

X. Concurrence of the Tendencies toward Reorganization and their Meaning for Higher Schools of the Future

Concurrence of tendencies. Among the most outstanding characteristics of the tendencies toward reorganization which have been disclosed in this chapter is their large degree of concurrence. Practically without exception they show the same general trend, indicating that, whatever the forces, these tendencies are all of a piece. The facts presented are to be regarded as links in essentially a single chain of evidence foreshadowing inevitable and ultimate reorganization which involves the acknowledgment of (1) the first two collegiate years as the typical termination of the period of general and secondary education for those who contemplate going on to higher levels and (2) the beginning of higher education proper somewhere in the vicinity of the present junior collegiate year.

Future organization of higher education. Some of our higher institutions (among them both colleges and universities), on account of the grip of tradition and a selected, persisting clientele, will doubtless be able to withstand for a long period the forces of reorganization to which attention has been directed. It is not unlikely, moreover, that there may be a place in the American system for a small proportion of institutions of the type that assumes the longer period of nonoccupational training before entering upon the work of the professional school. But in the face of the apparently inevitable tendencies of reorganization as disclosed, the consummation of the new type, bringing with it the upward extension of the secondary school by the inclusion of the junior-college years, will go far toward justifying those claims of the friends of the new unit who insist that it will place in the secondary school all work appropriate to it, foster the evolution of the public-school system, relieve the university, and make possible real university functioning. As pointed out in the concluding paragraphs of the preceding section, it will at the same time abate in considerable measure the present-day college-entrance controversy, which is the more acute because at present both secondary and higher institutions presume to give general training. For the current confusion will be substituted the clarifying influence of more unequivocally definable preparatory requirements of professional and other specializations.

The future of the university and other higher institutions of polytechnic type in this impending reorganization is much more clearly discernible than is that of its sister institutions—the separate four-year college and the normal school or teachers' college. Concerning these it is doubtless too early to essay prophecy that will approach realization in any significant degree, but at least some conjecture can be ventured. It is admitted that a small proportion of the separate colleges, especially those with a ballast of endowment and a host of well-to-do and tradition-loving alumni, may be able to withstand the inevitable trend and remain institutions which afford unspecialized training throughout a four-year period. Most of them, however, must make further accommodations to the trend, serving their generation in the way in which it insists upon being served. For the weaker units this will be as junior colleges that will draw their students from secondary schools in communities too small to warrant offering work on the junior-college level. In time, however, these junior colleges must go the way of the private academy in territory where the public high schools have seen a vigorous development. The remainder, in a better state of development than those just referred to, can for the most part serve in the dual capacity of (1) junior colleges and (2) senior colleges in which certain types of liberalized occupationalization and specialization are featured. Few such institutions will be able to compete with universities in the variety of opportunities for specialization, but they can devote their energies and resources to one or a few subjects —teaching, commerce, home economics, and the like. In the remoter future the junior-college division will atrophy, and these colleges will then devote themselves exclusively to the senior-college task.

If the future form and function of the separate college is problematic, that of the normal school or teachers' college is even more so. Perhaps, until standards of teacher preparation rise to appropriate heights, the normal school will recruit most of its students from communities too small to warrant offering junior-college work, as has just been predicted for the private junior college, and from among those who desire this type of semiprofessional training. As these standards are raised it is conceivable that the teachers' college with a four-year or five-year curriculum will come to articulate with the public junior college so as to encourage the prospective student to attend the latter for two years beyond the present high-school level and to transfer to the teacher-training institution at the opening of his third college year. It seems reasonable to expect that the general establishment of junior colleges will hasten the elevation of standards of teacher preparation to the strictly professional level.

Although we may question the validity of this prophecy of the future of the two types of institution last considered, one thing is certain, that the advent of reorganization of the secondary school and the university along lines involving the incorporation of the junior-college plan will be reflected in them, for the reason that they must adapt themselves to what is to become the dominant contemporaneous organization of the educational system.

VIII

OVERLAPPING IN HIGH SCHOOL AND COLLEGE

I. The Problem in General and the Approach in Canvassing It

The problem. As may be inferred from the introductory paragraphs of Chapter VII, at least two conceptions of the special purposes of the junior college frequently proposed imply a large extent of overlapping of work in high school and college. These are the claims which anticipate that the general establishment of the junior college will *place in the secondary school all work appropriate to it* and will assist in *economizing time and expense by avoiding duplication* (Chapter II, purposes 10 and 13). These beliefs are entertained by no inconsiderable proportion of those whose statements were included.

Something of the better type of thinking which characterizes the belief that the college is doing much work of secondary-school grade is illustrated in the following quotation,[1] although the excerpt is drawn

---

[1] J. R. Angell, "The Duplication of School Work by the College," in *School Review*, Vol. XXI, pp. 1–10 (January, 1913).

from a paper that was not used in the analysis of claims presented in Chapter II and is one without expressed intent of presenting any part of a case for the junior-college movement:

The wealth of subject matter offered in a high-school curriculum today often hopelessly outruns any possibility of mastery by a given pupil within a four-year period, and much therefore remains untouched which the student may possibly wish to attack at a later point in his career. The college has been willing in increasing degree to satisfy this demand, and as a result we find a wide range of identical subjects taught in school and college. The mere fact that the two varieties of institution offer the same work is not itself conclusive evidence of waste, but a careful study of the situation leads one to question whether the present practice is really defensible in all its aspects. . . .

. . . we may well remember that our colleges pursue two lines in their practice with regard to the school work which they duplicate. In the one case they do the seemingly obvious thing, and after a student has covered certain ground in school he is permitted to proceed in college to the next more advanced stage of the same subject. Work in the modern languages may illustrate this case. But in the second instance, where the colleges offer work which is nominally identical with that done in the schools and entrance credit is given for the same, the student, when once he is safely inside the college walls, finds himself set to doing right over again much which he has already done in school. This procedure is frequently justified on the ground that the work is carried on in college from a more mature and advanced point of view. Certain courses in science both physical and biological may illustrate this case. . . .

The only emendation one is moved to make in this description of duplication is that in many instances also secondary-school subjects are begun in the college. Cases in point are beginning courses in modern foreign language.

The plan of this chapter. The issues here concerned are of such a magnitude as to prompt the inclusion in this volume of some of the findings of an extended inquiry into the degree of overlapping in high-school and college work from the two standpoints of duplication of identical or similar curricular materials irrespective of repetition by an individual student and of duplication which is in the nature of such repetition. More specifically, this chapter will concern itself with (1) illustration of the extent and character of overlapping in the two fields of English literature and chemistry, (2) conclusions drawn from studies made of overlapping in other typical subjects, (3) a brief summary of such efforts as are made by colleges to obviate repetition, and (4) consideration of the extent of overlapping of high-school work in the first two years of college work as a whole. The chapter will close with a consideration of the significance of the extent of overlapping disclosed.

II. Overlapping in English Literature

The courses compared. The first of the comparisons the findings of which are here illustrated concerns those portions of the high-school offering in English devoted to the history of English literature and the course bearing that name (or names closely allied to it; for example, "survey course in English literature") as administered in colleges. The high-school material is not always presented as a separate course, but it is nevertheless a standard constituent of work in English in the lower unit. The historical portions of the high-school work in English literature most frequently come in the senior year, but are also to be found in the junior year in some of the institutions represented. In colleges the course is usually an offering to under-classmen. It is therefore almost always taken late in high school and early in college; that is to say, by students not often more than a year apart in classification.

The work here described is going forward in randomly selected institutions located for the most part in states of the Mid-West. The high schools represented are all in cities with populations in excess of seventy-five hundred, and the colleges are all on standard lists.

Textbooks. The two chief aspects of the content of the courses concerned are reading *about* English literature, usually in textbooks, and the reading *of* the literature itself. As all but a few of the high schools and almost three fifths of the colleges represented prescribe the study of a textbook in connection with the first aspect, a text from which only occasional omissions are made, it is pertinent to compare the courses by comparing the results of an analysis of the texts most frequently used. In the high school these were Halleck and Long; in the college, Moody-Lovett and Crawshaw. The medians of the amounts of textual content reported for both groups of courses are almost equal, being 549.4 pages for the high school and 535.3 for the college. These textual materials represent the following percentages of the courses: 29.3 for the high schools and 17.2 for the colleges. The high schools show some tendency to make more of this aspect than do the colleges, although the difference is not remarkable.

Division of the texts as to portions assigned to major and to minor writers shows in the college manuals a somewhat larger average percentage dealing with minor writers. The actual average difference between the two pairs of texts is that between a fourth and a third of the whole. The difference in this respect is really less notable than is the degree of similarity. Special inquiry was made on another point on which it was suspected that there might be a qualitative difference—the distribution of textual content between more strictly personal biography on the one hand and on the other the treatment of literary biography and works. Here again there is a tendency to larger proportions of the latter in the college texts, but the difference is at the same time not marked enough to disturb the conclusion of much more of identity than of distinctiveness in textual content.

A more nearly adequate comparison of the nature of the textual content is provided in a distribution to six major divisions—environmental influences, writings, biography, extracts, general considerations (usually introductory), and mechanical details (bibliographies, illustrations, etc.). The high-school texts devote proportions noticeably larger to biography, extracts, general considerations, and mechanical details, the college texts to the first two topics named. Once more, however, the distributions are not sufficiently different to warrant a conclusion of marked distinctiveness of textual content in the courses on the two levels.

Overlapping in the literature. The analysis of the other chief constituent of these courses in English literature in high school and college concerns the selections read. For the lower unit this includes all the classics (exclusive of those in the American field) read during the entire high-school course in English, extending through three or four years, and this comprehends also the selections read in that part of the full course concerned particularly with the history of English literature. For the college it includes only

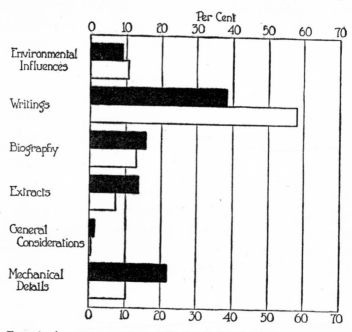

FIG. 36. Average percentages of high-school and college textbooks in the history of English literature devoted to certain topics. (Black, high school; in outline, college)

those selections read in the particular course which has so far been given consideration.

One of the measures of overlapping was drawn from a simple but extended table of frequencies with which each selection listed by all the institutions was read in each of the two groups, twenty-four high schools and twenty-four colleges. A total of 1792 different selections were reported by the forty-eight heads of departments. Of these, 546 only were not read in one or more of the high schools represented. Of the total of 1246 which were read in one or more high schools 118 were read in a half or more. Of the 118 selections 72 were read also in a half or more of the colleges, 35 with less frequency. Eleven only of this list of 118 were to be found in no college list. Another way of directing attention to the large extent of overlapping and apparent lack of distinctiveness of content for the courses on the two levels is to say that 575 selections, or 46.2 per cent, of all found in the high-school lists were also found in the college lists and that 575, or 51.3 per cent, of all the selections found in the college lists were also in the high-school lists.

The following is the list of seventy-two selections common to a half or more of both high-school and college lists. All seem to be gems held in such high esteem that few instructors on either level appear willing to leave them out of account.

Anon.: Beowulf	SHAKESPEARE: Sonnets
CHAUCER: Prologue	JONSON: Song to Celia
SPENSER: The Faërie Queene	BACON: Of Studies
MALORY: Morte d'Arthur	HERRICK: Corinna's Going a-
Anon.: Sir Patrick Spens	Maying

LOVELACE
To Lucasta on Going to the Wars
To Althea from Prison
BUNYAN
The Pilgrim's Progress
MILTON
L'Allegro
Il Penseroso
Lycidas
Paradise Lost
On his Blindness
DRYDEN: Alexander's Feast
ADDISON: Spectator
POPE: The Rape of the Lock
COLLINS: Ode to Evening
GRAY: Elegy
GOLDSMITH: The Deserted Village
BURNS
To a Mouse
The Cotter's Saturday Night
A Bard's Epitaph
Tam o' Shanter
Auld Lang Syne
John Anderson
To Mary in Heaven
Highland Mary
A Man's a Man
SCOTT: Marmion
BYRON: The Prisoner of Chillon
SHELLEY
Ode to the West Wind
The Cloud
To a Skylark
KEATS
On Chapman's Homer
To a Nightingale
On a Grecian Urn

The Eve of St. Agnes
La Belle Dame sans Merci
WORDSWORTH
We are Seven
She dwelt among . . .
I traveled among . . .
Three Years she grew . . .
My Heart leaps up . . .
The Solitary Reaper
She was a Phantom . . .
I wandered Lonely . . .
To a Skylark
Ode to Duty
Composed upon Westminster
Bridge
London, 1802
The World is too much . . .
Intimations of Immortality
COLERIDGE
Kubla Khan
Rime of the Ancient Mariner
TENNYSON
Ulysses
The Lady of Shalott
Morte d'Arthur
Locksley Hall
Break, Break, Break
In Memoriam
The Revenge
Crossing the Bar
BROWNING
My Last Duchess
Incident of the French Camp
Home-Thoughts from Abroad
Rabbi Ben Ezra
Prospice
ARNOLD: Sohrab and Rustum

Other measures of the extent of overlapping of literary content of the courses on the two levels were essayed, but probably as significant as any other is one which takes into account both the length of the selections and their frequency of appearance in the lists; that is, that weights the overlapping in terms of length and frequency. Computed in this way, the total number of equated pages read in twenty-four high schools was 119,848.4, of which the twenty-four colleges duplicated 42,344.9, or 35.3 per cent. This is an actual duplication in these college courses of well over a third of everything read in the high school.

Significance of the extent of overlapping found. A few additional aspects of the comparison of the two groups of offerings showed both differences and similarities. Examples of the differences are larger total reading requirements and larger numbers of pages of reading per clock-hour of class instruction in the college. These quantitative differences are not, however, far enough apart to make it impossible to achieve essentially the same ends on both levels on which they are given, especially as requirements in some high schools exceed those in some colleges. No evidence appeared to shake the conclusion of an undesirably large proportion of actual repetition for any group of students.

The findings of the study constitute a compelling argument for modifying the college courses and the high-school offerings in this field so that greater total progress can be achieved in the time spent by the student. They demonstrate unmistakably our error in distributing the task of giving this elementary instruction in English literature to two institutions, the authorities and instructors in the upper of which do not seem to be aware of what is going forward in the lower. Even if it is admitted that it is desirable for students to make more than a single contact with many of these selections during their school careers, there can be no point in having this accomplished under conditions which do not assure a different type of approach on each occasion. It may well be doubted whether this regrettable waste can ever be eliminated in the present organization of secondary and higher education, although steps should be taken in this direction without delay no matter what the arrangement of the system of schools. The logical step seems to be to bring the work together in the same institution where the duplication and repetition will more readily become apparent and be more promptly obviated. This means the establishment of junior-college work in connection with the high-school unit. This step is the more to be recommended by the outstanding fact of the similarity of the curricular materials concerned— a fact which marks those found in the upper unit as essentially secondary in character.

III. OVERLAPPING IN CHEMISTRY

The courses compared. The high-school courses in the field here reported upon bear such names as "chemistry," "elementary chemistry," "general chemistry," and "beginning chemistry," with a scattering of other titles. The college courses bear the names "general inorganic chemistry," "general chemistry," "Chemistry I and II," and "elementary chemistry," the last two titles appearing much less frequently than the first two.

Almost all the courses represented in both the high school and the college extend over a full school year. The numbers of recitation and laboratory periods per week tend to be identical in the two institutions, the difference in the total amount of time given to the courses arising from the longer periods in college.

The data on the classification of students who take the high-school course corroborate those of other investigations, showing that it is predominantly pursued by seniors, although it is also often taken by juniors. Students in these first college courses are mainly freshmen, although they are to some extent sophomores. We have here an instance of a subject taken predominantly by those in the last year of the lower unit and in the first year of the upper unit. This situation, combined with the approach to identity in the titles and duration of the courses, presages a large measure of identity of content.

The high schools represented are twenty-six in number and are distributed to cities of ten thousand and over in six north-central states. The forty-one higher institutions, of which all but four are of the separate college type, are located in the same general region as the high schools, but are scattered over eleven different states.

Content of high-school and college texts. The chief feature of the method of comparing the content of high-school and college courses in this subject is that of comparing the textbooks and laboratory manuals the use of which was reported by the heads of departments. This procedure has its justification in the fact that deviations from such materials are not at all commonly made; that is to say, the textbook and the laboratory manual usually constitute the course. That the analysis of the textbooks almost adequately represents the classroom content of the courses may be judged from what was ascertained touching the extent of omissions from them and from the infrequent recourse to collateral readings. Special inquiry on the former point brought the conclusion that nineteen of the twenty-six high-school courses made no omissions from the textbooks used, or practically none, the remainder excluding only a part or all of the organic chemistry. The situation, in so far as it concerns college courses, is even more than in the high school one of textbook domination.

The two larger headings under which the content has been divided are (1) the common elements and (2) subdivisions other than common elements. The former content is again distributed to occurrence, preparation, physical properties, chemical properties, history, uses, and the preparation, description, and uses of compounds; the latter content to the rarer elements, organic compounds, processes, principles, chemical laws, definitions, questions, problems, and summaries and restatements.

From what is generally known about the total amount of content in the two groups of textbooks it would not have been difficult to predict that the college texts would have *more* material in many of the subdivisions which high-school and college courses have in common. This prediction is borne out by the facts as to the averages in the two college and three high-school texts in most common use, since in all but four out of the eighteen subdivisions the average college amounts exceed the high-school amounts. The exceptions are the uses of the common elements, organic compounds, questions, and summaries and restatements. The second of the exceptions is to be explained by the fact that the college courses are more often designated as general *inorganic* chemistry than are the high-school courses, which aim to be even more general in character. The third and fourth exceptions are explicable through the greater emphasis upon pedagogical devices in the texts used in the lower unit.

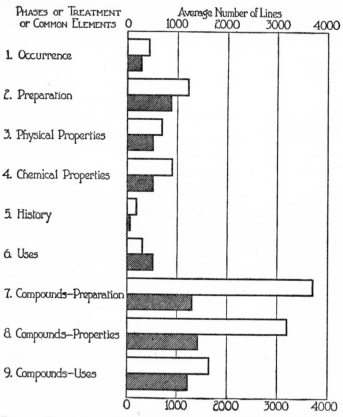

FIG. 37. Comparison of the distribution to the several subdivisions of the space devoted to the common elements in college and high-school textbooks in chemistry. (In outline, college; shaded, high school)

The largest differences in favor of the college texts are in the preparation and properties of compounds, the

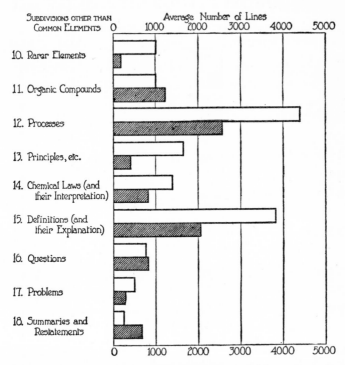

FIG. 38. Comparison of space devoted to subdivisions other than common elements in college and high-school textbooks in chemistry. (In outline, college; shaded, high school)

rarer elements, processes, principles, and definitions. Despite these differences all subdivisions are represented in both college and high-school texts.

The percentage distributions tend to emphasize the similarity more than do the data setting forth the actual space assignments in numbers of equated lines. The notable differences in favor of the college are reduced to four: preparation of compounds, properties of compounds, the rarer elements, and principles. On the other hand, one subdivision, the uses of compounds, is added to those in which high-school texts have an excess; for others the excess appearing in the first pair of figures is accentuated.

As far as can be concluded from the analysis of texts, it may be said that *although college texts are more extended than high-school texts, the relative recognition of the several subdivisions does not differ widely, except that college texts stress compounds (especially their preparation and properties), the rarer elements, and principles more than do high-school texts, whereas the latter make more of uses (both of elements and compounds), organic materials, and pedagogical features such as questions and summaries. Furthermore, the similarities far exceed the differences.*

It will be pertinent here to illustrate the nature of some of the differences found. The chief difference in favor of the college texts under the main head of common elements appears in the subdivisions dealing with *compounds*. For instance, the mean number of compounds of sulphur mentioned in college texts is 21; in high-school texts, 9.6. For nitrogen the means

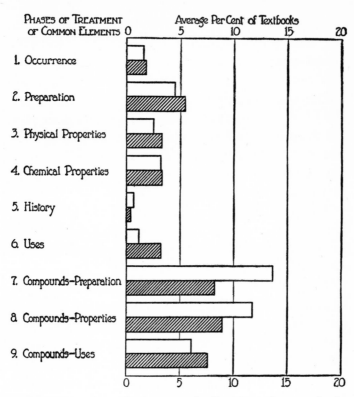

FIG. 39. Comparison of percentage distribution to the several sub-divisions of the space devoted to the common elements in college and high-school textbooks in chemistry. (In outline, college; shaded, high school)

are 13 and 8, and for iron 19 and 11.6 respectively. The difference in the matter of the *rarer and less common elements* may be made clear in brief space by stating that while one college text refers to at least

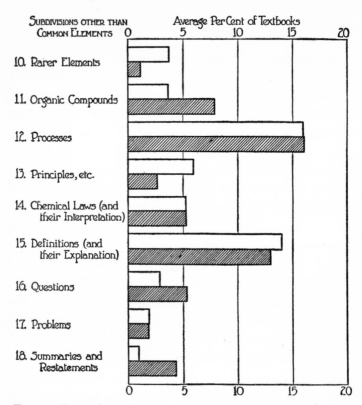

FIG. 40. Comparison of percentage of space devoted to subdivisions other than common elements in college and high-school textbooks in chemistry. (In outline, college; shaded, high school)

twenty-two and the other to at least twenty, the high-school texts refer to a much smaller number. Radium and helium are the only two of all these less common elements discussed in all the five texts analyzed.

If processes, principles, laws, and definitions are assumed to comprehend the more theoretical portions of the course in chemistry and are therefore considered for the time being as a whole, and if the average percentages of total content in these four groups are computed for college and high-school texts respectively, the percentages are found to be 41.33 and 37.34. The theoretical portions of the college texts can thus be said to exceed those of high-school texts by 4 per cent—an appreciable but hardly extraordinary difference.

A comparison of illustrations. Corroboratory testimony of some value on the extent of the similarity and difference of high-school and college texts is yielded by a comparative study of the illustrations to be found in them. The average number in the two groups of texts is almost identical, being 159 for the college and 164 for the high school. If the extent of the overlapping of the illustrations in the two groups of texts is computed, the procedure in computation assuming identity if the illustrations portray similar apparatus and are used to convey the same principle or idea, it is found to include roughly three fifths and two thirds of those appearing, respectively, in the college and high-school texts.

Overlapping in laboratory manuals. A count of the different experiments to be found in the laboratory manuals prepared to accompany the five texts analyzed results in a total of 99. Of these the two college manuals have 79 and 85, or a mean of 82. The mean for the three high-school manuals is $75\frac{2}{3}$, or only $6\frac{1}{3}$ less than the college average. This count of the large experiment heads does not, however, do full justice to the difference in extent of laboratory activity provided for, a difference which is somewhat accentuated when the comparison includes a consideration of sub-experiments (or parts of experiments). Data on this point, space for the presentation of which cannot be spared, give ground for the belief that although there is much overlapping in the larger features and content of the experiments introduced, the more extended detail in the college manuals means a more thoroughgoing experimental exploration of the fields represented.

Reverting to the overlapping computed in terms of space assigned to the large experiment heads, let it be said that the average percentages of overlapping turn out to be 72.59 for college experiments and 67.69 for high-school experiments. If to these amounts and percentages are added those of experiments found in both groups but not in each text of both groups, the totals mount to almost all the exercises, roughly 99 and 95 per cent, respectively, for the two groups of manuals. This leaves only about 1 per cent and 5 per cent, respectively, peculiar to college and high-school manuals. The larger per cent of materials distinctive of the high-school manuals arises out of the desire to emphasize the "practical" in the experiments, as well as to make the course more general by introducing simple experiments in the organic field. Even when any conclusion drawn is qualified by the fact of the larger number of sub-experiments introduced into the college manuals, it must be admitted that the laboratory portions of college and high-school courses in chemistry resemble each other vastly more than they differ.

Quantitative differences between high-school and college requirements. Some of the facts in the description of high-school and college courses in chemistry already cited point to appreciable and, in some instances, even notable quantitative distinctions. The average numbers of equated lines in the textbooks are respectively 15,875 and 27,343. The average number of topics per high-school text (the term "topic" referring to each common element, each rarer element, each "process," and so on) is 261.3 and per college text, 306.5; the average numbers of lines per topic are respectively 60.7 and 90.0. The median numbers of pages of text assigned per clock-hour of recitation or lecture are 7.9 and 9.2, showing a difference less marked than may be anticipated from the measures of gross content just presented. The reduction is accounted for by the considerably larger number of clock-hours of instruction in the college courses.

Conclusion. It is clear from the comparisons made that although there are some differences between high-school and first college courses in chemistry, they are much alike. Consequently, if the materials presented in high-school courses may be presumed to be secondary in character, there is relatively little in these first college courses which is not purely secondary. Moreover, if a student takes the course in general inorganic chemistry in college after having had the high-school course (which is often done), he is repeating almost all of it. Even in that relatively small proportion of higher institutions where such a student enters upon a course in general inorganic chemistry presumed to be administered for those who offered the high-school unit for admission, there must be a large amount of repetition.

The conclusions with reference to the proper means of effecting a reorganization of courses that will guarantee proper progress and obviate wasteful repetition must be identical with that presented in the section immediately preceding, which deals with overlapping in English literature: it must be through a regrouping of the years of school work that shall bring the present later high-school and earlier college years into intimate association. This is accomplished through the establishment of junior colleges.

IV. Overlapping in Other Subjects and Courses

Quantitative differences. The findings of extended investigations in five other fields—English composition, elementary French, algebra, American history, and economics—will be much more briefly epitomized than were those for English literature and chemistry. While the materials are no less pregnant with significance and hardly less striking as concerns the extent of overlapping, the trend of conclusions is very much in the same general direction, and this fact makes it possible to resort to an even briefer summary of tendencies.

In quantitative ways the high-school and college offerings in the five fields named differ, for the most part, in the same degree as do those in the two already dealt with. The total textual content for the median case in courses in "freshman rhetoric" exceeds by approximately a third that in all the composition portion of the full high-school course in English extending through three or four years, although the median number of clock-hours of instruction is almost twice as large in the latter. This means that the textual content in pages per clock-hour is considerably larger for the course on the upper level. The theme requirements of the college courses, when measured by the number of words per clock-hour of class time, are also about twice as large if the median here is compared with that for all four years of high school. There is not as great a difference when the college median is compared with that for the fourth high-school year, since, as is to be expected, requirements per clock-hour increase rather consistently as the student progresses from his freshman year to his senior year in the lower unit. The total textual and reading content and the number of pages per clock-hour of instruction in elementary French covered in college courses exceed those in high-school courses, although the difference is not so large as is assumed in admitting students to intermediate and advanced college courses. Comparison in quantitative ways is more difficult for algebra; but it may be said that in amount of theory the courses in college algebra exceed those in "higher" or "advanced" algebra as given in the high school, whereas in the gross number of exercises and verbal problems the high-school courses lead. Similarly, in both textual and collateral-reading content college courses in American history and economics far outstrip the high-school courses, some of which, however, exceed in these respects some college courses. What is referred to here is the trend of difference, which is clearly in favor of the courses in the upper unit.

Comparisons as to the nature of the content. Analysis of textual content of work in English composition in the high school and freshman rhetoric in the college discovers both similarities and differences.

Distributed to large groups, such as mechanics (grammar, punctuation, spelling, and pronunciation), diction, structure, forms of discourse, models, literary forms, and miscellaneous, the high-school courses show tendencies to large excesses over the college courses in the first, third, and fourth, whereas the college courses show a tendency to excesses only in the proportion devoted to models. If the constituent last named is omitted and recomputations of percentages for the remaining groups are made, the differences are less marked, but the portions devoted to diction and miscellaneous in the college courses notably exceed those in the high-school courses. The general conclusion is one of something of distinctiveness, but with much of similarity and even of identity.

This conclusion is much more nearly unequivocal for courses in elementary French, where the first two years of work in the high school were compared with the first year of work in the college. The chief difference is in the larger proportion of grammatical content in the college courses and the larger proportions of reading in the high-school courses. In other respects the content is more nearly alike than different, a finding corroborated by the common use in many instances of the same texts and readings.

Courses in higher algebra and college algebra are also both alike and different. Differentiation is shown, on the one hand, in the larger proportions of higher algebra devoted to more elementary topics, such as factoring, linear equations, radicals, etc., and, on the other, in the larger proportions of college algebra devoted to more advanced topics, such as permutations, combinations, probability, and determinants. The large extent of overlapping is shown both in the generous list of topics, such as quadratic equations, irrational equations, progressions, and the binomial theorem, in which the courses on the two levels have proportions of the total content approximately equal, and in the overlapping in the distributions of percentages when all higher and college algebra courses are compared.

In the majority of first college courses in American history, as in practically all high-school courses in the same field, the total period covered begins with discovery and ends with the present day. Moreover, if the textual content is distributed to nine periods, such as discovery and exploration, colonial development, colonial wars, pre-Revolutionary times, the Revolution, etc., the average percentages of the total course assigned to each in high-school and college courses are almost equal. When again, after a careful topical analysis, this textual content is classified as political, economic, social, or military, the proportions are found to be almost equal, the only exception being a somewhat larger percentage of the division last named in the average college course.

The high-school courses in economics are likewise, more often than not, reduced replicas of the college courses. When the textual content of representative groups of courses is distributed to the seven divisions of production, value and exchange, money and the medium of exchange, international trade, distribution, labor problems, and taxation, the percentages found to be devoted to each in the high-school and college courses are nearly equal, the only exceptions being a larger percentage in production in the high-school courses and compensating differences in favor of distribution and labor problems in college courses.

Undiscovered qualitative differences. It is to be conceded that although the methods of inquiry used are designed to discover some of the *qualitative* differences between the courses on the two levels represented, they have not found all. Nothing short of a comprehensive plan of measuring the results of the instruction given can meet the requirements of the situation. Among the factors certain to make for qualitative distinctions (at least as concerns results) are the larger extent of selection in the student-body of even the first years of the college as compared with the last years of the present high-school period and the more extended training in subject matter of college teachers. There are also other qualitative differences in detail of content which are not discoverable by the methods used.

Factors making for identity. But after all admissions of undiscovered distinctions have been made, the large extent of community of content remains as the salient feature of the curricular situation investigated. This conclusion of the large extent of identity is encouraged, moreover, by other facts summarized in this and the preceding chapter. In the last chapter we learned that much, if not most, of what is now offered in the high school is a heritage from collegiate curricula; that subject after subject has been depressed, usually without dilution, from college years to high-school years. Since this depression was accomplished by teachers trained in the colleges, it would have been surprising indeed if they did not transfer to the lower school, as nearly complete as possible, what had been in the work taken by them in their college careers. The same conclusion is anticipated also by facts concerning the proximity of classification of students taking the high-school courses examined, and the degree of similarity in the methods used, the latter being in turn anticipated by the negligible differences in the typical size of the class sections. For example, that part of the high-school course in English which is devoted to the survey of English literature is taken typically by seniors, whereas the college course is usually taken by freshmen and sophomores. The tendency to nearness of classification is characteristic of most of the courses scrutinized in this chapter. The subjects which in part form exceptions to this generalization are English composition (certain portions of which come in for emphasis during the lower high-school years only), and first courses in high-school French, which are in some high schools more frequently taken by students in the ninth or tenth grade than by those in the eleventh grade. The first college courses in most of the subjects investigated are thus typically pursued either in the year immediately following that in which the corresponding course is pursued in the high school, or with but a single school year intervening. Much less frequently is there a wider gap of time between them. Under such circumstances it is not to be expected that the courses would differ widely.

Another type of fact that points to similarity is the degree of similarity of methods. The chief difference here seems to be the more frequent use of the lecture method in the college courses, more especially in the survey course in English literature, in chemistry, and in American history. Even in these there is not as large a difference as traditional beliefs lead us to expect, the recitation mode being the typically predominant one in the college courses as well as in the high-school courses. This similarity of procedure is made possible by a relatively small average excess in the size of class sections in college.

The situation in courses and subjects not investigated in detail. Some comment will now be ventured on the degree of overlapping in fields and courses not subjected to such detailed analysis as was attempted for the materials on the subjects just summarized. On the basis of the earlier place of Greek and Latin in secondary-school programs there was relatively little overlapping of college upon high-school offerings in these languages. Beginning Greek has, however, become a course given almost exclusively in the college, and therefore we may say that although there is little in the way of repetition by the individual student, those who begin Greek are doing work of secondary-school character. Latin seems to be following its elder sister in this process of being relegated to the early college years, if we may judge by the appearance of elementary offerings in the college catalogues in the West and Middle West; and, to the extent that this is true, the same thing may be said of it as was just said of Greek. The situation as to Spanish is essentially the same as that for French; for German it differs only in the fact that instruction in this language is now practically nonexistent in high schools, elementary courses, like those in other modern foreign languages, being pursued in junior-college years.

In so far as students pursue courses in solid geometry and trigonometry in college they are doing work of secondary-school character, since solid geometry is typically given in the high school and trigonometry is often given. The courses in analytic geometry overlap to some extent upon high-school courses, but less than do the two thus far named, and courses in the calculus are even more markedly differentiated. College courses in science other than chemistry overlap less than do those in this subject upon corresponding high-school courses, sometimes because they are farther apart in the matter of typical student classification. There is, notwithstanding, a large amount of community of content in high-school courses and first college courses in biology, physics, physiography, etc.

There is no occasion to believe that the situation touching courses in history other than American history is essentially different from that shown for it, except where the student classifications for the corresponding courses are farther apart. The gap in this respect would usually be widest for courses dealing with the ancient world. Similarities and differences for political science and sociology and corresponding courses in the high school are probably somewhat analogous to those shown in economics. Certain fields, such as philosophy and psychology, are so infrequently represented in the lower unit that the content may be regarded as fully distinctive of the college.

This brief survey of the unanalyzed subjects and courses leads to conclusions not differing widely from those already drawn, but at the same time to such as acknowledge a somewhat greater extent of difference and less of repetition in some subjects and courses.

V. Current Efforts to obviate Repetition

In the face of all the overlapping and repetition which appears to be the rule in the subjects and courses represented in both high school and college, little is done to obviate it, as may be judged from the following summary of practices in a large number of colleges and universities.

1. Only a single catalogue among eighty-six selected at random gave evidence of attempting to avoid repetition in English: one college announces that it is possible for the student to be excused from freshman rhetoric by passing an examination at the opening of the school year.

2. The standardization of course sequences in older subjects, such as the ancient languages and mathematics, seems to satisfy the colleges on the score of overlapping, as no special adjustments appear in these fields despite what is almost a certainty of overlapping somewhat similar to that reported for higher algebra and college algebra.

3. In approximately 90 per cent of the colleges two units of high-school modern language are counted the equivalent of a year of college work, the student with the former amount to his credit being admitted to second-year college courses in the same language.

4. Chemistry is the only one of the college sciences in which there is any extent of effort to recognize the

fact of overlapping. In all others there is seldom, if ever, administrative acknowledgment, other than giving entrance credit, that the student has had a high-school course in an identical line. Even in chemistry only twenty-four, or less than 30 per cent, of a total of eighty-six colleges make such acknowledgment. Of these, thirteen reduce the number of semester-hours (by an average of 4.4) required for the completion of the college course in general inorganic chemistry. Among these are five colleges which save the student as much as one year in entering advanced courses, and three which save him a half-year. The principal remaining form of recognition is simply listing a separate course in general inorganic chemistry for students offering a high-school unit in this subject (the total number of credits for the course being the same as that for the regular beginning course) and concluding by putting those students no farther up in the department than others who have taken the course for students entering without high-school chemistry. There were nine such institutions represented in the group of catalogues examined.

In all the social subjects those students who have had no high-school course in a particular field enter the same courses as those who present half or whole units of admission in the same field.

There is thus an *all too common disregard in the college of what the student has compassed in his period of high-school training and, moreover, no notable tendency in the direction of proper recognition.* The situation is not likely to experience early improvement for the reason already mentioned in this chapter, that the work repeated is given in two separate institutions the upper of which is unaware, and making no effort to become aware, of what is going forward in the lower.

VI. The Overlapping Situation as a Whole

Overlapping in the offerings. Except for its introductory portions all sections of this chapter have been concerned with overlapping in specific courses and subjects. In the studies summarized the foundation was laid for an estimate of the extent of overlapping in all subjects combined. Such an estimate is here essayed, and follows three main lines: (1) a study of college offerings classified as secondary, partly secondary, and collegiate; (2) a study on the same basis of work actually taken by students in the first two college years; and (3) an estimate of the proportion of the work taken during the first two college years which constitutes repetition of that taken in high school by the same students.

The colleges whose offerings were examined for the first part of this study, which is in effect a comparison of college with high-school offerings, were eighty-six of those one hundred and fourteen whose catalogues were utilized in the study of college offerings reported in Chapter III, presenting the total offering to underclassmen. The shrinkage in number in the present instance was for the sake of economy in tabulation, omissions being made through a method of random selection.

Classification of a course as *secondary* for present purposes does not assume that the course is identical in level with a high-school course, but it does assume that there is a large measure of identity in the content of courses frequently listed in high-school offerings. In order to decide with something like assurance that such courses are or are not often found in high schools the investigator had before him a table of frequencies of appearance of subjects of study and courses in approximately two hundred and fifty high schools randomly selected and distributed over the entire country. A complete exposition of the bases of classifying courses as *partly secondary* cannot be presented on account of limitations of space, but these bases are illustrated: (1) courses which are sometimes but not frequently offered in high schools, for example the short story, intermediate course in the modern languages (that is, those beyond the second-year course in the high school); (2) courses in which there are many materials common to high-school courses but presumably fewer than for those classed as secondary, such as English poetry, inorganic chemistry for those

entering with a high-school unit, and elementary accounting; (3) introductory courses given in high
school more commonly as semester courses but more
often in college as full-year courses, such as principles
of economics; (4) courses in which the difference in
level between high school and college is rather wide,
owing to the fact that the high-school course is usually
taken in the earlier years, for example physiography
and botany; (5) introductory college courses having
their analogues in the high-school offering but administered with prerequisites which put them on a higher
level, like general physics. All other courses found
available for under-classmen were classified as strictly
collegiate.

The departments in which the college offers considerable work classed as secondary are English, most
of the foreign languages, chemistry and physics, history, art, music, and the engineering and industrial
group. Those in which it offers little or nothing on
this level are public speaking (grouped with English),
Greek, Italian, biology, geology, astronomy, the social
sciences, philosophy, psychology, Bible and religion,
education, and home economics. Several subjects falling within the groups just named—public speaking,
biology, geology, political science, economics, and
home economics—make their chief additions to the
total of the offerings classified as secondary and partly
secondary through the amounts and percentages of

courses placed under the latter category. Of a total
of twenty-nine departments of any considerable magnitude when measured by the total number of hours of
work offered, only sixteen contain no work on the secondary level, ten contain no work on the partly secondary level, and eight contain none on either the
secondary or the partly secondary level. *The salient
facts are that a generous fifth of all work offered to
freshmen and sophomores in these eighty-six colleges
is secondary and another generous fifth is partly secondary, as defined; in other words, between two fifths
and a half is secondary and partly secondary, the
remainder being more strictly collegiate.* While the
proportions in the several subject-groups differ, *except
for psychology, philosophy, etc., which include no
secondary work, all contain large proportions of work
below the distinctively collegiate classification.*

*Overlapping in work taken by two hundred college
students.* Merely tabulating the courses *offered* to
under-classmen, as was done in the study just reported, although it brings significant results, cannot
be regarded as furnishing a full description of the extent to which the work of junior-college years is of
secondary or partly secondary grade. A more complete account is provided by a study the results of
which are now to be summarized, which concerns the
work *actually taken* by a group of students during
their first two years in college. The students in this

instance were two hundred men and women who entered the College of Science, Literature, and the Arts in the University of Minnesota in the fall of 1920 and continued their residence during the two succeeding academic years ending in June, 1922. These students constitute an unselected group, being the first two hundred in alphabetical arrangement.

Here again large proportions of the work are seen to be of the secondary and partly secondary classifications. In fact, *the percentages of the lower classes of work actually taken are far in excess of those offered.* In five of the nine groups of subjects (that is, all excepting science, social subjects, and the philosophical, æsthetic, and occupational groups) there are larger proportions of secondary materials, in five groups there are larger proportions of partly secondary materials, and in all but three groups there are larger proportions of secondary and partly secondary materials combined. In most instances the differences are marked. In harmony with this are the percentages for all subjects represented, which are 29.8 secondary, 40.4 partly secondary, and 70.2 secondary and partly secondary combined, leaving in the distinctively collegiate classification only 29.8 per cent of the courses taken.

Overlapping in the nature of repetition. Up to this point in this section attention has been centered on the first type of duplication referred to in the quota-

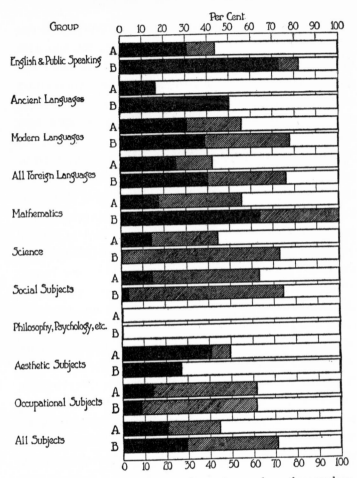

FIG. 41. Comparison of percentages of secondary work, partly secondary work, and collegiate work in (A) work offered in the first two college years and (B) work actually taken by two hundred college students. (Black, secondary; shaded, partly secondary; in outline, collegiate)

tion from President Angell's paper near the opening of the chapter; namely, the appearance in collegiate offerings of materials identical or partly identical with those available in the high school below. One aspect of the general situation still requires examination— that to which President Angell refers as "the second instance," where the student is required, after having been granted entrance credit for certain subjects, to repeat the materials represented in those subjects. Interest here focuses on the work taken in both high school and college by the same student or group of students. To ascertain the extent of overlapping that is in the nature of actual repetition, a careful study was made of the work taken in high school and in college (first two years) by the two hundred students, the content of whose collegiate curricula was canvassed for the paragraphs immediately preceding.

Very few of this group of students entered college with less than four units of English. Freshman English as administered in the College of Science, Literature, and the Arts in the University of Minnesota is composed of both rhetoric and literature, the latter not adhering closely to the content of a typical first course in this field in colleges. Such a course is usually designated as the "history of English literature" or the "survey course" in English literature. Since we are here concerned with the typical or general situation rather than with that in the University of Minnesota, overlapping will be estimated on the basis of what is typical, although the extent of repetition thus indicated is probably considerably in excess of the actual amount for the institution concerned. The writer feels that on the basis of the extent of over-lapping found in freshman composition and the history of English literature as summarized in foregoing sections of this chapter, he is safely within the truth when he assumes that these typical two first college courses repeat for students who have had four units of high-school English at least one and a half units per student, and three fourths of this amount for those offering three units for admission. This turns out to be an estimated repetition of 36.4 per cent.

On account of the standardization of courses in Latin—the predominant ancient language studied—there is little repetition in this field, although there is doubtless more than the fractional percentage (0.6) computed. On the assumption that two years of a modern language in the high school are the equivalent of as many quarters in the college, and that subsequent college work is a continuation,—not always a tenable assumption,—there is also little repetition in this field. Such as has been computed has its origin in demotion of the student to more elementary work where an instructor decides that preliminary work in the high school has not been well done, and this may at least in part not mean real repetition. The facts of the study of overlapping in French referred to in an earlier section do not lead to a conclusion of a large extent of repetition for the individual student, except where he has taken his elementary French in some high school that exceeds the typical amount of ground covered in course. There are such high schools.

TABLE V. TOTAL NUMBERS OF UNITS AND PERCENTAGES OF THEIR HIGH-SCHOOL WORK ESTIMATED TO BE DUPLICATED DURING THE FIRST TWO YEARS BY 200 STUDENTS IN THE COLLEGE OF SCIENCE, LITERATURE, AND THE ARTS OF THE UNIVERSITY OF MINNESOTA

Subject-Group	Total Number of Units Represented	Number of Units Duplicated	Per Cent of Units Duplicated
English	819⅓	298⅛	*36.4*
Ancient languages	333½	2	*0.6*
Modern languages	331½	39⅔	*12.0*
All foreign languages	665	41⅔	*6.3*
Mathematics	473	4⅙	*0.9*
Science	366⅚	34	*9.3*
Social subjects	507	102⅙	*20.1*
Philosophical subjects	6½	½	*7.7*
Æsthetic subjects	85	3⅔	*4.3*
Occupational subjects	341	1	*0.3*
All	3263⅔	485 7/24	*14.9*

The amounts and percentages of repetition found for mathematics are likewise based on the assumption that the courses taken in college are distinctly continuous with those pursued in the high school by the same students; for instance, that college algebra begins where higher algebra leaves off. This assumption may be true for some institutions, but it is rendered untenable for any large group of colleges by the study in this field summarized in an earlier section. This study justifies an estimate of larger proportionate repetition.

The estimate made indicates for those two hundred students a total extent of repetition of slightly less than a tenth of all science accepted for entrance. The three sciences most influential in this result are botany, zoölogy (animal biology), and physics, which were pursued both in high school and college by thirteen, eleven, and fifteen students respectively. As the University of Minnesota administers separate courses in general inorganic chemistry for those who have had high-school chemistry and for those who have not, reducing by one third the credit carried by the course taken by the former group, repetition was assumed in the case of one student only, who, having had chemistry in high school, took the longer college course. The assumption here is doubtless far short of the actual extent of repetition, as may be deduced from the section on overlapping in chemistry. Owing to the relatively small percentage of colleges making similar recognition of high-school chemistry, the extent of repetition in science for colleges generally must be much in excess of the 9.3 per cent computed.

The large extent of duplication estimated for the social subjects (20.1 per cent) arises in the repetition primarily of materials in modern and American history, civics, and economics, although there is an occasional repetition in English history. An earlier section on overlapping in American history and economics, although it does not cover all courses here concerned, lends full support to the extent of repetition assumed.

The estimated proportion of repetition in all subjects, on the basis of the assumptions described, turns out to be 14.9 per cent. However, owing to the conservative character of most of the assumptions, *the actual repetition of materials can hardly be less than a full sixth to a fifth of all the work taken in the high school by such a group of students. This is equivalent to from two thirds to four fifths of a high-school year. Even after allowance is made for some measure of review to add to such fixation of fundamental skills as can be accomplished only by means of extended drill, what remains is a big price to pay for our attempts to divide secondary education between two separate institutions.*

VII. Implications of the Extent of Overlapping Found

In brief the significance of the facts summarized in this chapter is that curricular offerings in the high school and in the college during freshman and sophomore years have much in common and, as administered, involve a large amount of repetition by the individual student. The community of content argues that if the work in the lower unit is to be characterized as secondary, the bulk of that taken by the student during his first two years in the upper unit is likewise secondary. There is much of artificiality and little of logic in our present line of demarcation between secondary and higher schools.

There are those who are disposed to contend that the individual student should repeat some of the work he has done in the high school. For grounds for this necessity they would resort to the traditional charges that high-school work of the present day is "inefficient," that its typical inadequacy obliges college teachers to cover the ground once more. It is conceded that some measure of renewed contact with materials already covered in the high school is desirable when a college student takes up again a subject to which he has given no thought for some months or a few years. It may even be that there are instances of some slight slump in efficiency of instruction in recent years because teachers in high schools are confused and baffled by a mental democratization which has brought into the high school a wider range of native ability than was formerly represented there, a democratization which has confused college authorities even more than those in high schools. As a whole, however, efficiency of instruction may safely be assumed to have held its own or even to have made substantial gains. The writer feels confident that the extent of repetition found is much in excess of the genuine necessities of the situation, and that a better organization of secondary and higher education would have obviated most of it. This confidence is increased when it is recalled that the high-school courses represented in the preceding chapters were those going forward in cities most of which had populations of ten thousand and over. Most of the large amount of repetition would not be found if contracts were at all frequent between instructors in courses on the two levels represented.

As it is, the repetition, going on unchallenged or with an inadequacy of adjustment to what the student has had in high school, must involve a staggering waste of time and demoralization of study habits. The types of adjustment now practiced have been seen to be at best only partial, the conclusion being that there is in the college an all too common disregard of what the student has compassed in his period of high-school training and no notable tendency in the direction of proper recognition.

The facts presented and the conclusions drawn all point in a single direction, and that is toward the inclusion of the junior-college years in a coherent plan of secondary schools. While some improvement can be effected through introducing junior-senior lines of cleavage in present-day higher institutions and through vigorous efforts at coöperation between those responsible for education on the high-school and junior-college levels concerned, these means will be inadequate to the needs of the situation. What is required is an organization of education that will bring into intimate and frequent contact the courses on the two levels and those presenting them. Only in this way can we have assurance of achieving in each field a realignment of courses that will promise the maximum of progress and training to students pursuing the sequences represented. For instance, it is unlikely that after junior-college reorganization brings these years of work into close association with the work in the unit below we shall go on having (as is now a too frequent practice) two courses in American history—one taken typically in the twelfth grade, the other in the fourteenth or fifteenth grade, both of them attempting to exhaust the possibilities of the outstanding movements from the period of discovery to the present day. The same may be said of high-school and first college courses in other fields, such as chemistry, economics, and so on. The realignment should and will bring profound modifications of content and character of courses and a standardization in these respects not now possible. Only through junior-college reorganization of the type indicated shall we eliminate in the college superfluous repetition of ground already covered in the high school.

Furthermore, only in this way shall we soon arrive at a place where educational advice to the student will assist in securing an approach to the proper distribution of work to the several fields during his full period of secondary education. With the present tendency to think of these two levels as distinct periods of education, there is too little likelihood of achieving anything like a satisfactory distribution.

Lest some may conclude that by introducing the junior college as proposed we shall merely be advancing by two years the point at which ill-considered repetition begins, let it be observed that there can be relatively little of this repetition if the junior year is made the place of first emphasizing one's specialty, as is now the predominant practice. With the period of general education concluded, most of the danger of superfluous repetition is removed.

IX

EVALUATING THE TYPES OF JUNIOR COLLEGES

I. THE MOVEMENT SUSTAINED

Summary of the advantages of the movement. **The** materials presented in the foregoing chapters of this volume afford ample justification of the junior-college movement. Only an occasional aspect of the many-sided study of the new unit has turned out unfavorable to it, and in most of these exceptions the inadequacy can be ascribed to the sheer immaturity of the movement. As it is believed that this conclusion of justification has been given adequate support at appropriate points in the preceding pages, there is no intention to do more at the opening of this chapter than to direct the attention of the reader again in the briefest manner to some of the more prominent of the findings sustaining the right of the junior college to a place in our school system.

1. It has been shown that in the extent of its offering the average junior college does not fall far short of the work actually taken by most students during their first two years in the colleges of liberal arts.

Although the new unit does not qualify so well on the requirements of the first two years of work in pre-professional curricula and in professional curricula opening with the freshman college year, it does not appear that sizable units cannot give all the general and special work needed by any considerable pro-portion of the total number of students in higher institutions.

2. In certain aspects of the instructional situation the junior college does not yet measure up to other higher institutions. This statement applies to the ex-tent of graduate training that the instructors have had and to the proportions of instructors adequately trained for the subjects they are teaching. In other respects the comparison is more favorable, as in expe-rience, in remuneration, and in the extent of training in education. Observation of the actual work of teach-ing corroborates the conclusion drawn from a study of training and experience: that, although instructors in junior colleges seem on the average less well equipped from the standpoint of subject matter, at the same time they tend to be superior in instructional proce-dure. The same observation indicated an approxi-mation to equality in the average level of student performance in accredited junior colleges and in other higher institutions, this judgment being supported by the results of a comparison of average marks earned in their third year of work in standard higher institu-

tions by junior-college graduates and by those who had earned the right to senior-college standing in an estimable state university. The progress of the junior college in these instructional matters during its brief history is an earnest of even more progress and of the ultimate attainment of satisfactory standards in all respects. There is no occasion to doubt that the junior college will achieve a type of instruction that is much more suited to students on this level than is much of the classroom procedure in present-day colleges and universities, in which there is too much effort to avoid lower-class teaching responsibilities to get wholesome and constructive results.

3. The junior college will not only be well suited to serve the needs of those who should or can aspire to higher levels of training, but it is clearly better designed than are our typical higher institutions to provide for those who should not or cannot go on. Its superiority in the solution of this problem rests in the fact that with the first two college years as terminal years in the school containing the junior college, there will be a marked tendency to look out for the interests of this group of students.

This interest in these years as culminal years will result in the development of general curricula as well as special occupational (semiprofessional) curricula ending with the close of the junior-college period. It is not to be expected that present-day higher institutions will manifest a constructive interest in curricula of less than four years' duration, because of their logically primary concern with students in curricula four or more years in length. Nor could students be induced to enroll in large numbers for such curricula, because of the loss of caste in aspiring to anything less than the completion of the typical length of curriculum in a given institution.

4. Through proximity and lowered costs the junior college is in a position to make more nearly universal the opportunities of education on this level. This in turn, by removing a large part of the cost in these years, will make it more nearly feasible for many to secure training beyond the junior-college level.

5. Judging from parents' opinions and from the more youthful age of freshmen in junior colleges and in other higher institutions when they reside in the community of location than when they come from outside, the new unit is looked upon by patrons as affording a continuation of home influences during the critical years of social immaturity. No matter what one's opinion may be touching the reality of the moral hazard to students away from home during these first college years, the attitude of parents is a social force to be reckoned with, since it postpones continuance of education and entails a deplorable loss of time. Moreover, few will doubt that there is an actual hazard, especially in institutions with large registrations and

staffs inadequate to the purposes of social and moral guidance important for young persons.

6. Not unrelated to this advantage is the greater attention affordable to the individual student in junior-college units. The marked difference as to size of class sections now obtaining between the new institution and the larger colleges and universities is likely in considerable part to disappear as we come to foster and maintain only sizable junior-college units. With a number of junior colleges in each state, however, there will be few so large as to parallel the situation that develops the attitude of unconcern toward the individual students and brings on the "depersonalization" which long since began to characterize the institutions affected by the "freshman flood."

7. Another element of superiority of the junior college is (and will be more and more) that it gives to students on this level better opportunities for laboratory practice in leadership, for there are no upperclassmen, who in other higher institutions are usually elected to most positions of student responsibility.

8. The junior-college movement has the support also of apparently inevitable forces of reorganization in higher education. Originating impulses here were the advancing age of the college entrant, the downward shift of materials of collegiate instruction, and the accompanying increase of entrance requirements, all of which provided the student with approximately

two more years of general training than he formerly received by the time he had reached any given year-point in his college career. Upon the heels of these changes have come others in harmony with them. One was the changing organization of college curricula, which moved from complete prescription to almost complete election and then to the prescription of a major subject which the student almost always looks upon as occupational specialization and in the majority of instances makes use of occupationally subsequently to graduation. Others are the accommodations that most colleges make to the desires of students for shortened periods of nonoccupational training; the trend of enrollment in higher institutions, which is reducing the proportions of students in the last two years of colleges of liberal arts whether these are in separate institutions or parts of universities, the line of cleavage appearing in universities between the sophomore and junior years; etc. Junior-college reorganization is also sustained by the argument of analogy with French and German school systems, since the latter include within the secondary school and the unit underlying it the whole of the period of general education, the university giving itself over entirely to specialization.

9. Finally, the materials presented in Chapter VIII constitute a cogent argument for the junior-college movement, since they show not only a large extent of

similarity and identity of work in the high school and on the junior-college level in colleges and universities but also a large amount of actual repetition for the individual student. To achieve such an organization and coördination of courses on these two levels as to economize time and assure proper sequence it is imperative that junior colleges be developed in intimate association with the high-school work below them.

Special purposes of the junior college. The rather extended list of advantages of the junior college as just epitomized are readily transmutable into its special or distinctive purposes, and will hereafter be so designated. As justified up to this point, these purposes may be restated as follows:

1. *To give the first two years of curricula (1) in liberal arts and (2) in preprofessional and professional work (where these professional curricula begin with the first college year).*

2. *To assure instruction as good as or better than that on the same level in other higher institutions.*

3. *To provide terminal general education for those who cannot or should not go on to higher levels of training.*

4. *To develop lines of semiprofessional training.*

5. *To popularize higher education.*

6. *To make possible the extension of home influences during immaturity.*

7. *To afford more attention to the individual student.*

8. *To improve the opportunities for laboratory practice in leadership.*

9. *To foster the inevitable reorganization of secondary and higher education.*

10. *To bring together into a single institution all work essentially similar in order to effect a better organization of courses and obviate wasteful duplication.*

It is desirable to point out that one of these purposes is not distinctive in the same degree as are the remainder. Reference is made in particular here to purpose 1. What subtracts from its distinctiveness is the fact that it is now being performed in our traditional types of higher institutions. There are grounds, however, for retaining it as part of the complete list, since, if it cannot be accomplished, there would be no point in the acceptance of attempts at the performance of most of the others.

II. Evaluating the Main Types of Junior Colleges

Plan of evaluation. As the type or types of junior colleges to be encouraged should be those which will most effectively perform the special purposes of the institution, the logical procedure in evaluation must be the examination of each type as to the likelihood of such performance. This procedure will here be followed. The measure of likelihood is afforded for the most part in the materials already used in this volume, but additional data will be introduced at several points at which pertinent materials are available. The first step will be a concurrent scrutiny of three main types of junior colleges: (1) junior colleges in city or high-school districts, referred to here as *public* junior colleges, (2) *private* junior colleges, and (3) those maintained in connection with normal schools and teachers' colleges, referred to as *normal-school* junior colleges. Certain considerations bearing on the desirability or undesirability of the second and third types will, however, be presented subsequently to the concurrent canvass. Evaluation of occasional additional types will also be separately accomplished.

Performing the special purposes in public, private, and normal-school junior colleges. 1. The stronger junior colleges in all three types may be judged from data presented in Chapter III to qualify on the former of the two aspects of the first special purpose, *giving the first two years of curricula* (1) *in liberal arts and* (2) *in preprofessional and professional work.* On the basis of average offerings public junior colleges lead the private junior colleges to some extent, the latter dropping somewhat more below the point of feasibility than the former. Special figures are not presented for normal-school junior colleges, but the writer's visits to institutions of this type assure him that they will tend to qualify as readily on this score as the better junior colleges in city and high-school districts. But to justify the tentative minimum liberal-arts offering of two hundred and twenty-five to two hundred and fifty semester-hours on economic and other grounds, Chapter X makes apparent the desirability of a minimum of approximately one hundred and fifty liberal-arts students, which is not attained by a large proportion of any type of junior college.

Strong junior colleges of all three types should also be able, if we may judge from other materials in Chapter III, to rise to the needs of the performance of the second aspect of this purpose. Public junior colleges are seen to have made more progress in this direction than private junior colleges. One reason for this is that the former are universally coeducational, whereas the latter are in a large proportion of instances segregated and, more especially, women's institutions. Since professionalization of women's training is lagging behind men's, private junior colleges have less of a problem in measuring up to requirements in this regard. At the same time the fact that private junior colleges are in such large proportions institutions for women only does not lead to an expectation of early and general performance of this purpose for *men*. The private coeducational junior colleges are less well equipped at the present than are the public to care for the preprofessional requirements of both sexes. The normal-school junior colleges, on whose course offerings no data have been presented, are fully as certain as the public group to be able to qualify on these requirements. Numbers again being necessary to justify such offerings, a sizable student-body is essential. On this score, as has already been indicated, the public and normal-school units are somewhat in advance of the private units, although there should be a marked increase in average enrollments in all units to bring the fifty to one hundred additional students to warrant the provision of the additional courses pointed out in Chapter III as needed for the special groups concerned.

2. The trend of the evidence in Chapter IV is that the public and normal-school junior colleges are in a somewhat better position than are the private units *to assure instruction as good as or better than that on the same level in higher institutions.* The advantage is in matters such as length of graduate training, experience, salary, and observed teaching. Some private junior colleges would make a better showing in certain of these respects than some public and normal-school units, but as a group they lag somewhat. This means, of course, that if the private junior college aspires to achieve the purpose, it has farther to go than the other types, but it does not mean that the latter have no further progress to make.

To provide teachers with even tolerably adequate preparation in all desirable fields of training, especially those like the social subjects, in which the total offering is now not as large as in English, French, etc., junior colleges will need either to have very large enrollments or to arrange for having teachers give instruction in their own or related fields in some other associated educational unit. This is practicable in public junior colleges because of their association with secondary schools below them. It is practicable also in normal-school units because of the need of work in some of these lines in teacher-training curricula. It is less so in many private junior colleges because, as will be shown later in evaluating types by means of the last purpose (purpose 10), there has been a marked tendency toward atrophy of the academies or high schools associated with them. In striving to achieve this purpose the private junior college will have this additional obstacle to overcome.

3. All institutions whose curricula end with the sophomore college year will be more disposed than are our colleges and universities *to provide appropriate terminal general education for those who cannot or should not go on to higher levels of training.* Therefore all types of junior colleges unassociated with institutions where work on higher levels is available can qualify on this requirement. This statement, however, implies only qualified approval of junior-college units with plans or aspirations for upward extension to include senior-college years. Responses on this point from heads of public and private junior colleges show that 16 and 42 per cent, respectively, entertain such aspirations. The proportion for the former group is

negligible and concerns only junior colleges in large cities, but for the latter it concerns a proportion sufficiently large to be discouraging. It is evidence that a large proportion of the heads of private units still look longingly at the four-year college status. To the extent that this is true it will tend to disqualify this type of unit for the performance of the special purpose under consideration, and this for somewhat the same reason that four-year colleges and universities are disqualified: their focus of attention is upon the longer curriculum and not upon the needs of students who are not going beyond the junior-college level. This same disqualification applies to normal schools with teachers'-college aspirations. In such of these normal schools as become teachers' colleges, however, until their students come to be enrolled predominantly in the four-year curricula—which will not occur for many years or even decades—the well-established habit of looking upon the first two years beyond the high school as culminal years will to some extent foster the performance of this purpose. Nevertheless the presence of the longer curricula must gradually lessen the realizability of this important special function.

4. The junior colleges unattached to four-year colleges and universities will also, and for the same reason (that they will hasten the provision of terminal general education for those who cannot or should not go on), be first in developing semiprofessional lines of

training. As between public and private units, the advantage in this respect will come to rest with public institutions, just as the development of vocational training has been more vigorous in public than in private secondary schools. Occasional public junior colleges have already made a beginning. Private junior colleges have, however, shown a larger development in home economics and teacher preparation. The growth in the former field is explained by the proportion of women's institutions represented.

The teacher-training function of junior colleges deserves special consideration. A study of the distribution of recent graduates of six public, seven Northern private (mostly in Missouri), eight Southern private, and two normal-school junior colleges shows the following percentages, irrespective of sex, engaged in teaching: 1.3, 43.3, 41.8, and 13.7 respectively. Corresponding percentages for women only are 2.0, 45.4, 55.1, and 16.7. Some private institutions send negligible proportions of their graduates into teaching immediately upon completion of the junior-college work, but these institutions can be matched by others almost all of whose graduates enter this work. More commonly it is elementary-school teaching into which these graduates go, but sometimes it is high-school teaching. For instance, two thirds of the graduates of one junior college entered teaching, and of this proportion fully two thirds went into high-school work.

Little can be said in favor of this semiprofessional-training function characteristic of private junior colleges, except that in the states represented it may be justified as a temporary expedient in view of a dearth of teachers properly prepared for the work upon which these junior-college graduates enter. As nothing short of four-year college graduation should be countenanced for high-school teaching, junior-college graduates should not be permitted to qualify for it without further training. For elementary-school teaching the training received in junior colleges is not suitable, and the two-year course in the normal school is much to be preferred. It is obvious that the semiprofessional teacher-training function of the private junior college, although at present its predominant one, is hardly legitimate and affords no satisfactory permanent field of service for that unit. As standards of teacher preparation become more discriminating, the best we may look for is that this function will become preprofessional in character.

5. The lower cost of education in the public junior college, as shown in Chapter V, puts that type of unit in a better position than the private institution *to popularize higher education.* Whatever is said for the public junior college in this connection appears to be just as applicable to the normal-school type.

The extent of popularization in the two main types was tested by essaying a comparison between the numbers in each thousand of the population represented by those from the local community enrolled in public junior colleges and by those enrolled in the first two years of standard four-year colleges in the Middle West. For this purpose, only institutions in cities of ten thousand to seventy thousand population were considered. The average of these measures for nine public junior colleges was 3.8, whereas the range was from 0.76 to 8.9. The corresponding measures for fourteen standard colleges, freshman and sophomore years only, were 3.1 and 0.4 to 5.8. This shows some tendency to larger proportions for the public institutions. At one point in Chapter X it is shown that in the present state of development of public junior colleges they hold into the sophomore college year smaller percentages than do four-year institutions. If it is assumed that the new unit will in time come to hold into this year as large a percentage as does the standard college, —a reasonable assumption for the time when junior colleges are more firmly established,—the typical difference between public and private junior colleges in the proportions of the population attending will be almost certain to be greater than the difference shown above, especially in view of the fact that there is typically no tuition charge for attendance upon the public junior college.

A factor operating to reduce the proportions of the population of the local community enrolling in private junior colleges is their denominationalism. This is reflected in a comparison of the denominational distributions of the mothers of students in public and private junior colleges. Data of this sort were available for fifteen public and seven private institutions. In the public junior college with the smallest proportion the most common church membership or preference represented (Methodist) was reported by fifty-seven, or 20.4 per cent of the students responding. More than two thirds of the students reporting from this institution—68.2 per cent, to be exact—reported seventeen other denominations. The largest percentage among the public junior colleges in the most frequently represented denomination was 36.1, or well over a third. The percentage for all public units was 27.9, somewhat in excess of a fourth of all mothers represented. Computations for the seven private units disclose a range of 27.3 to 93.9 per cent, with an average percentage of 51.1—slightly more than a half—for all students represented. The average proportion in a single denomination is almost twice as large as that for public junior colleges. In the private junior colleges the predominant denomination is in every instance the one under whose auspices the institution is operating.

The complete array of percentages for the predominant denomination in private junior colleges shows that in occasional instances they drop to something like those for public units. With the continued breakdown of denominationalism these lower percentages should become more characteristic, thus providing some assurance that the private institutions will in time be able to draw something like equivalent proportions of the local populations. At the same time it should be borne in mind that this breakdown itself will remove one of the most influential of the arguments for education under private control.

Before leaving the consideration of the three main types of junior colleges from the standpoint of the likelihood that they will perform the function of popularizing higher education, it is desirable to point out that if an institution is public it is almost certain that an increasing proportion of the population will avail themselves of its opportunities. This has been found true for other public educational institutions, such as the high school and the state university; and the force should be no less operative for the upward extension of public secondary education, especially, let it be repeated, since education in these public units is typically being provided free of cost or nearly so.

6. All types of junior colleges will make possible *the extension of home influences during immaturity* to the extent that they serve local constituencies. In this respect the public junior college, because it is at present almost exclusively locally patronized, is easily the leader. Judging from what was shown in evaluating the three types in terms of purpose 5, we may ex-

pect the public and normal-school types to continue to lead the private institutions in this respect. On the other hand, as is made clear in the following chapter, committal to a proper system of public junior colleges will call for units of such size as to take in from without the community of location larger proportions of the total student-body than they do at present, and to that extent will make it impossible for the junior colleges to preserve home influences for all students. This fact suggests the advisability of caution in the selection of cities in which such colleges shall be established, so that at least the majority of the student-body may be recruited from the immediate vicinity.

7. In terms of the enrollments of junior colleges as shown in Chapter I the possibility of *affording more attention to the individual student* than can be given in the larger colleges and universities places the three main types in the following order: private junior colleges, public junior colleges, and normal-school junior colleges. At the same time it is apparent that few if any units of any type are so large as to put adequate individual attention out of consideration. Furthermore, since the desirable minimum enrollment supported by the findings of this report—something like two hundred students—must apply to such institutions irrespective of type, the reduction in opportunities for this kind of attention to the student must come to all alike. To argue for a minimum student-

[331]

body much smaller than that named is to argue for a relatively prohibitive cost level or the reduction of desirable course offerings.

8. All three types of junior colleges here considered should be able to qualify on the requirement for *improving the opportunities for laboratory practice in leadership*, with the exception of those teachers'-college units in which the number of third-year and fourth-year students is large enough to prevent those in the first and second years from winning opportunities for leadership in student activities, or in normal schools in which the teacher-training enrollment is relatively so large as to overwhelm the junior-college group. Data have been presented to indicate that the development of these activities has gone somewhat farther in private units than in public units.

9. The three types of junior colleges are very unequally matched in their capacity *to foster the reorganization of secondary and higher education* toward which it has been seen that we are moving. The types unassociated with high schools below them will make some slight contribution in this direction, but much more is to be expected from those maintained in connection with strong secondary schools. The logic of reorganization is to administer these junior-college years as an upward extension of the units of our system now devoted primarily to general education and to avoid a multiplication of units in the system, rather

than to make it even more unwieldy than it is at the present time. Complexity would be added by increasing the problems of articulation. That type of junior college is to be preferred which encourages the development of closely articulating units in a *coherent system* of general education, and this is the public junior college developed in association with our public high schools.

Tested by this purpose the normal-school junior colleges do not qualify because the tendency to elevate normal-school standards has resulted in removing from most of them the high-school work they once had. Only recently have those which are developing into teachers' colleges taken steps to introduce high-school work, and in these instances the aim is to provide practice facilities for students training to be high-school teachers and not to reëstablish high-school courses in terms of their former function of providing the foundation of general training for prospective elementary-school teachers.

The private junior college also is handicapped in this respect, in that, as was foreshadowed in discussing purpose 2 and as will be made clear in dealing with the next and last purpose, the academy or high school associated with it has in most cases become of relatively inconsequential concern.

10. That we may *bring together into a single institution all work essentially similar in order to effect a*

better organization of courses and obviate wasteful duplication, it is just as necessary as in achieving the foregoing purpose (if not more necessary) to avail ourselves predominantly of a type of junior college that permits close association with the work of the high-school years immediately below the junior college. As already stated, this is the public junior college in city and high-school districts. The normal-school and private types cannot serve as well in this important respect. The reason for this inaptitude is, in the case of the normal school, that its high-school work is in most instances gone; in the private junior colleges if the high-school work has not gone it is going.

The fact that it is disappearing in the normal school is so well known as not to require mention. Some notion of what is happening in private secondary education may be had from the facts presented by Bonner,[1] who showed that the public secondary school has been gaining steadily on the private school since 1890. From that date until 1918, public high schools mounted from 60.8 to 87.2 per cent of all institutions of this grade, while the percentage of students enrolled in these public institutions increased from 68.1 to 91.2. With the trend so markedly in this direction it is hardly to be anticipated that the tide could be set

[1] H. R. Bonner, Statistics of Public High Schools, 1917–1918. *United States Bureau of Education Bulletin No. 19* (1920), pp. 11, 16.

sufficiently in the opposite direction to assure the large secondary-school enrollments that are desirable for the performance of the function in question.

A more direct measure of present possibilities in private institutions compared with public institutions is afforded by a computation that takes into account the number of students enrolled in senior high-school and freshman college classes. The data utilized were collected at the time of visiting the schools represented and pertain to the school year 1921–1922. Enrollments in the last high-school year in public units range from 87.8 to 841.5 per cent of those in the first junior-college year, with an average of 232.1 per cent for all represented. For private junior colleges the range is 7.4 to 300.0, with an average of 46.8. The average for all private units is not far from a fifth of that for public units. With the high-school enrollment relatively so inconsequential in private institutions and with the tendency of the public secondary school to gain consistently on the private secondary school, the chances are not strong that the private unit will be in a position to qualify on purpose 10. Some, however, are in a position to meet this requirement at the present time, although they will need a change of policy in the direction of encouraging rather than discouraging the development, enrollment, and work on the high-school level.

III. The Normal-School Type as a Special Problem

The problem. There has been such a battle of words over the junior college in the normal schools that no evaluation of types would be regarded as complete without giving this question some special consideration. The argument has not centered so much around the question of the *feasibility* of giving the junior-college work in normal schools as of the *desirability* of doing so, in view of an assumed violation of the teacher-training functions of institutions with which the junior-college units are associated. As this possible infringement on original functions has been said to express itself in several ways, it will be considered under two heads: the possible inroads of the junior college upon (1) the available source of a teacher-training student-body numerically and in mentality and (2) the dominance of the professional attitudes in teacher-training institutions.

Does provision of junior-college work cut in on the available supply of candidates for teacher-training? It is a matter of common knowledge that for a considerable proportion of their student-bodies higher institutions depend upon the youth of the community of location, and this dependence must characterize normal schools and teachers' colleges at least as much as other types. In an important sense the community of location of a normal school has an obligation to the state to provide a large proportion of the total number of candidates for teachers' certificates who should be trained in that particular normal school. This obligation must apply peculiarly at a time when there is a dearth of adequately trained teachers for elementary-school work, preparation for which is the primary concern of the normal school. There is some justification for the statement that, to the extent that the offering of junior-college courses attracts students away from the teacher-training curricula, the normal schools are not keeping faith with the purpose which brought them into existence, which *is* teacher-training.

TABLE VI. DISTRIBUTION BY SEX AND CURRICULUM OF FIRST-YEAR STUDENTS IN TWO NORMAL SCHOOLS IN WISCONSIN

CURRICULA	NUMBER		
	Men	Women	Total
Regular normal [1]	15	214	229
High-school teacher-training [2]	31	52	83
Special teacher-training [3]	90	63	153
Junior-college	66	21	87
Total	202	350	552

The question becomes one of the extent of the inroad. Certain facts assembled concerning the sex

[1] Preparing to teach in primary, intermediate, grammar-grade, and rural schools.

[2] Three-year curricula.

[3] Preparing to teach "special" subjects.

distribution of freshmen in two normal schools with junior colleges supply an illuminating indirect answer. The two significant facts in the distribution are the predominance of men in the junior-college group and the very small, almost negligible, proportion of this sex in the "regular" normal groups. The proportionate distribution of students from the local community is very similar. For example, of seventy-five students from the community of location in one of these institutions twenty-two are enrolled in the regular normal curriculum and twenty-eight in the junior-college curriculum. One only of the twenty-two is a man; only six of the twenty-eight are women. It is known to all those who are in touch with normal-school registration that the negligible proportion of men in the regular curricula is characteristic irrespective of the presence of a junior-college offering. This fact, joined with the relatively small proportion of women in junior-college curricula, leads to the conclusion that in these institutions the junior-college curricula can make at most only moderate inroads on a potentially available teacher-training student-body. Some inroads, however, they do make.

Does provision of junior-college work reduce the quality of candidates for teacher-training? This question has been answered in large part by inference from the foregoing discussion. If the junior-college enrollment is made up largely of men who but infrequently register for regular normal curricula, there can be nothing like a general tendency for the junior college to drain off the superior students, leaving the less capable for the regular normal course. Nevertheless, since the question is an important one, conclusions drawn from a study of test scores of students so far represented and of one other group will be set forth for as much of an answer as can be essayed here.

The distribution and the medians of test scores for men in the junior-college group are notably higher than those for women in the regular normal group, the difference being too large to be accounted for by the usual sex differences between men and women as shown by the army test. The difference between these two groups, moreover, is without doubt the chief factor of the difference in median scores for regular normal and junior-college groups, which vary from 120.4 for the former to 135.4 for the latter. While this is being admitted we should not lose sight of the high range of scores for women in the junior-college group. Of the twenty-one women represented not a single score drops below 120, which is almost identical with the median score for women in the regular normal group (120.3). At the same time the upper limits of the range are practically the same for the two groups of women. Certainly, although there are not many of them, women enrolling in the junior-college curriculum are a selected group. It would not be at all surprising if some, at least, of these women would, were junior-college work not available, register for regular normal work and thus tend to elevate in some measure the distribution of scores and median scores for the

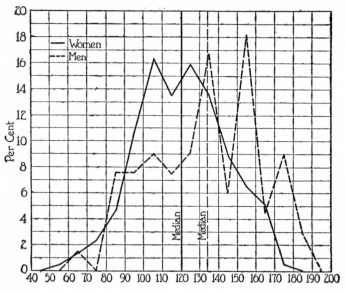

FIG. 42. Percentage distribution of scores obtained on the army alpha test by women in regular normal and men in junior-college curricula in two normal schools of Wisconsin

group representing the original and principal concern of these institutions. On the other hand, if it were assumed that all these twenty-one women would have registered in regular normal curricula, which not even the most ardent champion of unadulterated teacher-training functions in normal schools could claim, the new median would be only 122.9—not three points above that for women in regular normal work.

To find out whether the draining off of superior minds from regular normal curricula, which is assumed to follow the introduction of junior-college work, applies particularly to students from the community where they are located, students in regular normal curricula in one of the two normal schools so far represented in this section have been classified as coming from within and without the city of location, and the distributions and medians of their mental-test scores have been compared. Before passing judgment the reader should bear in mind that there is at least one other line of work besides the junior-college offering—the high-school teacher-training curriculum—which in these normal schools is also likely to make inroads on the quality of the regular normal group. The validity of the findings of the comparison is somewhat affected by the small number of students from the city where they are located, but there appears to be no such reduction in quality as suggested.

Comparison on the basis of mental-test scores of students in teacher-training and junior-college curricula in another institution similar in type to those of Wisconsin has also been made. The institution concerned is the State Teachers College in San Diego, California. The original scores obtained on the

Terman Group Intelligence Test (Form A) were made available to the writer by the authorities in charge, the giving and scoring of the tests having been done

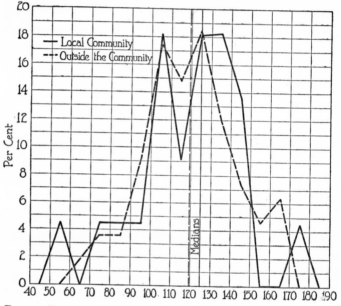

FIG. 43. Percentage distribution of scores obtained on the army alpha test by students in regular normal curricula from the local community and from outside the community

by Mrs. Gertrude S. Bell, director of tests and measurements. At the time the test was given there were no men in the teachers'-college group, but there were sixty-five women in this group, and fifty-six men and fifty-two women in the junior-college group. There

[342]

seems, thus, to be a larger proportion of women in the junior-college group than in Wisconsin, which suggests larger inroads on the available teacher-training student-body, on the assumption that teacher-training curricula would attract most of the women registering in a given institution. The distributions and medians show a marked superiority of junior-college men over women in both junior college and teachers' college. These measures for the two groups of women are notably similar, indicating that even if the provision of junior-college curricula cuts in numerically on the available supply of candidates for teacher-training, it does not affect the quality as indicated by the mental-test scores.

From the materials presented touching the two institutions in Wisconsin and the one in California the following conclusion is drawn: although there is some likelihood that the establishment of junior-college curricula in normal schools and teachers' colleges tends to affect somewhat unfavorably the number or the quality of candidates for teacher-training curricula, the testimony seems not to be particularly damaging to junior-college units of this type. This degree of detriment alone seems not to be sufficiently large to discredit the normal-school junior college.

Other considerations pro and con. Various objections other than those so far treated have been raised against the establishment of junior-college work in normal schools, and many arguments have been mustered in its behalf. Few if any of the claims made in the early stages of experience with this type of unit are to be accepted or denied on grounds objectively

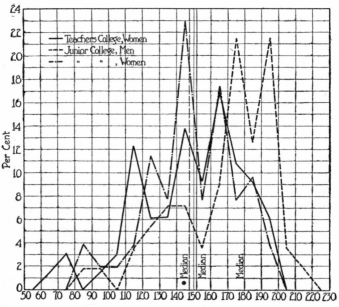

FIG. 44. Percentage distribution of scores obtained on the Terman Group Intelligence Test (Form A) by first-year students in teachers'-college and junior-college curricula in the State Teachers College, San Diego, California

ascertained, but this fact does not excuse us from giving some measure of scrutiny to those arguments commonly recurring. The complaints of those who oppose the movement as it affects normal schools center about the desirability of conserving the primary function of a teacher-training institution. Says one writer:[1]

> The normal school was created for a special purpose. Its existence is justified on the grounds of peculiar adaptation to the ends it serves, the preparation of teachers. . . . The normal-school activities should be a sort of specialized industry, not an educational department store.

All this writer's subsequent arguments are to the effect that introducing junior-college curricula impairs the performance of this primary function.

> The normal school should be an institution of characteristic professional atmosphere. . . . The junior college, as an adjunct, has nothing in common with the professional school for teachers. The student in the junior college probably has no well-defined, specific end in view; or, if he has, that end is far removed. . . . He is a bird of passage, a preparatory student for the university or senior college. . . . The normal school will lose prestige when it assumes to prepare for these.

Perhaps the most complete attempt to answer such objections which has so far made its appearance, and at the same time the briefest, is that by President Maxwell, from whose defense of the junior college in the normal school we quote on page 346:[2]

[1] E. L. Silver, "Should the Normal School Function as a Junior College?" in *National School Digest*, Vol. XL, pp. 582, 588 (May, 1921).

[2] Guy E. Maxwell, "The Junior College Question—The Other Side," in *National School Digest*, Vol. XL, p. 600 (June, 1921).

Our junior-college work supplements and aids the professional training of teachers in the following ways:

1. It provides a broader scholastic foundation for prospective teachers who plan to do departmental or higher grade work, or to teach in the junior high school. . . .

2. The prospective teacher with ambition to pursue special fields in later university study, seeks the privilege of beginning his studies in the normal school. . . .

3. Our junior-college work provides the opportunity and emphasizes the necessity for higher scholarship for teachers. . . .

4. The junior-college work leads naturally and effectively into the four-year professional curriculum for teachers and supervisors in elementary education. . . . The four-year teacher-training curriculum of the near future will therefore rest upon the two basic years of general culture which now form the junior college. *When the four-year teacher-training curriculum comes, the junior college will be superseded though not abandoned. During the transition period the junior college is a desirable means of making the curriculum or content subjects "pay for themselves." When normal schools become four-year colleges with power to grant degrees, their junior colleges, as such, will be absorbed.*[1]

5. Our junior-college work has brought three and four times as many young men into elementary education as were previously preparing for this form of service. . . .

6. The presence of young men in the normal school (brought about by the junior-college work) tends to

---

[1] The italics are not President Maxwell's but the present writer's.

promote a saner atmosphere [along social lines] among the young-women students. . . .

7. The junior-college group foster athletics and other school enterprises and develop and justify a school enthusiasm and *esprit de corps* that are a boon to every prospective teacher.

8. The junior-college work has a definitely stimulating effect upon the faculty of the institution. It enables the school to secure more scholarly men and women and to hold them longer against the competition of larger and stronger institutions. . . .

Before passing on to a critique of these arguments it is apposite to cite certain factual materials which have come to the attention of the writer. These materials, which relate to the fifth claim put forward by President Maxwell—the increase in the number of men entering educational work—and are in harmony with evidence that may be secured in all normal schools and teachers' colleges having some curricula more than two years in length, are as follows: of the fifty-one junior-college graduates of 1921 in the two Wisconsin normal schools represented elsewhere in this chapter, eighteen transferred at the opening of the next year to the third year of the high-school teacher-training curricula. All but two of these transfers were men. Other students, most of them men, transfer to these curricula before completing the two years of junior-college work.

Although the writer spent a number of days in visiting several normal schools and teachers' colleges in which junior-college units are maintained, endeavoring to discover, both in class and out, evidences of untoward influences on the teacher-training function, he became aware of few if any. Perhaps these detrimental effects are of a sort to elude observation during the brief stay of a day or two in each of five institutions, but nothing was seen over which to become exercised. Perhaps also the position of dominance in numbers and tradition which teacher-training groups still hold in these particular institutions is instrumental in checking any hurtful influences, and these may not manifest themselves until such time as the junior-college enrollment exceeds the teacher-training enrollment. Instead of detrimental influences the visitor felt that the junior college was, as a whole, beneficial in its effect upon the primary function of the institutions visited.

But even should all these arguments favorable to the establishment of junior-college units in normal schools be accepted at par, *they do not make a strong case for this type when compared with others from the viewpoint of junior-college functioning.* These arguments have one characteristic in common: they would convince us that the *junior college will make for an improved teacher-training institution.* While a teacher-training situation superior to our present one is to be desired, the primary purpose of the new unit is certainly not that which the champions of its establishment in normal schools (if we may judge by their emphasis) would make it. The junior college has fundamental purposes that far transcend this one, however important it may be regarded.

This tendency on the part of normal-school authorities to lose sight of the real functions of the junior college is strikingly illustrated in the italicized portions of the fourth point made in the quotation from President Maxwell's article. The junior college is there seen as a stepping-stone for the normal school on its way to the status of teachers' college. After the latter consummation the junior college is "absorbed." And after this absorption has taken place, where is this new unit which we have seen to possess qualities that warrant assigning it a *permanent* place in the school system?

That the opinion of President Maxwell works out as a tendency is shown in what is taking place in Wisconsin normal schools. Given authority in 1911 to establish junior-college curricula, they have relinquished their claims to being junior colleges and are asking to be made four-year teachers' colleges with power to grant degrees.

There is here no desire to deny the right to some stronger normal schools, as the need arises, to be raised to the rank of teachers' colleges. This development for many is doubtless inevitable in the evolution of the American school system and in the elevation of standards in the teaching profession. The objection raised is solely to the abuse of an institution which deserves to be established under auspices that will assure it a longer life. This ambition to extend curricula beyond the second-year collegiate level is common to the normal schools and to two fifths of the private junior colleges, as reported earlier in the chapter. To the extent that the ambition is entertained and realizable it disqualifies both types in the achievement of the special purposes of the junior college, since it encourages a focus of attention upon the longer curricula in much the same sense as is now the case in colleges and universities.

Concluding comment. Special examination of the junior-college situation (both present and prospective) in normal schools indicates that although some small inroads upon the teacher-training function are likely to be made by reducing the numbers and quality of those entering the teacher-training curricula, this disadvantage is almost certain to be offset by improvement in performing the function for which these normal schools were established. Simultaneously, however, because these institutions have their eyes on the four-year teachers' college as a goal, there must be a dwindling hope that they will look out for the continued performance of those special purposes of a junior college which depend upon regarding the first two college years as terminal years for an increasing proportion of students. The fact should not be overlooked, moreover, that this type of unit is disqualified because it cannot also perform the ninth and tenth purposes listed above, the achievement of which depends upon the close association of junior-college years with those immediately below. To carry out these purposes it would be necessary for these institutions to revert to the status from which they have for so long endeavored to be emancipated—the status of the secondary school.

IV. FURTHER CONSIDERATION OF THE PRIVATE JUNIOR COLLEGE

In the comparison involved in the evaluation of the three main types of junior colleges at a previous point in this chapter the private junior college did not fare very well, in terms of either its present state or its prospective development. Because of its relative character this degree of disparagement is likely to underrate the opportunities for service that this unit has in the current educational situation. In all fairness it should be admitted that many private junior colleges are in a position to render a really estimable service for decades to come. They will do this not only in the educational opportunities afforded but also in their contribution to the popularization of the junior-college idea or plan of organization.

Our gratitude for these benefits should not, however, blind us to the limitations indicated nor to the need of rectifying certain current untoward conditions. One of the chief hindrances to wider service of private junior colleges is the present cost to the student, particularly to the student who leaves home to attend. This cost is actually rather low in some private junior colleges, but we have seen that the trend is for attendance in these units to be more expensive than in standard higher institutions. The means of reduction must be through having sources of income other than student fees, such as endowments, with which private junior colleges are too meagerly supplied, or more generous church support, or both. And as endowments come, it is essential that the authorities in charge remain loyal to the junior-college idea and not yield to the temptation that we know exists to betray it by adding senior-college years just as soon as the financial conditions can be stretched to the point of warranting the move.

One element of cost in maintaining private junior colleges deserves special emphasis here, as under present financial conditions in these schools it is bound to be carried ultimately by the student in attendance or by some other person bearing the burden of such attendance. This is the cost of publicity. A large proportion of private junior colleges have extraordinarily heavy budget items to cover this charge. Expenditures along these lines as ascertained by personal inquiry in nine private institutions were found to total between $35,000 and $36,000, not including stenographic assistance. The items included are the cost of catalogues and view-books, advertising in church and secular periodicals, salaries and expenses of personal solicitors, and the like. As the total enrollment in high-school and junior-college departments in these nine institutions was 1434, there was an average expenditure for these items of between $24 and $25 per student. To include students who enroll for special work only would bring a somewhat lower average cost. For a few private units visited the cost for publicity was almost negligible; for others in this group it mounted to an average of more than $40 per student.

Some idea of the significance of such expenditures may be gained from comparing them with the cost of publicity in public junior colleges. For eight public junior colleges visited the total outlay for publicity items—almost exclusively for modest bulletins or catalogues—was $463. Since in these units this expenditure is made for junior-college students only, who numbered 666, the average cost is hardly 70 cents per student. This comparison suggests the need for efforts in private junior colleges to reduce expenditures along these lines, thereby making possible a reduction in costs to the student or a diversion to the educational functions of the school of a larger proportion of all the funds available.

Two occasional additional hindrances to performing in private institutions in any genuine way the special purposes of the junior college are to be found in the fact that (as mentioned in Chapter I) some of these are strictly private-venture schools, and the further fact that some still retain undesirable characteristics of the obsolescent "finishing school." Private owner-ship turns out to be an obstruction because of the obvious ineptitude to the performance of several sig-nificant junior-college purposes in schools which are looked upon as commercial enterprises by those who direct them. The second fact is a hindrance for rea-sons somewhat similar and because the finishing school never has been disposed to adjust itself to the perform-ance of legitimate educational functions. The private junior-college movement will do well to avoid these two influences incompatible to its best development.

V. Other Types of Junior Colleges

The remaining types. Up to this point only the three predominant forms of the junior college have been evaluated: the public type (in city and high-school districts), the normal-school type, and the pri-vate type. Occasional variations of form taken by the movement or proposed for it, however, demand consideration. Some have been listed as junior colleges on state foundations, and they were therefore grouped with the normal-school type in Chapter I. Most of these schools are either avowedly or essentially branches of other state higher institutions, either of universities or of colleges of agriculture and mechanic arts. Other types are those maintained as lower divisions of universities, state and private, as described in Chapter VII. In addition to these, one occasionally hears a proposal to provide a state system of well-distributed two-year junior-college units unassociated with other schools, either lower or higher, now in existence.

Their evaluation. Since the criteria have already been presented and applied to related types, evaluation of these additional forms taken by the junior college or proposed for it can be accomplished in brief space.

The "branch" unit is not to be commended as an appropriately *typical* junior college. It should be undertaken only where the ultimate goal of the branch is admittedly the paralleling of certain lines at least of the upper levels of work in the parent institution or where the distribution of population is such as to urge it in preference to the type that is a part of the public secondary school. Sooner or later local ambitions and political pressure may bring a demand for upward extension, and the state embarking on such a program will then face the necessity of supporting several co-ordinate higher institutions. Since the public type is almost universally closely associated with the high school, it is much more certain to be conceived of as a part of the lower school system and therefore cannot in most instances logically aspire to senior-college levels of training.

The branch type is especially to be deplored if it brings with it, as has been true in some instances, provisions for the high-school work below. The function of our higher institutions is certainly not to set up a system of secondary schools competing with and duplicating the work of the state's system of high schools already in operation.

On the other hand, if on this account the high-school work below should not be and is not maintained in connection with these branch junior-college units, we thwart the chances of reorganization and economy urged in purposes 9 and 10 (p. 320). This type of junior college would increase rather than diminish the problems of articulation of the several units of our school system. This last reason should just as emphatically preclude serious consideration of the separate type of junior-college unit sometimes proposed; namely, the type unassociated with other schools in the system.

Concerning the type of junior college that is a lower division of present-day colleges and universities it is scarcely necessary to say more than has been said in Chapter VII or is implicit in the need for performance of most of the distinctive purposes of the junior college. Even if this line of cleavage in higher institutions becomes more prevalent than at present, as seems certain, most of the functions peculiar to the junior college must remain unachieved unless other types maintained in connection with institutions terminating with the second college year are established and come in time to displace these years in our colleges and universities. This must apply especially to providing satisfactory terminal general education for those who cannot or should not go on, to popularizing higher education, to making possible the extension of home influences during immaturity, to affording more attention to the individual student, to improving the opportunities for laboratory practice in leadership, to fostering the inevitable reorganization of secondary and higher education, and to bringing together into a single institution all work essentially similar, in order to effect a better organization of courses and obviate wasteful duplication. Although there are several reasons for advocating the line of cleavage to which reference is made, the highest commendation for it is that it is a natural first step toward a surrender of work on this level to the enlarging secondary school below.

Many of the same considerations that urge the ultimate discontinuance of the first two years of work in the university and its provision in connection with strong secondary schools oppose maintaining one of a system of junior colleges in a state as a part of its existing universities or other higher institutions. If it is provided in the community where such institutions are located, it should be as a part of the community's lower school system, just as now the high-school work is not administered by the university but by the local community.

VI. The Logical Organization of Secondary Education

The problem of appropriate organization of the future secondary school. The foregoing evaluation having shown that the junior college maintained in connection with city and high-school districts is the one best designed to achieve the purposes of the institution, the problem next centers about the appropriate means of incorporating it in our secondary-school organization. It is obvious that this question cannot be settled without reference to other important tendencies toward reorganization of our systems of lower and secondary schools. Evidence shows that the older eight-four organization is rapidly passing, and that in its place is coming a regrouping which provides for beginning the period of secondary education two years earlier than formerly; that is, with the seventh grade. For instance, Superintendent Pratt of Spokane in a

[358]

recent article[1] gives reports from sixty cities in the United States with populations of 100,000 and over. Twenty-six have junior high schools in operation, and twenty more have them in various stages of preparation. As these sixty replies were received from a total of sixty-eight cities to which the blanks of inquiry were sent, there can be little doubt that, as Superintendent Pratt puts it, the "junior high school is . . . 'the coming plan of organization.'" His data indicate also that the almost universal grouping of the six high-school years is three in the junior unit and three in the senior unit. This movement is making rapid gains also in cities of smaller size.

The six-four-four organization. This marked tendency to extend the period of secondary education downward and to divide it into units raises the question of the practicability of adding still another unit of two years at the top, thereby making for a three-unit secondary school with three years in each of the two lowest units and two years in the last of the units. A much more sensible procedure seems to be the division of the full eight-year secondary-school period into two units of four years each and their administration after a manner similar to that being followed with respect to our present-day junior and senior high schools.

This concept of a six-four-four organization of edu-

[1] O. C. Pratt, "Status of the Junior High School in Larger Cities," in *School Review*, Vol. XXX, pp. 663–670 (November, 1922).

cation is not without precedent in thought and prac-
tice. It was proposed in 1915 by a committee of the
North Central Association of Colleges and Secondary
Schools, a part of whose report is quoted:[1]

The main subdivisions of elementary and secondary
education should therefore be as follows:

First—The Elementary School, six grades.

Second—The Lower Secondary, to include the Seventh,
Eighth, Ninth, and Tenth years of the usual school course.

Third—The Upper Secondary, to include the present
Eleventh and Twelfth Grades of the usual High Schools
and the Freshman and Sophomore years of the usual
American Colleges.

Whether it will take a student four or three years to
complete the curriculum of either of these stages of Secondary Education will depend upon whether he is able to
carry at one time three or four studies and whether the
school year consists of thirty-six or forty-eight weeks.

The Lower Secondary should be so organized and administered as to make it possible for one who is preparing
to enter the upper secondary to complete the curriculum in
three years—whether others should take three or four or
five years should depend on their individual needs and
attainments.

This report was adopted by the association.

Professor Miller of the University of Wisconsin,
principal of the Wisconsin High School, and Professor
Proctor of Leland Stanford Junior University have

[1] Proceedings of the Twentieth Annual Meeting of the North Central
Association of Colleges and Secondary Schools, pp. 77–78.

more recently advocated an identical organization of these eight secondary-school years,[1] the former proposing that the two resulting units bear the names now carried by the three-year units in the junior-senior organization.

The first public secondary schools to be organized in accordance with this plan were those of Hibbing, Minnesota. The school system in that city had since the opening of the school-year in 1916 offered junior-college work. Junior high-school reorganization had also been effected. The coincidence of two influential facts precipitated the change resulting in the redistribution of grades referred to: the resignation of the high-school principal and the removal from the old building into a new plant designed to accommodate all students from the seventh through the fourteenth grade. A junior high-school principal was appointed from the staff and placed in charge of the first four of these eight grades. The dean of the junior college was made head of the upper unit of four years. In this way the complexity of a situation involving three distinct educational units under three coördinate heads within the same secondary school was avoided.

Other approaches to precedents in practice of which the writer is cognizant are the length and arrangement

[1] H. L. Miller, "The Junior College and Secondary Education," in *Wisconsin Journal of Education*, March, 1922, pp. 47–51, and **W. M. Proctor**, "The Junior College and Educational Reorganization," in *Educational Review*, Vol. LXV, pp. 275–280 (May, 1923).

of curricula in certain Southern junior colleges and the two-cycle arrangement in the French lycée. Some of these Southern private schools, in shifting from their previous organizations, retained the name "senior" for the last class (which is now on a par with the sophomores of ordinary colleges) and the three names "junior," "sophomore," and "freshman" for the three classes next below. The Grubbs Vocational College[1] and the John Tarleton Agricultural College, which are maintained as branches of the Agricultural and Mechanical College of Texas, also have curricula of similar length, students bearing the same classifications as those in the private institutions referred to. These four-year units correspond in length with the proposed senior high school. The French lycée is to some extent similar in that it is constituted of two cycles: the first, of four years; the second, of three years.

Some advantages of the organization proposed. A glance at the accepted special purposes of the junior college will show that this method of incorporating the junior-college years in the new secondary school is better designed to achieve some of the aims than is a three-three-two organization. This superiority would apply particularly to purposes 3, 4, 5, 9, and 10. Certain other benefits would accrue, some of which should at least be mentioned. Related to purposes 9 and 10 would be the extent to which the plan will help to

[1] Recently renamed the North Texas Agricultural College.

solve the problems of articulating the several units of the system, and related in turn to this advantage is the opportunity for economy of time in the longer units in which this grouping results. This opportunity is anticipated in the quotation given above from the report of the committee of the North Central Association as well as in the proposals of Professors Miller and Proctor to which reference has been made. The economy suggested in both instances is the more rapid advancement of the more capable students. Such a consummation affords broad grounds for accepting as valid the claims classified in Chapter II, as "caring better for brighter high-school students." In view of the large extent of repetition shown in Chapter VIII and of an overlapping which must also obtain at other points in the full secondary-school period included, there is reason to believe that the typical length of stay can in time be shortened by a full year or even more, and that ultimately a seven-year or even a six-year secondary-school period will result. If this is not accomplished we shall cover more ground in the same time, enriching the extended secondary-school course, which is likewise a method of economizing time.

Both these types of economy are being achieved simultaneously at the present time in the laboratory schools of the School of Education of the University of Chicago, which have been taking over some of the work of the junior-college years. The interested reader will find these economies described in brief as one of the major lines of experimentation of these schools on pages 17–19 in a recent publication of the Department of Education of the University entitled "Studies in Secondary Education—I."[1]

This plan, providing as it does a terminal four-year unit, would compensate for the tendency of the junior-college movement to break across the student's four-year college course, a disruption deplored by those in charge of separate colleges. The four-year senior secondary-school unit will in time assure the desired continuity that will offset this loss—in fact, will more than offset it, since larger numbers will come to complete the full four-year curriculum than now remain throughout the college course. Although these values cannot be achieved at once, there is no occasion to fear that they are not ultimately attainable.

The last of the special values inherent in the four-year organization to which attention is directed is that looked for by those whose statements were classified under special purpose 18 in Chapter II, "improving high-school instruction." Some of the grounds for assurance on this score are the better teacher preparation in subject matter that must follow in the wake of close association of the work in junior-college years

[1] Supplementary Educational Monograph No. 24 (January, 1923). The University of Chicago. See also Studies in Secondary Education— II, Supplementary Educational Monograph No. 26 (February, 1925), pp. 12–13.

and the better laboratory, library, and other facilities that will be at hand for use in connection with these upper years of high-school work. At the same time the division into units at the point indicated, between the tenth and eleventh grades, will prevent that confusion of standards of work that sometimes now manifests itself because students in lower high-school and in junior-college years are too closely associated in the same educational unit.

Four-year unit not necessarily an immediate step. Although the four-four organization recommended by this scrutiny as the more desirable one is to be kept in mind as the final goal of a reorganized secondary-school period, it need not be the next step in communities which have not yet had experience with junior-college work; in fact, valid reasons can be given for first proceeding to establish units of the type now current, which provide at least a partial separation of the high school and the junior college. Among these reasons are the need of winning acceptance of the local constituency for the junior-college work provided. With our college-going traditions it is difficult at first to induce certain members of a community to believe that what they look upon as college work can really be given in a secondary school; and the maintenance for a time (at least until a new tradition of attendance at home has been established) of some lines of demarcation will assist in "selling" the work both to parents and to students. The traditional separation is like-wise temporarily desirable in some high-school situa-tions in order to establish a satisfactory pace of scholarship on the part of the student. The trend must inevitably be, nevertheless, toward welding the junior-college years solidly and intimately to those immediately below, the point of juncture becoming indistinguishable.

VII. The Junior College and the Remaining Claims made for it

Claims remaining undiscussed. Up to this point, directly or indirectly, all but a small number of the claims made on behalf of the junior college as reported in Chapter II have been subjected to examination in the light of such data as were obtainable for the pur-pose. Those still remaining undiscussed are claims 9, 11, 20, and 21. These are, respectively, that it allows for exploration, that it makes the secondary-school period coincide with adolescence, that it offers work meeting local needs, and that it affects the cultural level of the local community. Brief comment will now be made on the acceptability of these as special pur-poses and on the relation between their achievement and the types of junior colleges.

The *exploratory* function of junior-college years is probably to be accepted without debate. This is still a period during which students will make earlier contacts with materials of instruction that they have thus far in their school careers left untouched or have so inadequately explored as not to afford a sufficient basis of guidance as to future education and occupational destination. The admitted fact that these years of work are for most students enrolled in them a part of their general education implies that they are at the same time a part of the period in which educational and vocational guidance of this and other sorts is essential. In a significant sense the period of guidance is the period of secondary education, and, unfortunately, our present typical organization of education breaks across this period at two points, distributing the function to three distinct types of units. Our hope for adequate performance of the function must rest in bringing the responsibilities largely into a single period of the school system—the secondary. This will be possible with downward and upward extension of secondary education as here proposed.

Evaluation of the claim that the junior college aids in *making the secondary-school period coincide with adolescence* is not so easily accomplished. The reason is that we know so little about the characteristics of this period of life. What we do know is more pertinent to its point of onset than to its point of termination, with which a discussion of the junior college would be concerned. Therefore we have a better factual basis for deciding when secondary education should begin than when it should end, as far as it is to be determined by the period of adolescence. If the problem of the appropriate point for upper termination is broken up into the questions of when complete physical, mental, and social maturity arrives, and each of these is considered separately, we are only a little better off. On the first question we have evidence that growth in height, weight, girth of chest, strength of forearms, etc. in girls slackens notably from the fourteenth to the sixteenth year.[1] For boys the rapid increments extend beyond the typical ages of notable cessation for girls.

This difference in the typical ages for the arrival of physical maturity in the two sexes tends to discredit the claim under consideration, since boys and girls arrive at particular grades in the secondary and higher schools at ages which, if not accurately equivalent, are at least approximately equivalent. The determination of the ages of arrival at mental and social maturity is so hedged about by difficulties that no statement can be ventured which is dependable and which will throw light on the problem of the proper point of termination for the secondary-school period. The best that can be done is to make a loose general statement that only a small proportion of students seem to be socially ma-

---

[1] B. T. Baldwin, "The Physical Growth of Children from Birth to Maturity," in *University of Iowa Studies: Studies in Child Welfare*, Vol. I, No. 1, chap. v.

ture by the time of their graduation from high school, and that if higher education began with the third college year instead of the first we should be dealing in universities with men and women rather than with boys and girls.

Claim 20—*offering work adapted to local needs*—has some justification of acceptance in view of current junior-college offerings. In this respect the public junior college shows greater responsiveness than does the private institution. The last claim—*influencing the cultural level of the local community*—is admissible without extended argument, since the performance of this function is inherent in all worthy educational institutions.

Although most of these additional claims have some validity, for the sake of keeping our problem as simple as possible they will not be placed in what has here been used as a working list of special purposes of the junior college.

VIII. Summarizing the Evaluation of the Types of Junior Colleges

The method of summary. A means of summarizing the foregoing evaluation of the several types of junior colleges is afforded in Fig. 45, which presents at the left, in somewhat abbreviated form, the special purposes accepted earlier in the chapter and at the head the types of institutions offering junior-college work. It will be noted that the latter includes the "large college or university." The significant feature of the figure is that it shows the relationship of each type of institution to the achievement of each of the special purposes. The degrees of relationship are indicated by cross-hatching, by single-hatching, and by leaving in outline the intersections of the special purposes with the columns under the types of institutions. Cross-hatching signifies a high degree of assurance of achieving a special purpose; single-hatching, a moderate but not high degree of assurance; space in outline, relatively little or no assurance. For example, we have a high degree of assurance that the first part of purpose 1—giving the first two years of liberal-arts curricula—can be performed in all the types of institutions represented. The degree indicated has been determined by the facts given in this report and by the evaluation attempted in this chapter. The writer feels that only occasionally if at all can exception be taken to the degrees of relationship shown. Disagreement could at most be on a few purposes only and for but a single step in the gradation of relationships.

A few comments of a miscellaneous character will be made before summarizing the results of the comparison afforded. It should be noted that for Fig. 45 the two aspects of purpose 1 are separately considered. Reference has already been made to the fact that purposes 1 and 2 are not to be looked upon as essentially

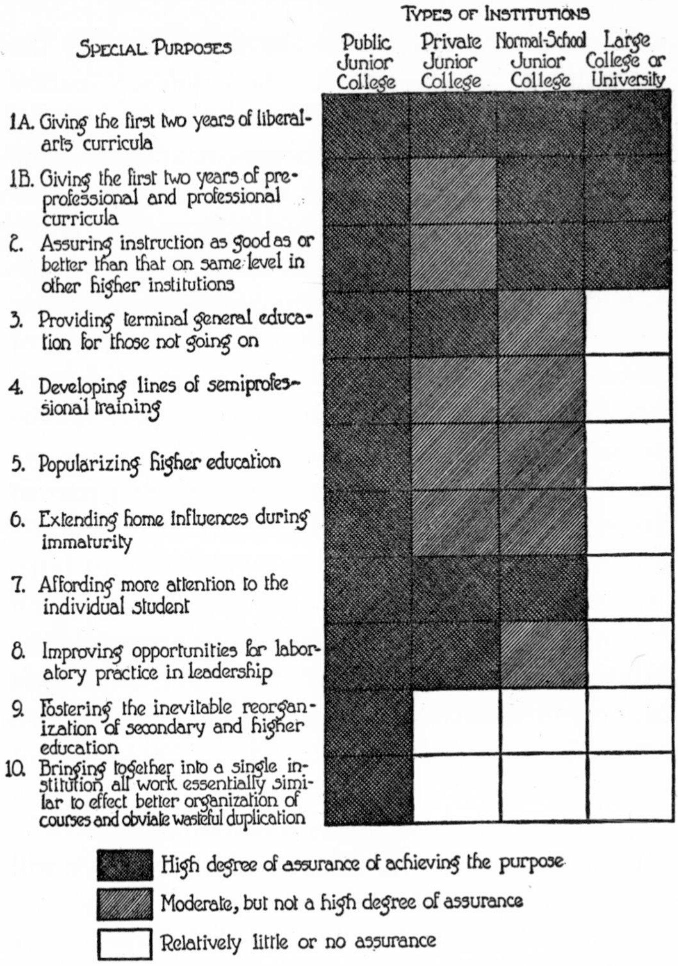

FIG. 45. Relationships of the types of institution giving junior-college work to the achievement of junior-college purposes

"special" or distinctive of the junior college, but that the likelihood of their effective performance is so vital to the pertinence of the remaining functions that it is desirable to retain them in the list. Although junior-college units on state foundations other than those maintained in connection with normal schools and teachers' colleges are not given separate consideration in the figure, the judgments rendered on the normal-school type are almost as applicable. The exceptions would tend to be for purposes 3, 4, and 5, for which the degree of relationship might justifiably be raised to the next higher step.

Results of the comparison. The continuity of cross-hatching in the columns of spaces for the public junior college in Fig. 45 indicates a high degree of assurance of its achievement of all the special purposes in the accepted list. The possibility of achieving all these purposes is not so complete for the private and the normal-school types, although one or the other of the two highest degrees of relationship is judged to apply in all but the last two special purposes. Emphasis has already been laid upon the desirability of assuring the achievement of these two purposes because of their profoundly significant bearing on the full meaning of the junior-college movement; reorganization would be inadequate indeed if it did not provide for their complete performance. The large proportion of un-shaded spaces in the column headed "Large college or university" calls attention again to the ineptitude of the typical present-day organization to the requirements of the situation. Only with reference to purposes 1 and 2, which have already been indicated as less distinctive of the junior college, do we find a high degree of assurance of achievement. It may be worth mentioning that if the type of unit here considered were the "small college" and not the large college or university the only additional purpose that would come in for recognition would be purpose 7—*affording more attention to the individual student.*

X

THE PROBLEMS OF LOCATION AND MAINTENANCE

I. THE SOURCE OF THE STUDENT-BODY

The problems. A conclusion with reference to the type of junior college to be fostered having been reached, the problem settles down to a question of where such units should be established. This in turn resolves itself into subproblems, two of which are of major concern: (1) the source of the student-body; (2) adequately financing the work. The second will be attacked in section II of this chapter; the first will be given consideration in this section. The particular question to be answered may be put as follows: How large must be the enrollment of a high school and the population of the community which it serves, in order that junior-college work may be established with assurance that the requisite student-body will be at hand to avail themselves of its opportunities?

The data utilized concern the numbers of graduates of high schools located for the most part in the north-central states who have enrolled in the first two years of higher institutions. It was believed best to secure the bulk of the data from a single section of the country, in order to make certain, as nearly as possible, that the conclusions should be adequate for the purposes to which they are put. The facts used were ascertained by means of an inquiry blank directed to the principals of high schools in communities representing a wide range of population—from small villages to cities in which there are no colleges and to those in which there are a small number of such higher institutions. The latter were included in order to determine the influence of the presence of higher institutions on the proportions of high-school graduates likely to attend them. The items of information asked for were the figures on enrollment during the academic years 1920–1921 or 1921–1922[1] by years (first or second years of higher institutions only), by sex, and by lines of work ("regular college work," pre-medical, pre-legal, the several engineering groups, architecture, dentistry, pharmacy, business, normal, education, agriculture, home economics, music, and other arts; blank spaces were provided for reporting the enrollment in other lines). Among other data requested was the enrollment of the high schools

[1] The study here reported is an extension of one published under the title "Where to Establish Junior Colleges" in the *School Review*, Vol. XXIX, pp. 414–433 (June, 1921). This study concerned enrollments for the school year 1920–1921 and pertained to high schools in the north-central states. For the purposes of this chapter the study was extended to include additional schools in this section as well as in other parts of the United States. All additional data are for the school year 1921–1922.

(Grades 9 to 12) for the year in which the report was made. Principals were asked to include in their report all their graduates "who are this year enrolled . . . irrespective of the year of graduation from the high school." For the purposes of the study a higher institution was defined as "one which requires for admission high-school graduation or its essential equivalent in earned units of credit." Approximately 250 of the blanks of inquiry were returned with data of some sort; 194 proved usable. Conclusions will be drawn almost exclusively from the 111 of these from high schools in the north-central states.

The distribution by lines of work. A total of 8885 graduates of all the 194 high schools represented in the study are enrolled in the first two years of work in higher institutions—an average of about 46 per high school. This large number is widely distributed as to the lines of work being followed. "Liberal arts" as here tabulated includes those in regular college work as well as pre-medical, pre-legal, and education (not normal-school) students. It is by far the largest group, including 5114, or almost three fifths of the total. For the problem in hand the significance of this predominance of students in liberal arts is in the direction of simplifying the task of providing in the junior college the work suited to the needs of those who are going on. The five other lines enrolling notably large numbers of students are, in order of predominance, normal, engineering, business or pre-business, agriculture, and home economics. The percentages of the totals in these lines are, respectively, 14.6, 9.5, 5.8, 2.8, and 2.4.

Enrollment in higher institutions as related to the size of high schools. The relationship between the numbers of graduates enrolled in the first two years of higher institutions and the high-school enrollment has been studied by computing the percentages of the former to the latter and then computing the average percentages after the high schools have been grouped by size. For this purpose high schools in communities in which there are no colleges or universities have been separated from those in which there are such institutions, to make possible a comparison of the percentages for these two groups. The percentages found demonstrate an interesting similarity for high schools of widely different enrollments, since they do not range beyond limits set by 10.6 and 12.8 per cent.

For the twenty high schools in communities with local higher institutions the average is 17.3, whereas the average for the group without a local higher institution is 11.8. This means that on the average the presence of a local higher institution adds more than two fifths and well up toward a half to the proportion of the high-school enrollment represented by graduates who attend a higher institution—a fact of large significance in establishing junior-college work.

TABLE VII. PERCENTAGES WHICH THE NUMBERS OF GRADUATES OF HIGH SCHOOLS ENROLLED IN THE FIRST TWO YEARS OF HIGHER INSTITUTIONS ARE OF THE ENROLLMENTS OF THESE HIGH SCHOOLS (NORTH-CENTRAL STATES)

PERCENTAGE ENROLLED IN FIRST TWO YEARS	NUMBERS OF HIGH SCHOOLS IN COMMUNITIES WITHOUT COLLEGES CLASSIFIED BY SIZE OF ENROLLMENT							COMMUNITIES WITH LOCAL HIGHER INSTITUTIONS
	51–150	151–250	251–350	351–450	451–550	551 and over	Total	
3.0–6.9	2	5	1	4	2		14	
7.0–10.9	3	8	7	5	2	5	30	3
11.0–14.9 . . .	1	4	8	7	5	4	29	6
15.0–18.9 . . .	1	1	3	1	1	1	8	2
19.0–22.9 . . .	1	2		1	1		5	3
23.0–26.9 . . .		2	1		1		4	5
27.0–30.9 . . .	1						1	1
Number of high schools . . .	9	22	20	18	12	10	91	20
Average of per- centages . .	12.8	11.7	12.2	10.6	12.7	11.4	11.8	17.3

Some corroboration of the validity of this finding is supplied by another approach to the estimate of the proportion of the high-school enrollment to be found in the first two years of higher institutions if junior-college work is established in connection with a high school. This is made possible by utilizing the percentages of students enrolled in each of the four years of large high schools on the accredited lists of the North Central Association as ascertained by Davis.[1] These percentages for the years from the first through

[1] C. O. Davis, Accredited Secondary Schools of the North Central Association. *United States Bureau of Education Bulletin No. 45* (1919), p. 34.

the fourth are, respectively, 39.98, 27.69, 18.64, and 13.67. This means that at the time of making the study 67.7 per cent were enrolled in the first two years and the remainder, 32.3 per cent, in the last two years. Assuming that the enrollment in an upward extension of two years in these high schools would bear the same relationship to the enrollment in the last two years as the latter does to the enrollment of the first two years, then from the proportionate relationship $67.7 : 32.3 : : 32.3 : x$ we obtain $x = 15.4$ per cent. This is seen to approximate the percentage found for high schools in communities with local higher institutions. There are grounds for assurance, therefore, that after the junior-college idea is fully accepted the proportion of the high-school enrollment represented by graduates enrolled in the local junior-college unit would not often be less than a sixth.

Enrollment in higher institutions as related to local population. A second relationship of significance is that of the numbers and proportions of the total populations of the cities represented by those of the high-school graduates who are enrolled in the work of the first two years in higher institutions. The figures are taken from the 1920 census. The average numbers in each thousand of the population thus enrolled show a marked tendency to equivalence, except for the groups of smallest and largest communities represented; that is, those with less than two thousand and those with more than fifteen thousand. For the four groups with population lying between these figures the averages range only from 4.6 to 6.3 per thousand of the population. For the smaller communities the average is somewhat higher. On the other hand there is a somewhat smaller average proportion in communities of fifteen thousand and over. This situation is in harmony with that found when proportions of the population enrolled in high schools have been computed, and therefore seems attributable to the same causes. One of these is the fact that nonresident enrollment in small high schools is larger proportionately than in large urban high schools.

Again, the distribution of the figures for communities in which there are higher institutions is toward the larger proportions; the average of the proportions is 10.9 in each thousand of the population. This is a difference of 5.3 per thousand, or an increase of about 95 per cent, owing to the presence of the local higher institutions.

The minimum junior-college unit. At other places in this volume data are presented which provide a basis for arriving at a minimum approvable junior-college student-body. One determinative relationship is that of cost per student as canvassed in subsequent sections of this chapter. Data there presented indicate that this cost is likely to run unreasonably high for units which do not enroll as many as from one hundred and fifty to two hundred students. Another important consideration is the restrictions that must be placed upon the curricular offering in units enrolling less than this number of students. The desirable minimal offerings have been given attention in Chapter III and are so extended as to discourage the establishment of units enrolling less than the larger number of students referred to. The discouragement is in part that of high costs and in part that of classes too small to provide the emulation necessary to effective scholarship. Again, it was shown in Chapter IV that without enrollments of good size it will be out of the question to provide in the junior colleges instructors with adequate specialization in certain essential fields. Another consideration in support of sizable units is the restrictions upon the socializing value of attendance if total enrollments are too small to provide a wide variety of student contacts. The tentative minimum accepted for consideration here is two hundred students. It is not assumed that experience may not in time lead to the approval of a smaller number, nor that inaccessibility of opportunities for higher education may not recommend occasional units that are marked exceptions, just as it sometimes justifies the establishment of very small high-school units. Present indications are, however, that enrollments should extend from two hundred students upward.

THE JUNIOR–COLLEGE MOVEMENT

The size of high-school enrollment and of population assuring feasibility. Assuming a minimum unit of two hundred students and a proportion enrolling in any local junior college equal to a sixth of the high-school registration, it becomes apparent that if all students were drawn from the graduates of any local high school the enrollment in the latter would need to be in the neighborhood of 1200 students. Bonner shows that in 1917–1918, of almost 14,000 high schools in the United States reporting, only 278 enrolled more than 1000 students.[1] Since we are, for the sake of illustration, giving particular attention to the north-central states, it should be stated that of this number slightly less than 100 (98, to be exact) were in this region— less than 100 in a total of 6618 reporting. Recent tendencies toward an increase in high-school attendance have without doubt brought this number well up above the century mark, but their relative infrequency in a territory as large as that represented, extending from Ohio to Nebraska and from Minnesota and North Dakota to Missouri and Oklahoma, makes it clear that if junior colleges were established only in connection with high schools having enrollments of 1000 or more this region would not be well served by them.

The proportion of the population enrolled in the first two college years is not as constant as is the ratio of those so enrolled to the high-school enrollment.

[1] *United States Bureau of Education Bulletin No. 19* (1920), pp. 19 ff.

Whatever may be the causes, there is an observable decline in the proportions by size of cities in proceeding from those of smaller population to those of larger population. On this account and because the study does not include data touching very large populations, it is impossible on the basis of populations to predict with as much certainty as in the foregoing instance whether a minimum student-body of two hundred will be at hand. There is, however, a sufficient basis of assurance in the materials to warrant the attempt. It has already been indicated that the proportion of the population attending is practically doubled by the presence of a local higher institution. Accepting the proportion in cities of 15,000 and over which are without higher institutions as 2.7 per 1000, this means that the proportion would rise to something like 5 or 6 per 1000 in cities of this size with local colleges. A population of 35,000 to 40,000 would therefore be required if the total enrollment of two hundred junior-college students were to be drawn from within the city of location only. Because of the inconstancy of the proportion as shown, the feasible minimum population might in some instances drop to 25,000 or 30,000, whereas in others it would rise above 40,000.

The census figures for 1920 show for the north-central states a total of ninety-eight cities with populations of twenty-five thousand and over. By checking over the list of cities it is found that approximately half of them are already provided with one or more higher institutions of one sort or another. Although this fact would not always remove the desirability of establishing junior-college work in such cities, it would, owing to the draft of the institution already in existence upon the potential junior-college student-body, tend to discount the feasibility of the junior-college work.

A study, not to be reported here in detail, designed to ascertain the average percentages of the populations of cities represented by those enrolled in high schools, affords support for the conclusion that cities with a population of 35,000 to 40,000 are likely to have high-school enrollments approximating 1100 or 1200. This indicates a likelihood that communities meeting the requirements of population as just set will be identical with those having high schools with the requisite enrollments, and vice versa.

It may be gratuitous to emphasize the fact that the rough prediction here made is based for the most part on central tendencies and that in many particular situations deviation from it is to be anticipated. The variation leads to the admission, for instance, that there will be some high schools with enrollments of 1100 or 1200 or communities with populations of 35,000 to 40,000 from which it will not be possible to recruit the desirable minimum of two hundred students for junior-college work. On the other hand, the same variation makes clear that there will be high schools with smaller enrollments and communities of smaller populations where this minimum may be secured.

Junior colleges in smaller high schools and communities. It is clear that insistence that the junior college of practicable size must draw its students exclusively or almost exclusively from the city where it is located would be certain, to a large extent, to place the movement beyond the pale of serious consideration. However, since most colleges and universities, whether on public or private foundations, draw large proportions of their students from without their communities of location, we have a precedent of long standing to justify us in planning a system of public junior colleges that will make up their minimum student-body of two hundred in considerable part from beyond the immediate environs. The writer has elsewhere[1] presented data showing the percentages of students who had enrolled in the first two years of certain Mid-Western colleges and who reported as their residences the communities in which the institutions are located. An examination of these percentages for the fourteen colleges located in cities with populations ranging from 10,139 to 71,227 shows them to lie between the limits

[1] "The Residential Distribution of College Students and its Meaning for the Junior-College Problem," in *School and Society*, Vol. XIII, pp. 557–562 (May 7, 1921).

of 5.1 and 57.7. The median percentage for this group is 37.7. This means that the median percentage of students from *outside* the city of location is 62.3, somewhat short of two thirds. There is no reason to believe that an efficient state system of junior colleges properly located would be unable to draw an equally large proportion from outside. But there are vital reasons why such a state system should aim at so placing these units that a majority at least of the students can live at home while they are in attendance. Among these reasons are the advantages of lowered cost, which has been shown to be a powerful factor in democratizing higher education (see Chapter V) and which should be kept in mind in planning a system of junior colleges. Another is the more youthful age at which students under such circumstances will enter upon the work of these school years (see Chapter VI).

If as large a proportion as an approximate half (or a bare majority) of the minimum desirable junior-college student-body could be drawn from other high schools and from beyond the limits of the local community, it would markedly lower the point of feasibility of establishing junior colleges. It would cut in half the necessary high-school enrollment of 1200, reducing it to something like 600. Average proportions lead us to expect that in cities with populations of 10,000 to 15,000 the number enrolled in junior-college years in each 1000 of the population would be approximately 9. This in turn means that a majority of the minimum desirable student-body would be likely to be at hand in cities of 12,000 population or thereabouts, although on account of the larger variation from community to community this measure has less of predictive value than the proportion of the high-school enrollment that will go on.

Lowering the point of feasibility by assuming only a majority of students from the local high school and the local community increases, of course, the numbers of communities in which introduction of junior-college work could be justified. Referring again to Bonner,[1] we find that if we include with the 98 high schools in the north-central states which have enrollments of more than 1000 those with enrollments ranging from 551 to 1000, this increases the total number to 214, more than double. Similarly, adding to the number of cities with populations of 25,000 and over in the same states those with populations between 10,000 and 25,000 brings the total up to 256, whereas the group of larger cities included only 98. Although only a careful study of the distribution of the high schools and cities represented could indicate how well the region would be served by junior colleges established in them, the total numbers are sufficiently large to warrant the belief that enough of such high schools

[1] H. R. Bonner, Statistics of Public High Schools, 1917–1918, *United States Bureau of Education Bulletin No. 19* (1920), pp. 11, 16.

and cities are available to assure adequate systems of junior-college units in most states.

It should be of interest to note in passing that two states—Michigan and California—have passed laws attempting to regulate the location of junior colleges in such a way as to have some bearing on the problem of the source of the student-body. In Michigan any school district having a population of more than thirty thousand may provide two years of collegiate work.[1] The California statute insists that high-school enrollments in districts maintaining junior colleges be not less than four hundred.[2] Whether the former restriction was placed with the intent to assure an adequate student-body or adequate support, or both, is not clear.

Junior colleges not now attracting and holding all local high-school graduates who go on. An assumption underlying the foregoing predictions is that all graduates of high schools who go on to higher levels of training would attend a local junior college during the first two years. It should be frankly admitted that such an assumption does not accord with the facts in the present state of development of junior colleges. The situation in this regard may be illustrated by stating that

[1] General School Laws, State of Michigan, Revision of 1921: Section 1 of Act 146, Public Acts, 1917. State Printers, Lansing, 1921.

[2] Statutes of California: General Laws, etc., Passed at the Regular Session of the 44th Legislature, 1921: Section 2 of Chapter 495, p. 756. State Printing Office, Sacramento, 1921.

for thirteen public junior colleges for which data were available the percentages of the high-school graduates going on who attend the local junior college ranged from 37.8 to 95.8—from three eighths to almost all. The lower percentages indicate that in some junior colleges the proportion falls far below the assumption referred to. At the other extreme, however, there are junior colleges which attract almost all who continue their education. The average percentage for all thirteen units was 70.6. It is manifest that if the prediction as made is to be realized, junior colleges must all come to hold at least as large a proportion as the highest reported.

The public junior colleges at the present time fall short of the assumption in one additional respect— the proportion of first-year students held into the second year. This fact became apparent in a comparison of the percentages of retention into the second year in public junior colleges and four-year colleges of the Middle West. The average proportions in junior colleges was as low as a half of the total or slightly less, women being retained somewhat better than men. In the four-year colleges the percentage of retention was nearer two thirds.

Both types of facts just presented—those showing that the new unit draws less than the total number of those who go on to higher levels of training and those indicating the relatively small proportion of students remaining for the second junior-college year—are evidence that the movement is not yet thoroughly established. It takes time and effort to win acceptance of a new institution or to place it on a foundation that will justify its holding all students who go on through two years of residence. Even if we set aside for the moment the question whether all necessary work is now going forward in these new units, it must be admitted that only after some years can the new unit become a part of the educational tradition of all the possible constituency. This is the experience, of course, of every novelty and must be especially characteristic where the older traditions of "college life" are prevalent in a community. It will be difficult for some people to associate even a part of what they regard as the period of collegiate training with the secondary unit below. These persons will be prone to look upon the movement disparagingly because it *is* an upward extension of the high school. In such a situation there will be among both parents and potential junior-college students those who either will not look with favor upon attendance to any extent or will countenance at most a single further year in such an institution. A second factor must be the meager curricular offerings in some of the junior-college units. With little in the way of option and a much more restricted range of courses available in the second year than in the first, the former factor of a lack of understanding or appreciation of the junior-college movement has something at least in its support.

These factors are, however, not permanently inherent in the situation. It has previously been indicated that some junior colleges have already been able to remove these obstacles almost entirely. There is no occasion to fear that, given sizable junior-college units on state foundations and with generous curricular offerings meeting the requirements of a wide variation in the student-body, these obstacles should not be entirely removed and predictions of the sort made at an earlier point in the chapter become completely realizable. To attract such numbers and proportions as have been predicted it will not be necessary to provide in the junior college all the lines of specialization previously mentioned, for students will gravitate toward the curricular materials available. At the same time such an offering could not be restricted to the first two years of work in colleges of liberal arts. Some opportunities of differentiation must be provided, such as engineering, business, home economics, etc. There is, again, no occasion to doubt that under such circumstances these junior-college units would attract practically all students ready for work on this level, just as the public high school in most of our communities has come to draw to it all or almost all students who enroll in work on the traditional secondary-school level.

[391]

The point of feasibility likely to lower. It is much more likely that a lowering of the point of feasibility as measured by the size of the high-school enrollment and of the population will take place than that anything more than temporary obstacles to the realization of the predictions will arise. As all those conversant with the situation in secondary and higher education are aware, high-school and college attendance has been gaining rapidly on the population during several decades. If junior colleges become at all common in our school system, even more rapidly increasing numbers and proportions will avail themselves of the opportunities afforded. This will be due to the rising tide of popular education itself, to sheer availability, as already indicated, to the public character of the institution, and to the tendency that must come to merge the high school and the junior college. The increase in attendance will be accompanied by an enrichment of curricula in these years, and this in turn will accelerate the increase.

II. THE FINANCIAL PROBLEM

Why and how studied. As admitted at the opening of the chapter, the establishment of a system of junior colleges is not merely a problem of securing a sizable student-body but is also one of adequately financing the work. To some this requirement may seem the more important of the two, and there are excellent grounds for such a conviction.

Although there can be no endeavor here to make a complete canvass of all financial aspects of junior-college establishment and maintenance, the volume could not be regarded as complete without giving some attention to the fiscal aspects of providing the work. This section will therefore present materials bearing on the teaching-cost in junior colleges, the total cost per student, the burden that would need to be carried by a local community providing the work if the cost is borne entirely by such community, the relationship of this burden to that already being carried by communities of different populations to support education on lower levels, and inferences from these financial data toward an appropriate procedure in fostering the movement.

The problem of cost to the student or the person bearing the burden of expense for his attendance will not be considered here, as it has been scrutinized in Chapter V.

Teaching-cost. It was possible to secure from as many as fifteen public junior colleges visited enough data to compute the annual cost of teaching per student enrolled. Although the figures on average cost are not to be regarded as fully accurate, they are sufficiently so to warrant the confidence that they are at least approximate. The method of computing average cost was simple. It consisted merely in obtaining the total cost of junior-college teaching and dividing it by the number of students enrolled.[1]

The average cost of instruction ranges as widely as from $83.26 to $223.54, the highest being almost 2.7 times as great as the lowest. A tendency for lowered costs with increased enrollments is shown in the following arrangement of average costs:

LARGE (MORE THAN 200 STUDENTS)

Junior college H	$117.48

MEDIUM (100–200 STUDENTS)

Junior college A	$83.26
Junior college C	106.61
Junior college E	*108.31*
Junior college F	114.30
Junior college M	207.15

SMALL (LESS THAN 100 STUDENTS)

Junior college B	$103.47
Junior college D	107.81
Junior college G	116.19
Junior college I	146.93
Junior college J	*168.75*
Junior college K	169.63
Junior college L	170.33
Junior college N	216.89
Junior college O	223.54

[1] The standard practice in such computations is to divide by the number of students in average daily attendance. If this method had been followed here, the number of junior colleges represented would have been reduced because of the difficulty in securing data on average daily attendance in some units.

In this arrangement the numbers in each of the three groups are seen to be one, five, and nine respectively. In the groups of medium and small junior colleges the arrangement is again from least to greatest average cost, the middle case being indicated in italics. The median cost in the group of smallest units is more than 1.5 times the median cost in the group of units of medium size.

The wide variations within each group may be ascribed primarily to the influence of the salary paid to junior-college teachers. This may be illustrated for junior colleges A and N, which had enrollments respectively of ninety and one hundred and twelve; that is, approximately equal. The difference in average teaching-costs in these two units is that between $83.26 and $216.89; and it is a difference determined for the most part by a large difference in salaries paid, although it is also to some extent attributable to the more extended offering and consequently smaller classes in junior college N. The same factors account for the difference between average teaching-costs in junior colleges E and M, which have almost equivalent enrollments.

After making a number of experimental computations of average annual costs and of average costs per student-hour, assuming enrollments of varying sizes and salary schedules just as high as, or somewhat higher than, those paid for the same work in four-year colleges, to make it possible to compete for teachers with such institutions, the writer has concluded that satisfactory instruction can be provided at from $115 to $135 per student enrolled per year and that a tentative middle figure, variable to a considerable extent above and below, is $125. To make such a figure possible, however, it is necessary to keep the minimum enrollment at something like one hundred and fifty to two hundred students. As the enrollment drops below this minimum the average annual cost of teaching must rise, so that a comparison of costs with those for the same work in other standard higher institutions is less favorable to the new unit. By keeping the offering meager, large classes would be encouraged and the average cost be kept low, but such a practice would itself militate against the maximum enrollment. The assumption in the matter of breadth of work offered is a practice no less generous than that suggested in Chapter III.

The writer admitted in the first section of this chapter that certain special considerations, such as the relative inaccessibility of opportunities for education on this level, will sometimes justify providing junior-college work to smaller numbers than the typical minimum suggested, much as we sometimes defend a similar provision of opportunities of education on the high-school level for smaller numbers in remote territory. Such provisions should be made, however, with a full understanding of what they mean in additional cost per student. In the long run we cannot defend an average annual teaching-cost very much greater than that for which the same education can be given in the larger educational units now in existence, although in view of the lowered cost to the student who can attend near home some increase in annual cost will at times be defensible.

To ascertain teaching-costs is a simple matter when compared with obtaining other costs of providing education on the junior-college level. In few if any systems in which junior-college work is maintained are there anything like satisfactory methods of school accounting which attempt to separate the junior-college costs along nonteaching lines from those for other parts of the system. Even where this separation is attempted the practices vary enough to prevent comparison from unit to unit.

Although this situation is discouraging as concerns the complete analysis of the financial problems of instituting and maintaining the work, access was had to sufficient pertinent data to justify a fairly dependable estimate of nonteaching costs per student in units of the size approved in the foregoing section as a desirable minimum. The method of presentation to be used will be that of illustrating the computation for a single junior college (F), one of the units in southern California with an enrollment approximately a fourth smaller than that approved as a desirable minimum. It is a part of the school system in a city with a population and high-school enrollment not far from adequate when measured by standards applied in foregoing portions of the chapter. Although the results of the computations are not to be regarded as accurate, they are sufficiently so to warrant their use in connection with the problem here under consideration.

All items of cost are as follows:

1. Teaching	. . . .	$125.00
2. Other instructional	. . . .	21.09
3. General control	. . . .	1.49
4. Operation of plant	. . . .	10.92
5. Maintenance	. . . .	1.73
6. Fixed charges	. . . .	1.19
7. Auxiliary agencies	. . . .	1.62
8. Plant replacement	. . . .	24.61
Total	. . . .	$187.65

The estimate for teaching-cost, it will be noted, is not that for junior college F as reported but that tentatively arrived at as necessary in public junior colleges.

The items other than teaching will require some explanation. *Other instructional* covers expenditures for special salary additions for the services of the dean, apportionment of the salary of a registrar serving both high school and junior college, printing, apportionment of expenditures for the library used in common by high-school and junior-college students, and similar apportionment of general and consumable instructional supplies. *General control* is synonymous with overhead expenses—the superintendent's salary and the expenses of his office, maintenance of offices of the Board of Education, etc. The amount charged to the junior college was determined by the proportion of its enrollment to the total in all public schools of the district. *Operation of plant* covers fuel, light and power, water, janitors, janitors' supplies, and telephones; *maintenance*, the repairs on buildings and grounds; *fixed charges*, insurance; *auxiliary agencies*, medical inspection etc.

One of the most important costs, and at the same time one of the most perplexing items to compute, is that for the provision of the plant in which the junior-college work is to be carried on, especially when it is required to put this expense in terms of the cost per year. The steps in the present attempt to arrive at an approximate figure are as follows: (1) ascertaining the total value of the housing and equipment in common use by the high school and junior college, (2) computing the portion of this capital outlay which may properly be assumed to be assigned to the use of the junior college, and (3) computing the annual cost per student per year to cover this portion of the capital outlay and the quota of the interest charge during the period over which the payments on capital extend.

From figures concerning the amount and the proportion of insurance protection and supplementary estimates of value it is safe to put the value of the housing and equipment under consideration at $450,000. This is exclusive of the value of the site, which would hardly differ in size if no junior college were being maintained. On the basis of the proportion of space used, as followed in the instances of certain other items of cost, 13.97 per cent, or $62,865, of this outlay is for the junior college. A prevalent practice in payment will be assumed; that is, that bonds are issued for this sum and that equal parts of the indebtedness will be discharged each year for thirty years—the probable period of usefulness of the building. Since the rate of interest on most bonds issued by this district is 5 per cent, the interest at this rate on all unpaid balances must be included as a part of the total outlay for the plant for the junior-college unit. This interest is the equivalent of 5 per cent per year for fifteen years, or 75 per cent of $62,865, so that a total interest charge of $47,148.75 must be paid by the district. This in turn will require during the thirty-year period a total expenditure of $110,013.75 for the plant, which is equivalent to $3667.12 per year, or $24.61 per student per year. Should such a community see fit to pay the full cost of such a building by one large tax levy at the time of construction, the virtual cost of housing and equipping the junior college would be as just computed, because, although not actually paying an interest charge, the taxpayers are deprived of the use of the amount they have invested, this amount decreasing of course as the plant depreciates. Although it may be argued that the estimated cost per student per year is probably high because the life of well-constructed buildings is likely to run beyond the limit of thirty years, it is easily conceivable that costs of construction in certain sections of the country where heavier walls must be built will tend to keep the average somewhere in the vicinity of this figure.

It is to be noted that the total for all items is $187.65. From what has been said of the conservative character of the estimates on certain items it does not appear to be especially hazardous to assume that in cities of the size represented a reasonable approximate average cost over all per student is $185, with a division of something like $125 for teaching-items and the remaining $60 for nonteaching-items. It is easy to conceive of situations in which this average cost will and should rise to $200 or beyond, with $135 for teaching-items and $65 for nonteaching-items. A safe range of cost where conditions are satisfactory is probably somewhere between $175 and a little more than $200.

To those who have been in actual contact with the movement to establish junior colleges in particular communities it will long before this have occurred that most persons who have urged this expansion have not referred to the items of cost other than 1 and 2 in the foregoing list, except perhaps to point out that in the initial stages the district would by such establishment be put to no additional outlay for items like 3, 4, 5, 6, 7, and 8. And, let it be said on behalf of these advocates of the junior college, there is seldom if ever real misrepresentation of the situation at the time financial feasibility is discussed in this way. Usually a small unit only is contemplated at first, one which can be accommodated with small additions to the teaching staff, with only minor increases in instructional facilities, and without significant additions to overhead costs or an enlargement of space provisions that would involve further cost in operation, maintenance, etc. It has been fortunate during earlier experimental stages of the movement that beginnings under these relatively inexpensive conditions have been possible.

But this facility of initiating the movement should not prevent our being alert to all the aspects of financial responsibility involved when a unit is well established and of a size not far from that proposed as a desirable minimum. In most situations, long before' a junior-college student-body of this size can be assembled the high-school student-body with which it is associated will have outgrown all the space used by the junior college. The provision of additional space will therefore be necessary, and this in turn is certain to increase the cost of operation, maintenance, fixed charges, auxiliary agencies, and plant replacement. Such increases must in time affect also the cost of general control. Certainly if a state system of junior colleges is contemplated, the neglect of noninstructional factors of cost will eventually militate against the efficiency of the plan or, at least, against the willingness of communities to bear the junior-college burden.

Curricular distribution of students. The estimate of junior-college costs per student was worked out without special reference to students pursuing or intending to pursue professional or preprofessional curricula during these two collegiate years. A considerable number of students in several of the junior colleges represented were registered for work pertaining to such curricula, but it was not possible to consider specifically the extent to which providing the courses they need affects the average cost per student. It is correct to assume, however, that the proportion is smaller than that which would be found in any random sampling of students enrolled in the first two years of work in all types of higher institutions.

A study of the proportionate distribution to the several lines of work of 63,724 students enrolled during 1919–1920 in a dozen Western and Mid-Western universities warrants the expectation that from two thirds to seven tenths must during their first two years pursue curricula falling within the liberal-arts field.

[403]

To arrive at this proportion, there have been added to the percentage in liberal arts proper those in graduate departments and schools of law, medicine, dentistry, education, divinity, journalism, and library training, all of which will soon, if in essence they do not already, prescribe work in liberal-arts lines during at least the first two years in college. This proportion is almost identical with that found for the liberal-arts group in the distribution of students referred to earlier in this chapter. A total of 8885 graduates of one hundred and ninety-four high schools who were going on to higher institutions were there concerned, of whom 1297 were enrolled in normal schools. Of the 7588 remaining, slightly more than two thirds were enrolled in liberal-arts groups, including pre-medical, pre-legal, and education. The findings seem to warrant the belief that under normal conditions, and with a satisfactory offering available, not far from two thirds to seven tenths of a junior-college student-body can be expected to enroll in liberal-arts courses or lines closely related; the remainder—a third or less—will register in other special curricula provided. This means that for the desirable minimum of two hundred students proposed, somewhat less than one hundred and fifty will be enrolled in liberal-arts or general curricula, the remainder in specialized curricula.

Guidance in the precedence to be given in providing these specialized curricula is afforded to some extent by the proportionate registration in such curricula. First would come the engineering group, enrolling approximately a seventh of the total of 63,724 students; next in order would come (to mention only the courses more frequently elected) commerce, with a tenth of the student-body, agriculture with a sixteenth, and home economics.

The most important conclusion from these distributions is that since the estimated cost per student is based on a student-body rather largely in the liberal-arts group as here classified, it is to be regarded as pertinent for the overwhelming majority of the probable junior-college enrollment. A second conclusion, in the nature of a corollary, is that the proportion of other than liberal-arts students is relatively small and cannot therefore bring the average cost far above the estimate ventured. This group will rise to larger proportions as the junior college comes to provide training in the semiprofessions. Additional mitigating circumstances are (1) that expenditures for some of this work have entered into the estimate made, (2) that in such lines as commerce and home economics, if classes are kept at good size, the average costs are not likely to be much higher if higher at all, (3) that a great deal of the work taken by students in some of the special curricula represented is of the liberal-arts (or nonspecial) type, and (4) that the lower or junior-college levels of work in most of these specialized curricula (engineering for example) are less expensive than are the upper or senior-college levels.

It must be apparent that in order to keep the cost per student near a reasonable figure it will not be practicable to attempt to provide in all junior-college units the first two years of all preprofessional and professional curricula beginning with the first college year. As with the high schools, it will be found necessary to restrict the smaller junior colleges to fewer of these specialized curricula than can be economically maintained in the larger junior colleges. It will be possible to defend the introduction into a single larger unit of all or nearly all types of curricula to be found in the first two years of our present university organization. Certainly the introduction of all necessary types will be feasible and also essential in any complete state system of junior colleges.

The discussion of this subject should not be dropped without reference again to the simplification of curricular problems that is almost certain to follow the general adoption of the junior-college plan which involves the upward extension of the secondary school. The popularization of these school years that will in this way be achieved will encourage the setting up of preprofessional curricula ending with the sophomore college year in some professional lines: such an innovation has sometimes been desired (for example, in engineering), but has not seemed practicable.

LOCATION AND MAINTENANCE

The financial problem of establishing junior colleges in two states. Having procured an estimated annual cost per student enrolled, the logical next steps are in the direction of considering the financial responsibilities involved in establishing junior colleges in communities of different sizes in two Mid-Western states which have already made notable beginnings in the movement; namely, Michigan and Minnesota. Throughout this aspect of the study the desirable minimum of two hundred students has been assumed.

The study included cities of a wide range of size, the aim being to scrutinize this aspect of the financial problem as fully as necessary so that some indication of the most suitable size of city might have the opportunity to emerge in the process of inquiry. Some cities already provided with higher institutions were included, although the problem of junior-college establishment is not likely soon to arise in them. In Michigan all cities with populations of seven thousand and over have been included; in Minnesota, because of its lesser number of municipalities of good size, those included reach down to five thousand. The numbers of cities represented were thirty-seven and twenty-six respectively. All predictions of numbers of junior-college students in the local population likely to avail themselves of the opportunities were computed from high-school enrollments in these cities, since this method of estimate has been found more dependable than is the proportion of the total populations likely to go on to this level of training.

The types of estimate made of the cost burden of maintaining junior colleges in these cities will be illustrated for city A, which is credited by the Census of 1920 with a population of 7419 and which has the lowest local school-tax levy in a group of twelve Michigan cities with populations ranging between 7000 and 10,000. This local school-tax rate for 1920 has been computed at 4.22 mills. To ask this district to foot the entire bill for maintaining a junior college with the minimum desirable student-body of two hundred would entail an increase of this local rate to 6.17 mills, a percentage increase for junior-college purposes of 46.2, or almost half. If it is assumed that the district would pay the full cost for students from the local community only and that reimbursement for nonresident students would come from other sources such as state aid, the levy would be increased to 4.69 mills only, or by 11.1 per cent. If in addition to assuming the burden for all nonresident students the state would distribute aid for local students in the same proportion as districts are now being aided in maintaining the lower schools, the rate would need to be raised to 4.59 mills, or by 8.8 per cent.

Tendencies are best represented not by this individual case but by the medians for cities of different size in the two states. Examination and comparison of these measures divulge several important findings, among them the following: (1) the smaller the city the larger the local tax rate for the maintenance of lower schools; (2) the smaller the city the larger the total and proportional increment for maintaining junior-college units with the minimum desirable student-body. The median increment in the smaller cities of Michigan is almost exactly a half, and for those in Minnesota it is well over a fourth. Although no absolute criterion of what is practicable in this connection is at hand, it is too obvious for argument that increments of such magnitudes are not to be thought of. (3) When it is assumed that the local district will bear the cost for resident students only, being fully reimbursed for the nonresidents necessary to make up the total of two hundred students, the median increment is much more for the smaller than for the larger cities, this larger subtraction being directly attributable to the small total number and the relatively small proportion of junior-college students for which the local district would be assuming financial responsibility. (4) The chief conclusion to be drawn from the data showing the effect of having the state bear the same proportion of the burden for local students that it now bears of the cost of maintaining the lower schools in the same districts is that only a small proportion of the additional burden will be lifted from the local community, a proportion so small as to be relatively inconsiderable. In the three groups into which cities of 100,000 and less in Michigan have been divided this median amount would turn out to be $31.27, $29.78, and $24.79, and in the two groups in

TABLE VIII. Effect of Junior-College Establishment on the Local Tax Rate for Schools in the Cities of Michigan and Minnesota

STATE AND GROUP OF CITIES	Median Local School-Tax Levy in Mills[1]	DISTRICT ADDING TOTAL COST FOR 200 STUDENTS		DISTRICT ADDING COST FOR LOCAL STUDENTS ONLY		DISTRICT AIDED FOR LOCAL STUDENTS AT PRESENT RATE	
		Median Total Mill Levy	Median Per Cent Increase	Median Total Mill Levy	Median Per Cent Increase	Median Total Mill Levy	Median Per Cent Increase
Michigan							
7000 to 10,000	10.73	17.31	50.1	11.95	12.7	11.74	10.7
10,000 to 20,000	9.54	11.82	30.5	10.62	12.4	10.45	9.9
30,000 to 100,000	8.78	9.58	8.3	9.58	7.7	9.46	6.6
Minnesota							
5000 to 10,000	37.52	50.23	28.2	42.68	8.4	41.96	7.5
10,000 to 20,000	31.52	36.37	14.4	34.34	8.4	34.12	7.4

Minnesota with less than 20,000 it would be $20.72 and $16.83—small parts of an average annual total cost of from $185 to $200 per student. Similar computations for the five cities in these two states with populations in excess of 100,000 bring conclusions similar to those already drawn.

[1] The rates in Minnesota are levied on a percentage only (for the most part 40 per cent) of the total valuation, whereas in Michigan assessed valuations are understood to correspond with total valuations.

Besides constituting an argument for generous state subsidy rather than almost exclusively local support

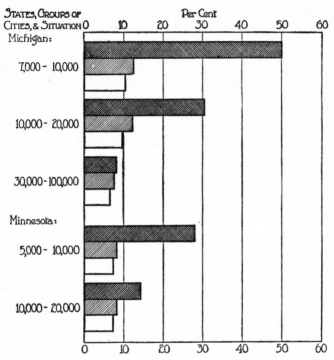

FIG. 46. Percentages by which maintaining a junior college would increase the local tax rate for schools. (Cross-hatching, if district adds total cost for two hundred students; single-hatching, if district adds cost for local students only; in outline, if district is aided by state at present rate for lower schools)

of junior colleges, these findings point to the location of the junior colleges in cities of good size.

[411]

The argument for a more generous policy. Perhaps the most telling consideration in support of a much more generous policy toward junior colleges than seems to be the present policy toward the lower schools in these two states arises from a comparison of these proportions and amounts with what the state contributes to the education of a student taking work on the junior-college level in a state university. The latter amount would not have been obtainable directly for the two states represented without including in the investigation a special study of costs on this level in the universities of Michigan and Minnesota, and this was not practicable. It is possible, however, on the basis of certain figures available for the University of Minnesota, to make an estimate that may be accepted as at least an approximation. The average cost over all per student per year in the College of Science, Literature, and the Arts has been computed for 1920–1921 at $219.15.[1] This figure was obtained, of course, by including the registration of all students, both in the junior college and in the senior college. It must therefore be somewhat higher than that for junior-college students only. The cost per junior-college student could hardly be more than $200 and is probably somewhat less. From this should be subtracted

[1] Report of Survey Commission V, Table XVI. *Bulletin of the University of Minnesota*, Vol. XXV, No. 7 (April 20, 1922), p. 57. The materials for this number were prepared by Dr. J. B. Sears of Stanford University.

the tuition fee of students who are residents of the state, amounting in this college to $60 for the three quarters of a school year. This leaves an amount not far from $130 to $140 per year that is being contributed directly or indirectly by the state to the education of each student in the first two years of this college. As the cost in the freshman and sophomore years in other colleges of the university is in all probability somewhat higher, the difference not being offset by an equivalently higher tuition charge, it is almost certain that this estimate of the average contribution of the state to the education of the individual student in attendance upon work in the first two college years at the university is a conservative one. In such a situation it can hardly be regarded as logical for the state to undertake to subsidize any less generously those communities which provide junior-college education, as it would do if such aid were to be in the same proportion as for the lower schools that are now subsidized. It is worth noting that education on higher than junior-college levels in state universities, on account of its higher cost per student, is being subsidized in even larger proportions. Again, it may be judged from the conclusions in the treatment of economic democratization (see Chapter V) that the subsidy is being distributed to those who are on the average somewhat better prepared to carry a larger proportion of the full burden of cost than students who would avail themselves of the education if it were brought nearer their places of residence through the establishment of junior colleges.

A second consideration arises out of the certainty that in many of the cities where the provision of junior-college work can be justified as far as the number of students from local sources is concerned, any attempt to foot all or most of the junior-college bill locally will endanger the interests of education on the lower levels. No plan of establishing junior colleges can be defended if it involves a large element of hazard to efficiency of levels of school work which may be regarded as having prior claims to adequate support.

A state policy of generous subsidies for junior colleges is supported, moreover, by any admission that the movement is in accord with the inevitable forces of reorganization in secondary and higher education. Chapters VII and VIII have presented some of the results of the operation of these forces, and, among other things, have disclosed the important fact that for most students enrolled the two junior-college years may be rightly looked upon as the concluding years of the period of general or of secondary education. Universal practice in this country indicates that we have committed ourselves to a policy of providing the school patron with secondary education free of cost. It would therefore be difficult to show why, anticipating the evolution of the secondary school to include the junior-college years, any policy should be followed which is likely to oblige the communities maintaining the work to levy a tuition charge against those in attendance. Without generous subvention by the state, it would be difficult to avoid this charge, as is evident from any facts that illustrate the widely differing resources where junior colleges are otherwise feasible and from the imperativeness of safeguarding the interests of education on lower levels.

What one state is doing. In California (a state in which the public junior college has made more progress than in any other) state support has within the last few years arrived at a much more desirable stage than that which would characterize a policy of assistance in proportion to current conditions of state aid for lower schools in Michigan or Minnesota. To each junior college maintained in districts organized in accordance with a law passed in 1921 there is paid an allotment of $2000 per annum and an attendance grant of $100 per student in average daily attendance, one condition being that "no junior-college district shall receive any state allotment unless it has provided during the preceding school year an amount for maintenance at least equal to the amount apportioned by the state."[1] Assuming a student-body of one hundred

[1] F. H. Swift, Studies in Public School Finance—California and Colorado. Research Publications of the University of Minnesota, Education Series, No. 1, p. 115.

from local sources, the allotment is equal to $20 per student per year. This, together with the attendance grant of $100 per student, is not far from the estimated amount the state of Minnesota is, without reimbursement, paying for the education of the average student in junior-college years of the College of Science, Literature, and the Arts at its state university. It is, however, in excess of the amount of aid being paid to those districts of California which still maintain junior colleges under the law that authorized their establishment prior to 1921, and there are several of these districts.

Differentiating aid for residents and for nonresidents. The data of the first main division of this chapter make it evident that in order to recruit the minimum desirable unit many communities will need to draw considerable proportions of their junior-college student-bodies from beyond the borders of the district. Materials in the financial portions emphasize the often impossible increase in the local tax rate that must be imposed for schools if these communities endeavor to carry the burden of providing education on this level for both resident students and a large number and proportion of nonresident students. If we grant the desirability of having a state policy of junior-college encouragement that opens up opportunities of education on this level in much the same manner in which it has been achieved in many states on the conventional high-school level, we have the need of taking away from the community in which the junior-college is maintained all or nearly all the burden of cost for nonresidents. The fact that a junior-college establishment, on account of its demands in the way of population and high-school enrollment, can properly be accomplished in a relatively smaller number of communities than those in which high-school work can and should be given, makes the need more imperative. The district in which the junior college is maintained must be fully willing to accept all nonresident students.

California has taken steps in this direction, as may be seen in the following digest of the statutory provision:[1]

The act providing for the organization of junior-college districts and for the maintenance of junior colleges therein, approved May 27, 1921, endeavors to make junior colleges accessible to students residing in counties wherein no such college is located. The provisions in the present case are similar to those relating to high schools. In each county wherein there is not a junior college, the county superintendent is required to certify annually to the Board of County Supervisors and to the county auditor the total net cost, less state aid, for educating, during the next preceding year, all junior-college pupils residing in such county

[1] F. H. Swift, Studies in Public School Finance—California and Colorado. Research Publications of the University of Minnesota, Education Series, No. 1, pp. 71–73.

but not in any junior-college district, and the estimated amount needed for that purpose for the current year.

A special tax upon all taxable property within the county not situated in any junior-college district must be levied by the County Board of Supervisors. This tax must be sufficient to defray the net cost of educating [less state aid], for the current year, students attending a junior college in an adjoining county.

If the Board of Supervisors fails to make a levy, the county auditor must make the same.

What makes these provisions fall short of the full needs of the situation is that they do not apply to all types of junior-college districts and that they apply only to students in counties outside the one in which the junior college is maintained. Some may object that this net cost is borne by a local political unit— the county—rather than by the state; but it must be remembered that the state is already contributing $100 per student plus the annual allotment of $2000, and that it is only the net cost less state aid that is being paid by the county. Nevertheless, there will be those who would be disposed to prefer state subvention up to the full amount or almost the full amount of the cost for nonresidents.

Final comments on where to establish junior colleges. Before a state system of junior colleges is instituted it will be essential to keep constantly in mind, besides the factors so far recognized, the important question of such a geographical distribution of the units as will serve best the whole state. They should not be placed so near together as to tend to reduce too far below the desirable minimum the number of students in any unit. On the other hand, to serve the entire state it might be found necessary to encourage the introduction of the work in a small proportion of districts where the cost per student to the state might turn out relatively high because of the small number enrolled. The work of establishing them should be done very guardedly so as to serve the youth of the state as economically as possible. A condition complicating an adequate solution is to be found in those communities in which higher institutions, some public and others private, are already in existence. Their presence cannot be ignored. In several states this fact will remove from the feasible list a number of communities that would otherwise be desirable localities for establishing junior colleges.

Doubtless the most significant admonition to be made where state encouragement or establishment is contemplated is to urge scientific rather than "political" location. Experience has often shown that location by log-rolling results too much in mislocation, as is demonstrable in certain instances where normal schools or other higher institutions have been established without regard to sources of student-body etc. Scientific location of junior-college units requires that among the facts to be assembled and used are the numbers of students who shall be served, their distribution as residents or nonresidents of the locality, transportation facilities, the financial situation in each district under consideration, the degree of efficiency of the lower schools, and the support of the lower schools. Unless there is a thoroughgoing study of the state in these and allied respects before a program of junior-college establishment is ventured upon, a few years of experience might result in more to regret than to commend.

APPENDIX

SELECTED BIBLIOGRAPHY

NOTE. The following list contains only references bearing directly on the junior-college problem. Space could not be spared for many items having important meaning indirectly for the movement, and for the titles, dates of appearance, etc. of the thousands of catalogues and other documents to which access was had in assembling the materials of the volume.

ALEXANDER, C. C., and WILLETT, G. W. "Some Aspects of the Junior College," in *School Review*, Vol. XXVIII, pp. 15–25 (January, 1920).

ANGELL, JAMES R. "The Junior-College Movement in High Schools," in *School Review*, Vol. XXIII, pp. 289–302 (May, 1915). Also in Proceedings of the North Central Association of Colleges and Secondary Schools, 1915, pp. 80–94.

ANGELL, JAMES R. "Problems Peculiar to the Junior College," in *School Review*, Vol. XXV, pp. 385–397 (June, 1917).

BABCOCK, K. C. "Standard Colleges and Junior Colleges," in Report of the United States Commissioner of Education, 1912, Vol. I, pp. 97–102.

BARROWS, DAVID P. "State Provision for Junior Colleges," in Transactions and Proceedings of the National Association of State Universities, Vol. XX, pp. 56–77 (1922).

BLAUCH, L. E. "Reorganization on European Lines appears Imminent," in *School Life*, Vol. IX, pp. 77–79 (December, 1923).

BLISS, F. L. (chairman). "Report of the Committee on the Revision of the Definition of the Unit," in Proceedings of the North Central Association of Colleges and Secondary Schools, 1915, pp. 27–30.

BOLTON, FREDERICK E. "Some Probable Effects upon Higher Education Due to the Development of Junior Colleges," in *Educational Administration and Supervision*, Vol. V, pp. 85–93 (February, 1918).

THE JUNIOR-COLLEGE MOVEMENT

BOLTON, FREDERICK E. "What should constitute the Curriculum of the Junior College or Extended High School?" in *School and Society*, Vol. VIII, pp. 726–730 (December 21, 1918).

BROWN, J. S. "Present Development of Secondary Schools according to the Proposed Plan," in *School Review*, Vol. XIII, pp. 15–18 (January, 1905).

BRUSH, H. R. "The Junior College and the Universities," in *School and Society*, Vol. IV, pp. 357–365 (September 2, 1916).

California State Board of Education, in its Report of the Commissioner of Secondary Schools, 1916, pp. 19–26.

California State Board of Education, in its Report of the Commissioner of Secondary Schools, June 30, 1914, pp. 20–23. State Printing Office, 1914.

CAMMACK, I. I. "The Legitimate Range of Activity of the Junior College in the Public School System," in N.E.A. Proceedings, 1917, pp. 724–729.

CLAXTON, P. P. "Better Organization in Higher Education," in Report of the United States Commissioner of Education, 1913, Vol. I, chaps. xxxix–xlii.

CLAXTON, P. P. "The Junior College," in Proceedings of the Association of American Colleges, Vol. II (1916), No. 3, pp. 104–112.

CLEMENT, J. A. Curriculum Making in Secondary Schools, chap. xi, pp. 222–239. Henry Holt and Company, New York, 1923.

COLTON, ELIZABETH A. "Standards of Southern Colleges for Women," in *School Review*, Vol. XX, pp. 458–475 (September, 1912).

CORSON, D. B. "Claims of the New Type Junior College," in *Education*, Vol. XL, pp. 327–339 (February, 1920).

COURSAULT, J. H. (editor). "Circular of Information to Accredited Junior Colleges issued by the Committee on Accredited Schools and Colleges," in *University of Missouri Bulletin*, Vol. XIX, No. 4, Education Series 12. Columbia, Missouri, February, 1918. 182 pp.

COURSAULT, J. H. "Standardizing the Junior College: an Experiment by the University of Missouri," in *Educational Review*, Vol. XLIX, pp. 56–62 (January, 1915).

APPENDIX

CUBBERLEY, E. P. "The Junior College," in Monroe's Cyclopedia of Education, p. 573. The Macmillan Company, New York, 1912.

DUNIWAY, C. A. "The Separation and Development of the Junior College as Distinct from the University," in N.E.A. Proceedings, 1911, pp. 660–664.

ELLIFF, J. D. "College Credit for High School and Junior-College Work—the Missouri Plan," in *High School Quarterly*, Vol. IV, No. 2 (January, 1916).

ELLIFF, J. D. "The Junior College, the Missouri Plan," in Proceedings of the Association of Colleges and Secondary Schools of Southern States, 1915, pp. 52–54.

FELMLEY, DAVID. "The New Normal School Movement," in *Educational Review*, Vol. XLV, pp. 409–415 (April, 1913).

FITZPATRICK, E. A. "The Case for Junior Colleges," in *Educational Review*, Vol. LXV, pp. 150–156 (March, 1923).

FOLWELL, WILLIAM WATTS. "The High School as the People's College," in *Minnesota Educational Association News Letter*, Vol. VII, pp. 26–30 (April, 1920).

FOLWELL, WILLIAM WATTS. University Addresses (especially I, "Inaugural Address," pp. 1–76, and II, "The Minnesota Plan," pp. 77–141). H. W. Wilson Co., Minneapolis, 1909. 224 pp.

FRAZIER, C. R. "The Junior College," in N.E.A. Proceedings, 1917, pp. 271–274.

GOULD, A. L. "Can the Junior College be made to serve its Community primarily and be an End in itself?" in *Sierra Educational News*, Vol. XII, pp. 116–118 (August, 1916).

GRAY, A. A. The Junior College (master's thesis). University of California, 1915. 160 pp.

GRAY, A. A. "The Status and Service of the Small College," in *School and Society*, Vol. III, pp. 586–594 (April 22, 1916).

GRAY, A. A., and ZUEBLIN, CHARLES. "Brief Symposium on the Junior College," in *Journal of Education*, Vol. LXXXV, pp. 39–40 (January 11, 1917).

HARBESON, JOHN W. "The Place of the Junior College in Public Education," in *Educational Review*, Vol. LXVII, pp. 187–191 (April, 1924).

THE JUNIOR-COLLEGE MOVEMENT

HARPER, WILLIAM RAINEY. "The High School of the Future," in *School Review*, Vol. XI, pp. 1-3 (January, 1903).

HARPER, WILLIAM RAINEY. Trend in Higher Education (see especially chap. xxiii, pp. 378-383, "The Situation of the Small College"). The University of Chicago Press, Chicago, 1905.

HEADLEY, LEAL H. "The College and the Junior College," in *Carleton College News Bulletin*, Vol. III, No. 5, pp. 6 ff.

HEDGEPETH, V. W. B. "The Six-Year High School at Goshen, Indiana," in *School Review*, Vol. XIII, pp. 19-23 (January, 1905).

HILL, A. R. "The Junior College," in Transactions and Proceedings of the National Association of State Universities, Vol. XIII, pp. 122-130 (1915).

HINES, H. C. "The Status of the Public Junior College in the United States," in *Educator-Journal*, Vol. XVIII, pp. 180-186.

HOLLIDAY, C. "Junior Colleges—If—," in *School and Society*, Vol. XI, pp. 211-214 (February 21, 1920).

HUGHES, W. H. "Junior-College Development," in *Educational Administration and Supervision*, Vol. V, pp. 189-196 (April, 1919).

JAMES, E. J. "The Function of the State University," in *Science* (new series), Vol. XXII, pp. 609-628 (November 17, 1905).

"Johns Hopkins drops the College"; editorial in *New Republic*, Vol. XLII, pp. 113-115 (March 25, 1925).

JOHNSTON, C. H. The Modern High School (especially Appendix, pp. 829-839, on "The Upward Extension of the High School"). Charles Scribner's Sons, New York, 1914.

JONES, J. C. "The Junior-College Movement in Missouri," in Transactions and Proceedings of the National Association of State Universities, Vol. XX, pp. 77-82 (1922).

Junior College Bulletin, The. *University of California Bulletin* (third series), Vol. XI, No. 12 (May, 1918). University of California Press, Berkeley, California. 56 pp.

Junior College in California, The. A circular prepared by the Committee on Courses of Instruction of the Academic Senate. University of California Press, Berkeley, California, July, 1915. 56 pp.

KEMP, W. W. "The Junior-College Movement in California." Eighth Yearbook of the National Association of Secondary School Principals, 1924, pp. 82-94.

APPENDIX

Kolbe, P. R. "The Junior College and Municipal Universities," in *School and Society*, Vol. XIII, pp. 451–456 (April 16, 1921).

Koos, Leonard V. "Current Conceptions of the Special Purposes of the Junior College," in *School Review*, Vol. XXIX, pp. 520–529 (September, 1921).

Koos, Leonard V. "Junior-College Courses in 1920–1921," in *School Review*, Vol. XXIX, pp. 586–592, 668–678 (October, November, 1921).

Koos, Leonard V. The Junior College. Research Publications of the University of Minnesota, Education Series No. 5. Minneapolis, 1924. xxxii + 688 pp.

Koos, Leonard V. "The Place of the Junior College in American Education," in Transactions and Proceedings of the National Association of State Universities, Vol. XX, pp. 44–56 (1922).

Koos, Leonard V. "The Residential Distribution of College Students and its Meaning for the Junior-College Problem," in *School and Society*, Vol. XIII, pp. 557–562 (May 7, 1921).

Koos, Leonard V. "Where to establish Junior Colleges," in *School Review*, Vol. XXIX, pp. 414–433 (June, 1921).

Koos, Leonard V., and Crawford, C. C. "College Aims, Past and Present," in *School and Society*, Vol. XIV, pp. 499–509 (December 3, 1921).

Lange, A. F. "The Junior College," in N.E.A. Proceedings, 1915, pp. 119–124.

Lange, A. F. "The Junior College—with Special Reference to California," in *Educational Administration and Supervision*, Vol. II, pp. 1–8 (January, 1916).

Lange, A. F. "The Unification of our School System," in *Sierra Educational News*, Vol. V, pp. 8–15 (June, 1909).

Leonard, Robert J. "Suggestions for the Place and Function of Junior Colleges in a System of Schools." Eighth Yearbook of the National Association of Secondary School Principals, 1924, pp. 106–111.

Liddeke, Frederick. "The Extension of the High-School Course," in *School Review*, Vol. XII, pp. 635–647 (October, 1904).

Liddeke, Frederick. "The Junior-College Department in the Fresno High School," in *Sierra Educational News*, Vol. X, pp. 409–413 (June, 1914).

THE JUNIOR–COLLEGE MOVEMENT

McDowell, F. M. The Junior College. Department of the Interior, *Bureau of Education Bulletin No. 35* (1919). Government Printing Office, Washington. 134 pp.

McLane, C. L. "The Junior College, or Upward Extension of the High School," in *School Review*, Vol. XXI, pp. 161–170 (March, 1913).

Magruder, William T. "The Junior College as a Relief," in *Educational Review*, Vol. LXI, pp. 286–297 (April, 1921).

Maxwell, G. E. "The Junior College Question—the Other Side," in *National School Digest*, Vol. XL, p. 600 (June, 1921).

Miller, H. L. "The Junior College and Secondary Education," in *Wisconsin Journal of Education*, March, 1922, pp. 47–51.

O Brien, F. P. "Report of a Survey in Atchison Dealing with the Establishment of a Junior College," in *Bulletin of the University of Kansas*, Vol. XXIV, No. 16 (October 1, 1923). 42 pp.

Pearse, Carroll G. College Courses in Normal Schools. A brief submitted to the Board of Regents of Normal Schools (Wisconsin), February, 1920. Printed and distributed by the Committee for the Preservation of the Two-Year College Courses and the Fine-Arts Course in the Normal School. 15 pp.

Proctor, William M. "The Junior College and Educational Reorganization," in *Educational Review*, Vol. LXV, pp. 275–280 (May, 1923).

Proctor, William M. "The Junior College in California," in *School Review*, Vol. XXXI, pp. 363–375 (May, 1923).

Sachs, J. "The Elimination of the First Two College Years—a Protest," in *Educational Review*, Vol. XXX, pp. 488–499 (May, 1905).

Shideler, J. W. "The Junior-College Movement in Kansas," in *School Review*, Vol. XXXI, pp. 460–463 (June, 1923).

Silver, Ernest L. "Should the Normal School function as a Junior College?" in *National School Digest*, Vol. XL, pp. 558, 582 (May, 1921).

Van Dyke, J. A. "Should the Course of Secondary Education be extended to include the Work in the Last Two Years in the Grades and the First Two Years in College?" in Minnesota Education Association Proceedings, 1902, pp. 134–139.

APPENDIX

VINCENT, GEORGE E. "The Junior College," in *School Education,* Vol. XXXVI, pp. 3–6 (February, 1917).

WILBUR, RAY LYMAN. Annual Report of the President for 1919–1920. Supplement to the *Stanford Illustrated Review*, Vol. XXII, pp. 1–146 (especially pp. 10–26, including the report of a sub-committee on the Reorganization of Undergraduate Instruction). Stanford University, 1920.

WOOD, JAMES M. "The Junior College," in N.E.A. Proceedings, 1916, pp. 151–157.

ZOOK, GEORGE F. (editor). National Conference of Junior Colleges, 1920, and First Annual Meeting of American Association of Junior Colleges, 1921. Department of the Interior, *Bureau of Education Bulletin No. 19* (1922). Government Printing Office, Washington, 1922. Pp. vi + 73.

ZOOK, GEORGE F. "The Junior College," in *School Review*, Vol. XXX, pp. 574–591 (October, 1922).

INDEX

[429]

INDEX

INDEX